THE OAKWOOD PRESS

The Essentia
to French
Heritage and
Tourist Railways

by
Mervyn Jones

THE OAKWOOD PRESS

© Oakwood Press & Mervyn Jones 2006

British Library Cataloguing in Publication Data
A Record for this book is available from the British Library
ISBN 0 85361 648 5

Typeset by Oakwood Graphics.
Repro by pkmediaworks, Cranborne, Dorset.
Printed by Cambrian Printers Ltd, Aberystwyth, Ceredigeon.

About the Author

Mervyn Jones began his interest in railways in the early 1950s spending much of his free time in that decade on the northern side of Preston railway station in London Midland Region days, enhanced in the summer months with 'Blackpool Specials' drawn from all over the United Kingdom.

However, this was all left behind when he joined the British Police Service and over the following 35 years he served in various forces, retiring as Chief Constable of Cheshire towards the end of 1997. Since then he has travelled the world extensively on behalf of the Foreign and Commonwealth Office teaching developing governments how to cope with natural and man-made disasters. On one occasion he taught in Mongolia travelling there and back by the Trans-Siberian and Trans-Mongolian railways.

He is the holder a Master of Science degree in Social Policy from Cranfield University, is a Serving Officer of the Order of St John and a recipient of the Queen's Police Medal for Distinguished Service and the Police Long Service Medal. He is a member of the UK's SNCF Society, France's FACS-UNECTO and an honorary member of AGRIVAP in the Auvergne.

He has published previously a book and numerous articles on academic subjects.

He lives with his wife, Caroline, half the year at their home on the North Wales, Shropshire and Cheshire borders and the remainder in the south of France between Avignon and Nîmes.

Title page: Pacific No. 231 G 558 preserved by the Pacific Vapeur Club at its base at Rouen in Haute-Normandie. *Daniel Briot*

Front cover: CITEV's Corpet-Louvet 030 T No. 8158 crosses the viaduct over the River Salindrinque near to St Jean-du-Gard in the Cévennes. *Author*

Rear cover: The 'little yellow train' of the Pyrénées crossing the Pont Séjourné viaduct. *Author*

Published by The Oakwood Press (Usk), P.O. Box 13, Usk, Mon., NP15 1YS.
E-mail: sales@oakwoodpress.co.uk
Website: www.oakwoodpress.co.uk

Contents

The Regions

030 T No. 3 type 'le Progrès' of Le Train des Mouettes railway in Poitou Charentes (*see entry on page 149*).   *Didier Lebrun and Xavier Léoty*

Introduction

This guide is intended not only to appeal to railway enthusiasts but to those holiday-makers and travellers, francophiles perhaps, who love France and wish to see this beautiful country from a different perspective. The book has identified in every corner of France a total of 160 locations where heritage and tourist railway activity can be found. In summary, identified in these pages is a collection of 81 heritage and/or tourist railways. Of these, the situation at the end of 2005 was that 71 are fully active, four have temporarily (hopefully!) suspended their operations, a further four are active development projects and not yet fully operational and, finally, there are two railways, one of which straddles the border between France and Luxembourg and the other, very close to it just in Luxembourg. The latter, whilst obviously not in France, is so close to the border and is just too good to miss, hence its inclusion (*see Train 1900 shown in the Lorraine Region*). Also listed are 19 of the most scenic TER-SNCF railway routes and 24 museums, one of which is closed (AMTUIR in the Île de France region) but it does open on special occasions and possibly on request. A further 19 locations and/or organizations have been identified where *matériel roulant* - locomotives, autorails, carriages and wagons - have been preserved and are exhibited or in some instances are stored. Much of this rolling stock, lovingly restored and maintained, has been approved for excursions on Réseau Ferré France (RFF) - Société Nationale des Chemins de Fer Français (SNCF) tracks, usually on Sundays when regular services are reduced. Included in this number are some other organizations which organize excursions using preserved locomotives or autorails. Seventeen places are listed where vélorail facilities are available. Finally, to clarify the current position in France, a further nine tourist railways have been briefly listed (not part of the total of 160 mentioned above) which are no longer in business.

Many of the railways identified here travel on routes, long and short, invariably through outstandingly beautiful countryside with a few others operating on purpose-built track laid in country amusement parks, thus offering something for all the family. In addition, the vélorail, for example, is a recent phenomenon in France and another facility that has universal appeal to families. There are two basic types of 'locomotion' – one form is effectively two pedal cycles (vélos) welded together by a metal frame to which is fitted a bench seat for the non-pedalling passengers or for luggage; and the other, a *cyclo-draisine* with wheels between 10 and 20 centimetres diameter and is a variation on a traditional self-propelled railcar. Both types of machine require human energies to be expended, but the benefits a vélorail journey brings is a worthwhile form of exercise and a pleasant group activity, as well as an opportunity to appreciate the countryside as viewed from a former local railway route.

France geographically is a large country having 543,965 sq. km, thus making it just over two and a quarter times the size of the United Kingdom and the second largest country in area in Europe. Two-thirds of France's relief is mountainous or hilly, which in the 19th century presented special problems for railway engineers laying track. At just over 60 million, its population is about the same as that of the United Kingdom, the two countries sharing the distinction of being the fourth most populous in Europe. For government

Corpet Louvet 030 T No. 8 *Ilena* heading for Ambert on the AGRIVAP railway. *Author*

purposes France, a republic, is divided into 22 regions each of which have a number of *départements* (departments akin perhaps to our counties). There are 96 departments many of which are named after local rivers. They are numbered from 01 to 95 in an order alphabetically; for example, the department of Ain is 01, Gard 30 and Val d'Oise 95. There is no number 20 but the designations 2A and 2B are used for the two departments on the island of Corsica. The numerical identification of departments, a legacy of Emperor Napoléon Bonaparte, is also used for identifying postcodes in France – the departmental numbers are the first two numbers in every five-number postcode. The system is also used for vehicle registrations in that the last two numbers indicate the origin of the current owner of the vehicle, although this system is in the process of changing to fall into line with European Union requirements.

A Short History of Railways in France and their preservation

As in other parts of Europe in the Industrial Age, railways in France had their origins in the 18th century mining industry for the transport of minerals. The development, however, of the earliest, albeit primitive, railways is credited to the Ancient Egyptians who built their great edifices by moving stone on planks laid out as track. Great Britain, though, takes the honour for the building of the first 'iron' railway line in 1825 between Stockton and Darlington. In France, following a Royal Decree by Louis XVIII in 1823, the first railway line was built in 1827 between St Etienne and Andrézieux, a distance of 18 km using standard gauge (*voie normale*) of 1.485 metres – the horsepower of the first traction literally being horses to haul wagons of coal. The horses were replaced at the beginning of the 1830s with the first steam locomotives. Incidentally, the 1.485 metre gauge became the standard at that time for all France's main lines, the only variations being for local lines built on metric or sub-metric gauges. Four years later, in 1831, this line started carrying its first passengers, as did a newly built line between Lyon and Givors. In 1837, the first truly modern line was constructed between Paris and Saint-Germain. However, in developing its rail network France failed to keep pace with its neighbours in Germany, Belgium and Switzerland, for example, nor with the huge expansion going on in Great Britain and the United States. The reasons for this slow development – as much as 10 years behind the others – are complex and varied. It is a fact that France, at that time, had a lower level of industrialisation compared with say Great Britain, agriculture still being seen as the priority. Furthermore, the ravages of the Napoléonic Wars meant that the priorities were those of reconstruction rather than the embracing of the 'new technology'. Attitudes to the railways were also different in France; for example, in 1832 the Rouen Chamber of Commerce refused to support the building of a rail link between Rouen and Paris because it would be 'detrimental to agriculture, hurt the traditional way of life and impinge on the business of canals and rivers'!

Notwithstanding such attitudes and the consequent late start, by 1838 there was 550 km of railway track in various parts of France. A year earlier, the French Government, with its strong centralist outlook, had appointed Monsieur Alexis Legrand as an Under Secretary of State for Public Works to oversee the development of a rail system radiating from Paris to the whole country, priority being given to routes to its ports and frontiers. Five years later legislation was enacted to ensure that private interests, unlike those in other developed countries, had a limited role in railway development. This meant that the state took responsibility for the railway infrastructure and the engineering works whilst private interests were allowed to lay the tracks, build the stations, offices, water towers and outbuildings, etc., and provide the rolling stock. Consequently, the French railway model fell between two conflicting types – on the one hand, the free market system as was operating in Great Britain, and on the other, the state-built and state-controlled model, as was the case in neighbouring Belgium. The French compromise led to conflicts and disagreements which were only resolved by the government taking greater control, an inevitable outcome given that the private companies were only given leases for 36 years. Although these leases were later extended by Napoléon III in the 1870s there was strong feeling that nationalisation of the railways was always on the agenda and only a question of time.

However, before nationalisation eventually did come, just before the onset of World War II, France was divided between a number of dominant railway companies, themselves the results of earlier amalgamations and take-overs of smaller companies. The big six were Compagnie de l'Est, the Compagnie du Nord, the Compagnie de l'État, Compagnie Paris-Orléans (PO), the Compagnie du Midi and the Compagnie Paris-Lyon-Méditerranée (PLM). These reduced to five when the PO merged with the Midi network in 1934. Interestingly, given the centralist nature of the country's government, all the companies saw fit to have their respective headquarters not in their respective geographical region but rather in Paris. All these company names, and many earlier ones, are still to be seen amongst the many preserved or reconstructed railways and rolling stock throughout France.

The French network continued to develop in the mid and late 19th century. By 1870, the national network had 25,000 km of track which was set to expand further following the publication of the Freycinet Plan in 1879. This allowed for the construction of thousands of kilometres of branch lines. The Plan, written by Monsieur Charles de Freycinet, the then Minister of Transport, paved the way for the construction of 150 new lines serving France's sub-prefectures, many being in isolated locations. As the 20th century dawned, the French railway network was still growing and even as late as 1914, just before the beginning of World War I, track was still being laid much of it by then being metre or 600 millimetre gauge. As war broke out France's railway system had become the most dense and highly-developed in the world with over 60,000 km of track, a third of which was, by then, narrow gauge.

After the end of World War I, much of France was in a poor state not least of all its railways and therefore the construction of new lines was halted in favour of repair. The rail industry about that time started to enter a decline not helped by the strikes and social upheaval of the 1920s and the Great Depression that followed in the 1930s. These factors, together with the growth of road transport at the expense of the railways and the unprofitable nature of many of the railway companies which had to be subsidised by the state, led to what many had predicted was the inevitable - Nationalisation. It was on 1st January, 1938, therefore, a landmark in the history of the railways in France, that the French railway companies were nationalised and overnight the Société Nationale des Chemins de Fer Français was formed. The first priority of SNCF was to rationalise the network by redistributing the rolling stock and closing uneconomic lines. However, World War II interrupted this policy of rationalisation and had the effect of setting back the achievement of their plans for a full 10 years.

After the war ended, as had been the case in 1918, there was much devastation throughout France, all in urgent need of re-building. This was especially so for the railways, given the importance they had been to military operations, they had taken a heavy hammering. Many were so badly damaged that they had to be closed being considered uneconomic to repair. Rolling stock was also much depleted, a situation which was overcome by the significant help that came through the delivery of the Marshal Aid Plan by the United States of America. For example, the Americans were able to supply many newly built locomotives, most notable being the Mikado 141 R class of locomotive of which 1,340 were delivered in the closing days of the war and immediately after (more information about this class of locomotive is contained in the section in this book on the Cité du Train museum at Mulhouse, Alsace region, *pages 18-19*).

In the late 1940s, electrification of the main line network began and was continued through to the 1960s. The next decade saw the beginning of the construction of high-speed LGV (*Ligne à Grande Vitesse*) track linking Paris to France's major cities using TGVs (*Trains Grande Vitesse*). Another major milestone was in 1994 which saw the introduction of rail services to and from France and the United Kingdom using the English Channel (La Manche) railway tunnel (see *The Channel Tunnel and its High Speed Links*, Nicholas Comfort, Oakwood Press, 2006).

Railway preservation in France had its origins in the late 1950s and early 1960s when enthusiasts (*passionnés*) formed and or joined an organization called Fédération des Amis des Chemins de Fer Secondaires (FACS) which had been created on New Year's Day in 1957. One of the objectives of FACS was to bring together like-minded people to safeguard the history of French railways and tramways by preserving equipment and, through a later-formed sister organization UNECTO (Union des Exploitants de Chemin de Fer Touristiques et de Musées) to encourage the development of railway museums and heritage lines. FACS-UNECTO today is the organization in France actively supporting its members in railway preservation acting as a pressure group on the French Government, SNCF and now including Réseau Ferré de France who are responsible for the track. A key responsibility for FACS-UNECTO is to ensure, and indeed strengthen the professionalism and quality of service provided by its members. A Charter signed in 2001 enhanced the role of FACS-UNECTO - more of this later. FACS-UNECTO links to other enthusiasts in other European countries by being a member of la Fédération Europennée des Chemins de Fer Touristiques (FEDECRAIL). Unfortunately, not all French heritage and tourist railways are represented as members of FACS-UNECTO which, in the author's view, is to their decided disadvantage.

The first lines to be safeguarded were the mountain railways followed by other narrow gauge lines, both metric and sub-metric. These became, and still are, the most popular of all the preserved lines in France, many of the enthusiasts who run them having taken notice of the experience and success of the Festiniog narrow gauge railway in North Wales.

Going back to the history of the development of French railways for a moment, with the coming of the extended rail network, most local railways took advantage of installing narrow gauge lines, but not all did. In the 1870s, for example, the first French local lines used standard gauge and many of these are still operating today albeit not necessarily all in SNCF ownership. Up until the 1980s the existence and preservation of these standard gauge lines was critical to the safeguarding of standard gauge locomotives and autorails. Prior to 1981, no 'amateur' trains were allowed to run on SNCF tracks restricting their use for those in '*état de marche*' (working order) to those few preserved non-SNCF controlled lines. However, all that was set to change when the socialist government came to power at the beginning of the 1980s. The then Minister of Transport, Monsieur Charles Fiterman, asked SNCF to explore the handing over to local authorities of closed lines and sections of track open only to goods traffic. The intention was that the lines could be used by railway and locomotive preservation organizations for tourism purposes with the stipulation that for safety reasons they should be under the technical supervision of SNCF. Whilst this appeared to be a generous offer in reality it proved not necessarily to be so. Those lines that had been closed to traffic turned out to be, as one might expect, the most expensive to maintain and, therefore, very few, i.e. those without sound financial backing, ever made it, especially where the local authority did not take over the running of the line or guarantee significant financial support. Those organizations, however, which utilised lines kept open for goods traffic fared better. With the greater use of the lines by freight traffic, the better the track was maintained thus reducing the overheads for the tourist railways. One of the outstanding successes of this changed policy was and still is the Chemin de Fer du Vermandois (*see entry under the Picardie Region*) which was the first tourist railway to operate on a SNCF goods line. An agreement with SNCF was signed in February 1982 to permit this arrangement which was subsequently strengthened by another agreement with the two local government authorities in 1989.

The first non-SNCF owned locomotive to venture out on to SNCF track took place in November 1981. Then, after nearly a year of negotiations with the legal representatives of SNCF, a Mikado steam locomotive No. 141 R 420, owned at that time by Monsieur André Presle, travelled between Gray and Vesoul. Six months later saw a 'Great Gathering' when another Mikado No. 141 R 568 and locomotive No. 140 C 27 joined 141 R 420 at the Gray depot. That is all history for it is not now uncommon for non-SNCF owned rolling stock, steam, diesel and autorail, to take excursions out on to RFF (SNCF) track at non-peak times in the SNCF timetable, and long may it continue!

Another important breakthrough, which further aided this opening up of SNCF lines, occurred in February 2001 with the signing of the National Charter for the Development of Tourist and Historic Railways. This recognised the importance of such railways to a country which is the world's most popular tourist destination. The charter clarifies the relationship between the interested parties through its objectives which are: the promotion and enhancement of railway lines through publicity in France and overseas; the guarantee of quality services; most importantly, the safety and proper control of the infrastructure; the preservation of the expertise of railway staff; and, of course, the contribution of all this effort can make to the development of local economies. FACS-UNECTO and SNCF are the major signatories to this charter.

Getting the best out of this Guide

To assist the reader in orientating him or herself relative to what is available and perhaps for planning a visit or visits to France, the locations in this guide have been organized on a regional basis. All 22 regions in France have something to offer the rail enthusiast, the traveller or the family holiday-maker. Within each region the entries have been organized in eight thematic sections, i.e. firstly, heritage and tourist railways; secondly, tourist railway routes run by TER-SNCF; thirdly, railways where operations have been temporarily suspended; fourthly, railways which are in project form; fifthly, brief details of railways which have ceased operation; sixthly, locations where locomotives, other traction and rolling stock are stored, sometimes exhibited and/or used for excursions on RFF (SNCF) tracks; seventhly, museums of railway interest; and, finally, locations where vélorail services are offered.

The guide has avoided becoming too detailed about the rolling stock which is held, in favour of listing, where known, of what may be seen and indicating where more information may be found. Those who do want more detail will invariably find that a good starting point is the organization's website where experience has shown a wealth of information can often be found. To assist in this respect, where known, website and e-mail address have been listed for each entry. It has also been the author's experience that there is a tremendous enthusiasm amongst the members of these organizations for their railway interest, coupled with a great willingness to share irrespective of national, cultural or language differences. Having said that, language can be something of a barrier and therefore to assist those who have some understanding of French, a glossary of the more common railway terms has been included. Incidentally, on a question of detail, especially as it relates to locomotives, it may help to know that the French adopt a slightly different system for identifying wheel configurations. Where, for example in the United Kingdom we would describe the *Flying Scotsman* as being a 4-6-2, the French would call it a 231, in other words they only count the wheels on the one side of the locomotive. That number also always forms part of the locomotive identification number. For example, a large class of locomotives was the Mikado which in United Kingdom terms has a 2-8-2 configuration but in France would be described as 141, followed by the sub-class letter and then the actual number of the locomotive. One such example is Mikado 141 R 840 which is kept by AAATV (Centre) at Cosne-Cours-sur-Loire in the Bourgogne (Burgundy) region. Incidentally, this locomotive is fully restored and periodically undertakes excursions on SNCF lines. It has not been a common practice for the French to name their individual locomotives although some can now be found amongst the preserved stock. More common was the naming of a service such as *La Fleche d'Or* (The Golden Arrow) and *Le Train Bleu* (The Blue Train). For a worthwhile understanding of this subject of naming French train services read *Named Trains of France* by Derek Wilde published by the United Kingdom's SNCF Society.

Almost all of the entries in this guide relate to organizations which are fully active; however, there are a few which, for a variety of reasons, often finance related, have suspended their services or perhaps are at an early stage in their development. Nonetheless, those which it is felt will resume activities in the not too distant future, or are in an advanced stage of building their operations, have been included. As with heritage and tourist railways elsewhere in the world, invariably they are sustained by the efforts of mainly volunteers. Sadly, they are not always successful and some ventures have to close or suspend operations.

Each entry identifies the location by town or city, its department and proximity to a major regional centre of population. Simple route directions together with other useful information such as contact details, including, as already said, websites and e-mail addresses where they exist, are also provided. A note of caution: websites are a very helpful means of obtaining current information but it is worth noting that some have not always been maintained or have been changed leaving the web browser at a loss. Similarly, some e-mail addresses are not always effective. At the time of going to print (in 2006) all the sites and addresses had been checked, found to be active and to be what they purported to be. The dates of opening, the hours of operation and examples of the charges levied are also included as are the train journey times which are for a single direction unless otherwise indicated. The year in brackets after the entry indicates the date of the latest information.

Every attempt has been made to ensure that all the information in this guide is correct and up-to-date, but it is important to render a health warning. Before travelling any distance in France to any of the locations listed here, it is wise in order to avoid disappointment, in all instances, to check the accuracy of current operations information beforehand. There are many factors in heritage and tourist railway operations, short of closure or suspension, which can change the availability of a service, not least the changing condition of many of the ageing locomotives and other rolling stock. Similarly, much of the French preserved railway rolling stock can and does move around the country so if one wishes to see a particular item, then check beforehand that it is where it is supposed to be. This applies particularly to those locomotives and autorails which are in a state of working order (*état de marche*) and approved for occasional use out on to RFF (SNCF) railway tracks.

Contact details have been provided including telephone numbers and fax numbers. Incidentally the telephone numbering system is a useful indicator to where the railway or museum is in France; the 01 prefix is for Paris and its environs, 02 the north-west, 03 the north-east, 04 the south-east and 05 the south-west. The prefix 06 is used for mobile telephones (portables) and 08, as in the United Kingdom, for non-geographic numbers some of which are charged at a premium rate. It will be noted that the numbers given herein are those as if one was dialling from within France. If dialling from abroad start the call with the international dialling code - in the UK it is 00 - followed by the code for France which is 33; then drop the first digit - the 0 - then follow it with the number. For example, the number in France for Train à Vapeur des Cévennes (CITEV) is 04 66 60 59 00 but if calling from the UK dial the following: 00 33 4 66 60 59 00.

The author is always keen to keep the information correct and up-to-date, so, if any inaccuracies are identified in this book, changes are found to have been made to the operating circumstances or new facilities have become available, then such information would be most welcomed by the author who can be contacted c/o Oakwood Press or by e-mail at trains@french-leave.com

Acknowledgements

The author wishes to acknowledge all the help, support, advice and, indeed, friendship, he has received during the research for and the writing of this guide. It is not practical to identify all those who helped by name but, nevertheless, their individual contributions are very much appreciated. Throughout the research, both in France and later in the United Kingdom, the author has been impressed with the high degrees of enthusiasm, commitment and sheer hard work displayed by all those involved in French heritage and tourist railways. The majority of those are unpaid volunteers, and, as in the UK, most of their worthwhile projects just would not happen without their dedication. They have the right to be proud of their achievements not least of all for the part they play in improving their country's economy. France is the most popular country in the world for tourism and there is no doubt that railway ventures such as those listed herein make an important contribution to the appeal of the country for the visitor.

One organization which does deserve special mention is FACS-UNECTO which is the key organization in France looking after the interests of heritage and tourist railways. The author is particularly indebted to them for all the help and advice provided, not least of all the up-to-date information about the activities of many of their members running tourist railways. Incidentally, anyone, including those living outside France, can join the organization, one of the many benefits being that they will be recipients of their useful quarterly review - *Chemins de fer régionaux et tramways*.

Important sources of information in compiling this guide have been by making visits to many of the railways and museums and learning at first hand about their history and current operations. Discussions enjoyed with organizers, enthusiasts and travellers, who were always found to be willing to share their valuable knowledge, proved most fruitful.

Other sources of information found to be important to building this guide were the many websites which have been written on the subject of French heritage railways. The FACS-UNECTO site proved to be an excellent starting point, as were the individual websites for many of the locations listed. The author, therefore, is indebted to the webmasters of FACS-UNECTO and all the other sites visited as are listed herein with each of the entries. Whilst all copyright (*les droits d'auteur*) has been observed, it is acknowledged by the author on an individual basis, the contributions of all those involved in utilising such a modern and powerful means of communication.

Another source of support and, indeed, at times, fresh ideas has come from Oakwood Press and in particular Andrew Kennedy and Ian Kennedy who both patiently helped the author with useful comments and suggestions for improvement.

Finally, the author wishes to give special thanks to his wife, Caroline, who uncomplainingly, supported him throughout the development of the project, accompanied him on numerous site visits waiting for yet another train to pass and, during the writing, gave much needed encouragement, advice and, most importantly, regular sustenance.

Alsace

The Alsace Region, comprising the Departments of Bas-Rhin (67) and Haut-Rhin (68) is located in the north-east of France adjoining the Lorraine Region and bordering Belgium, Germany and Luxembourg. Its regional capital is Strasbourg and Colmar and Mulhouse are other important centres. This region has three heritage/tourist railways, one discontinued railway and two active museums, including the French National Railway Museum - Le Cité du Train.

Railways

Chemin de Fer Touristique du Rhin (CFTR)

030 TB 134 standing at Vogelsheim station.   *Sebastién Keiffer*

Member: FACS-UNECTO
Location: Volgelsheim, near to the River Rhine, 19 km east of Colmar and 92 km south of Strasbourg.
Departments: Haut-Rhin (68) and Bas Rhin (67).
Getting there: The nearest SNCF station is at Colmar. By road take the RN415 from Colmar towards the River Rhine.
Route: Volgelsheim – Marckolsheim (12 km).
Journey time: 2 hours 45 minutes round trip.
Gauge and type of traction: Standard; steam, autorail and diesel.

Rolling stock: Two 030 TB steam locomotives formerly of Alsace and Lorraine built in 1900 and classified of historical interest, a Fives-Lille steam locomotive built in 1923, a Henschel steam locomotive built in 1901, a Decauville steam locomotive built 1922, a Cockerill steam locomotive, a Winterthur steam locomotive of 1917 preserved as a static exhibit, a Billard autorail, a diesel locomotive A1A-A1A 62029, a variety of locotracteurs, and a good selection of carriages and wagons. All rolling stock is kept at the railway's depot at Port Rhénan. Also located there, as a static exhibit, is an unusual l'Hispano-Suiza locotracteur No. 3245, a company name more usually associated with the manufacture of high class automobiles.

Contact details: 26 rue des Cordiers, 68280 Andolsheim. Telephone: 03 89 71 51 42 (weekdays) 03 89 72 55 97 (weekends) Fax: 03 89 71 51 42 E-mail: cheminferhin@worldonline.fr

Website: http://cftr.evolutive.org

Operating dates: From May to October on Sundays and French public holidays departing at 1500 hours and returning by 1745 hours.

Tariff: An adult return ticket for the train and a boat journey is 15€ and for a child (4-14 years) 7.50€. An adult ticket for the train journey only is 7.50€ and for a child 3.50€. Animals can travel on the train (2006).

History: CFTR was formed in 1983 and with support from the *Chambre de Commerce et d'Industrie* (CCI) of Colmar the line from Volgelsheim to Marckolsheim, originally opened in 1868, was made available to the association. In July 1983, the Fives-Lille undertook the inaugural journey. In 1984, an agreement was made with two local proprietors of *bateaux mouches* (river pleasure boats) to run combined rail and river tours. Every year since its formation, the railway has gone from strength to strength in spite of occasional setbacks. In a number of seasons special events and anniversaries have been celebrated and other interesting locomotives have been brought to the line both for the long and short duration. For example, from 1992 to 1998, steam locomotive 141 TB 424 operated on the line as did the 231 du Ulmer Eisenbahn Freunde (UEF) from Stuttgart for a short visit in May 1999.

Comments: The rail trip can be combined with a one and a half hour sailing from Sans-Soucis on the River Rhine on a 1930s pleasure boat. The 1878 railway station at Volgelsheim has been lovingly restored by the local commune, the late Mayor being a great supporter of the railway. This railway every year receives visits from UK groups of enthusiasts who invariably hire a special train for themselves. CFTR is keen to foster relationships with other *passionnés* in other countries of Europe. A local place to visit of transport interest not far from here is the Maginot Line (*see entry under the Lorraine Region*). A visit to this railway is a 'must-do' for rail enthusiasts and holidaymakers alike.

Local Tourist Office: 13, rue du Maréchal Foch, 67390 Marckolsheim. Telephone: 03 88 92 56 98 Fax: 03 88 92 56 07. E-mail: marckolsheim@tourisme-alsace.info website: www.grandried.free.fr

Chemin de Fer Touristique de la Vallée de la Doller (CFTVD)

Mallet 020+020 T at Sentheim station.   *Romain Tricot*

Member: FACS-UNECTO
Location: Cernay, 21 km west of Mulhouse and 114 km south of Strasbourg.
Department: Haut-Rhin (68).
Getting there: The nearest SNCF station is at Cernay on the Mulhouse to Thann line. By road take the A36 autoroute and exit for Thann then the RN66 and exit Porte-d'Alsace then the RN83 in the direction of Colmar.
Route: Cernay – Sentheim (14 km).
Journey time: 1 hour each way.
Gauge and type of traction: Standard; steam, autorail and diesel.
Rolling stock: Four steam locomotives which include a Mallet 030 T Meuse No. 51 ex-CSNE, a Henschel 020+020 T classified as of historical interest (*Monument Historique*) and recently restored to operational order in 2005 and a 030 T Couillet. There are also two diesel locotracteurs, two light autorails (ex-SNCF X 5852 and a Billard) four wooden carriages dating from 1892 formerly of the Palavas-les-Flots train, four other coaches ex-SNCF and HBL and a variety of goods wagons.
Contact details: Chemin de Fer Touristique de la Vallée de la Doller (CFTVD) 10 rue de la Gare, 68780 Sentheim. Telephone: 03 89 82 88 48
Fax: 03 89 82 88 48 E-mail: cftvd@train-doller.org
Website: www.train-doller.org
Operating dates: June to September on Sundays there are two services (steam and diesel) each way departing from Cernay at 1100 and 1530 hours and departing from Sentheim at 1400 and 1730 hours, plus two additional steam

services every Wednesday in July and August departing from Cernay at 1000 and 1400 hours and departing from Sentheim at 1245 and 1615 hours. Special excursions for groups can be arranged for any day of the week and Sundays. The trip, which can be tailored to the precise requirements of the group, can include stops for photography. Group reservations can be made by telephoning 03 89 82 88 48 or by E-mail.

Tariff: Not advised (2006).

History: The original line received its first traffic in June 1869, the line at time being just over 13 kilometres long but later was extended to Sewen in 1901 by the German Reich, Alsace at that time being part of Germany. Freight transport on the line was very important to the area with wine, mineral water and wood transported from Sentheim, coal from Guewenheim, bricks and wood from Burnhaupt and fertiliser from St-André. World War I broke out in 1914 and as one would expect the area and the railway suffered. The French military's front line reached Burnhaupt which is on the railway route and 11 kilometres beyond Sentheim. Between the end of World War I and the beginning of World War II, the railway flourished with as many as eight return journeys per day. Of course, with the onset of World War II traffic declined, a situation from which, after the end of hostilities, it never really recovered. Eventually, passenger traffic stopped in 1967 and goods traffic followed in 1973 and the line was declassified. Happily the line was re-opened in June 1976 for tourism using its 030 T Meuse No. 51 ex-CSNE. Unfortunately, the Sentheim to Sewen section of track no longer exists.

Comments: The train travels through beautiful countryside with mountain rivers, streams and lakes. The railway architecture is of a particular local style known as *la ferme sundgauvienne*, a region of southern Alsace. Local places to visit of transport interest are the French National Railway and Automobile (Schlumpf Collection) museums at Mulhouse. There is also the Wine Route of Alsace linked closely to the railway - see the website www.alsace-route-des-vins.com

Local Tourist Office: 1, rue Latouche, 68700 Cernay-St-André. Telephone: 03 89 75 50 35 Fax: 03 89 75 49 24. E-mail: info@cernay.net website: www.cernay.net

Discontinued Railway

Train Touristique Rosheim – Ottrott

Location: Rosheim

Department: Bas-Rhin (67).

Comments: From 1954 the local quarries of St Nabor operated a branch line, originally constructed in 1902, for the carriage of freight. In 1969, local tourist offices came together to run the railway, le Bimmel Bahn, as it was called, between Rosheim and Ottrott, a distance of about 12 kilometres. Unfortunately, the poor condition of the track and the lack of the necessary funds to repair led to its closure at the beginning of the 1990s. (Source: FACS-UNECTO.)

Museums

Musée Français du Chemin de Fer now known as the Cité du Train

No. 241 P 16 'Mountain' on display at Mulhouse Museum.   *Author*

Location: Mulhouse, 113 km south of Strasbourg.

Department: Haut-Rhin (68).

Getting there: By SNCF train direct to Mulhouse and then take No. 17 bus which circulates all the Mulhouse museums including the National Automobile (Schlumpf Collection). NB: The TGV Est is due to open in 2007. By road take the autoroute A36 exiting at the Mulhouse-Dornach turning. The museum is five minutes from the autoroute and a similar travelling time from Mulhouse city centre.

Exhibits: The museum has a total of 221 items of which 45 are steam locomotives, 36 electrically driven locomotives, 7 diesel locomotives, 13 electric automotrices, 10 automotrices thermiques and autorails, 56 passenger carriages, 37 goods wagons and 17 various other items. Given so much material it is difficult to list it all but well worth seeing are the 121 A Forquenot 340 ex-PO, the Hudson 232 U1, 232 Baltic (Nord) 3.1102, *L'Aigle* built by Robert Stephenson and put into service on the Avignon-Marseille line, Pacific 3.1192 (Nord), Atlantic 221 A 30 ex-2670 (Nord), Bugatti ZZy 24408 'Wagon Rapide' autorail, the 1954 electric locomotive BB 9004, the world speed record holder (331 kph) CC 7107, the 210 Crampton No. 80 'Continent', the E1 PO, 1936 built La Micheline XM 5005 (Est) autorail, the Voiture salon présidentielle PR1 and the Voiture Pullman 4018 saloon car. A particularly impressive exhibit is in the wartime section of the recently completed new part of the museum where the 140 A 259 (Consolidation) locomotive is laid on its side in a simulation of sabotage by members of the French Resistance. Also worthy of mention is the

Mikado 141 R 1187 which is preserved as a static exhibit at the museum. No. 141 R 1187, built by Baldwin in the USA and still owned by SNCF, started life out at Le Mans in July 1947 and was retired at Venissieux in November 1975 having travelled a total of 1,604,707 kilometres. It was one of the Mikados that was converted from coal to heavy oil-fired. There are 12 Mikados preserved out of the original 1,340 locomotives which were shipped to France at the end of World War II as part of the Marshal Aid Plan. Seven 141 Rs including No. 1187 are retained in France of which just four are active on RFF (SNCF) tracks. Those are Nos. 420 (working out of Clermont Ferrand), 840 (out of Cosne-Cours-sur-Loire), 1126 (out of Toulouse) and 1199 (out of Basse-Goulaine near Nantes). There was a fifth 141 R active in France, coal-fired No. 568 kept at Capendac, north of Toulouse, but towards the end of 2005 this was bought by British business man Andrew Cook with a view to it being moved to Embrach in Switzerland. Interestingly, Switzerland is the home to four other 141 Rs, Nos. 73 (coal), 1207 (coal), 1244 (heavy oil) and 1332 (heavy oil). None of these is active.
Contact details: Cité du Train, Musée Français du Chemin de Fer, 2 rue Alfred de Glehn, 68000 Mulhouse. Telephone: 03 89 42 25 67 Fax: 03 89 42 41 82 E-mail: message@citedutrain.com
Website: www.citedutrain.com
Operating dates: All year round except Christmas Day. Opening hours from 1st April to 31st October are 1000 hours to 1800 hours; the rest of the year the museum closes one hour earlier. Allow at least half a day for the visit.
Tariff: An adult ticket is 10€ or if combined with a visit to the Automobile Museum 15.50€. There are reduced rates for families and over-60s (2006).
Comments: The Museum was subjected to a major facelift in 2004 and re-opened to the public in April 2005. It is now known as the Cité du Train. The staff members are particularly helpful and many speak excellent English. The website has also been re-designed and is well worth visiting. The French National Automobile Museum (Schlumpf Collection) is also located not far away in Mulhouse and the Ecomusée d'Alsace is located 16 km away between Bollwiller and Pulversheim.
Local Tourist Office: 9, avenue du Maréchal Foch, Annexe au Musée Historique, place de la Réunion, 68100 Mulhouse. Telephone: 03 89 35 48 48 Fax: 03 89 45 66 16 E-mail: info@tourisme-mulhouse.com website: www.tourisme-mulhouse.com

Ecomusée d'Alsace also known as Clair de Mine

Member: FACS-UNECTO
Location: Bollwiller and Pulversheim, 16 km north of Mulhouse.
Department: Haut-Rhin (68).
Getting there: By SNCF train to Mulhouse and Bollwiller. By road, leave the autoroute A35 at the Ensisheim exit and for the next 10 km follow the direction arrows to the *ecomusée*; from Colmar and Belfort take the RN83; from Mulhouse take the RN430 in the direction of Guebwiller and exit where signed to Ecomusée Aéroport de Mulhouse-Bâle.
Route: Bollwiller (4 km).

Gauge and type of traction: Standard; diesel.

Rolling stock: One Moyse 20 TDE locotracteur and two carriages one from the 1930s and the other of the 1950s.

Contact details: Ecomusée d'Alsace, 68190 Ungersheim. Telephone: 03 89 74 44 74 Fax: 03 89 74 44 65. E-mail: contact@ecomusee-alsace.fr

Website: www.ecomusee-alsace.fr

Operating dates: May to October open every day on Mondays to Saturdays afternoons from 1400 to 1700 hours and 1000 to 1700 hours on Sundays and on French public holidays; in July and August the *ecomusée* is open every day from 1000 to 1800 hours.

Tariff: An adult combined ticket for the train, village and the mine is 19.50€ and for a child (4-16 years) 10€ (2005).

Comments: An imaginative project depicting life in a local village where many inhabitants worked in the local mines. This area is where the world's largest potassium deposits were found in 1904. Originally there were 11 mines but all have been closed including the Rodolphe which ended its days in 1976 but its pit head has been preserved as an outstanding example of 20th century engineering. Cité du Train and the National Automobile Museum both are nearby at Mulhouse.

Local Tourist Office: 9, avenue du Maréchal Foch, Annexe au Musée Historique, place de la Réunion, 68100 Mulhouse. Telephone: 03 89 35 48 48 Fax: 03 89 45 66 16. E-mail: info@tourisme-mulhouse.com website: www.tourisme-mulhouse.com

Moyse 20 TDE locotracteur and carriage at Ungersheim.   *Ecomusée d'Alsace*

Aquitaine

Aquitaine is in the south-west of France and borders to the south Spain and the French regions of Poitou-Charentes to the north, Limousin to the north-east and Midi-Pyrénées to the east. It comprises the departments of Dordogne (24), Gironde (33), Loir-et-Cher (40), Lot-et-Garonne (47), and Pyrénées-Atlantiques (64). Its regional capital is Bordeaux and other important cities are Perigueux, Mont-de-Marsan, Pau, and Agen. This region has eight heritage/tourist railways and one TER-SNCF tourist railway.

Railways

Chemin de Fer de la Rhune (CFTA) also known as Le Petit Train de la Rhune

A morning train departing Col de St Ignace station.   *Author*

Member: FACS-UNECTO
Location: Col de St Ignace, 17 km south of St Jean-de-Luz and 33 km from Bayonne.
Department: Pyrénées-Atlantiques (64).
Getting there: By SNCF train to St Jean-de-Luz on the Bordeaux-Hendaye line then by local coach (Autocars Le Basque Bondissant – Tel 05 59 26 30 74 or 05 59 26 25 87) or by taxi. By road from Bayonne take the RN10, the D918 and the D4 to Col de St Ignace.
Route: Col de St Ignace - La Rhune (4.2 km).
Journey time: 35 minutes at an average speed of 8 km/h to the summit of La Rhune. There is a passing point midway.

Gauge and type of traction: Metre gauge, rack-worked, electrified 3000V 50Hz three-phase.

Rolling stock: Six motrices (trams - five in service) and six carriages finished in beautifully varnished wood; four trains are in regular service.

Contact details: Chemin de Fer de la Rhune, Col de St Ignace, 64310 Sare. Telephone: 05 59 54 20 26 Fax: 05 59 47 50 76. E-mail: train.rhune@wanadoo.fr

Website: www.rhune.com also see www.connex-tradition.com

Operating dates: Mid-March to late October every day except certain holidays. In October, open every day except Mondays and Thursdays. It is essential to check operating dates before making a visit. Departures are regularly every 35 minutes. The station opens for the sale of tickets and souvenirs at 0830 hours. It pays to arrive early in high season.

Tariff: An adult return ticket is 13€, for a child (4-10 years) 7€ and for a dog 7€. An adult single ticket is 11€, for a child 6€ and for a dog 6€ (2006).

History: With development of tourism towards the end of the 19th century and the beginning of the 20th, the company Chemin de Fer du Midi created a number of important lines to access tourist sites and also their hotels, in particular at Font-Romeu and Super-Bagnères. Another one of these lines was at La Rhune. Construction begun in 1912 but owing to the onset of World War I (1914-18) the line did not come properly into service until June 1924.

Comments: It is operated by Connex-Tradition on a contract which at present runs until 2013. Certainly not the longest line on which to travel but very exhilarating although perhaps not one for those who have a fear of heights! The summit is 905 metres above sea level. Subject to the absence of cloud which is not uncommon, the view from the top of La Rhune, especially of the coastline, is *magnifique*. The wind at the summit can be cold even in the summer months so taking warm clothing is advised.

Local Tourist Office: place du Maréchal Foch, BP 265, 64500 St Jean-de-Luz. Telephone: 05 59 26 03 16 Fax: 05 59 26 21 47 E-mail: infos.tourisme@saint-jean-de-luz.com

Tramway du Cap Ferret (TCF)

Location: Cap Ferret, 70 km west of Bordeaux.

Department: Gironde (33).

Getting there: By road take the autoroutes A10 and A63 and exit at 24 and then the D216 to Cap Ferret.

Route: Gare Jetée de Bélisaire to l'Horizon (2 km).

Journey time: 12 minutes.

Gauge and type of traction: 800 mm; tram.

Contact details: Tramway du Cap Ferret, 33970 Le Cap Ferret. Telephone: 05 56 60 62 57 & 06 13 21 86 73 Fax: 05 56 60 60 20.

Website: via the Tourist Office: www.ville-lege-capferret.fr

Operating dates: In April, May and early June in the afternoons and in July, August and to mid-September in the mornings and afternoons.

Tariff: An adult return ticket is 5€ and for a child (up to 10 years) 3.65€. An adult single ticket is 3.35€ and for a child 2.15€. Special rates for groups (2006).

Comments: A lovely way in which to discover this interesting peninsular of the Presqu'île with its flora and fauna. The terrain is flat allowing easy access on pedal cycle to the 50 km of locally signed routes.
Local Tourist Office: 33950 Lège-Cap-Ferret. Telephone: 05 56 03 94 49
Fax: 05 57 70 31 70 Website: www.ville-lege-capferret.fr
E-mail: office.de.tourisme.lege.cap.ferret@wanadoo.fr

Train Touristique Guîtres Marcenais (TTGM) also referred to as Chemin de Fer Touristique de Guîtres

A line up at Guîtres.   *Alan Cassagnau*

Location: Guîtres, 49 km north-east of Bordeaux.
Department: Gironde (33).
Getting there: By road take the autoroute A10 and exit at 40A and then the D10 to Guîtres.
Route: Guîtres – Marcenais (12 km).
Journey time: 1 hour 30 minutes.
Gauge and type of traction: Standard; various.
Rolling stock: 45 locomotives, autorails, wagons and draisines (rail track inspection cars) dating from 1880 to 1950, 16 of which are classified as *Monuments Historiques*. Of particular note is one of only four examples in France of a 241 P Mountain locomotive, this No. 9 which was constructed in 1947. The other three are located as follows: No. 16 is on display in the Cité du Train museum in Mulhouse, the second, No. 17 is at Parc des Combes at Le Creusot undergoing restoration as is No. 30 in Switzerland by the Association Vapeur Val-de-Travers. At Guîtres there are three other steam locomotives, an 1890 020 T SACM, 1924 020 Meuse (*Monument Historique*) and a 1949 030 T 501 Fives Lille. There are the following diesels, a 1944 BB 4033 General Electric (*Monument*

Historique), a 1956 Decauville 020 locotracteur, a Moyse type 20 T and a locotracteur pousse-wagon called 'Locofox'. Two autorails complete the collection – a 1935 M7 De Dion-Bouton type MY and a 1938 M104 De Dion-Bouton type NT (both *Monuments Historiques*).
Contact details: Train Touristique Guîtres – Marcenais, c/o A. Leger-Bonalgue, 33750 St Germain-du-Puch. Telephone: 05 57 24 58 78. E-mail: train-guitres@wanadoo.fr (NB: do not use English words in the 'subject' of the e-mail – anti-spam software will reject it!).
Website: http://cf-guitres.rail-france.org
Operating dates: From 1st May to 31st October on Sundays leaving Guîtres at 1530 hours and returning from Marcenais at 1730 hours; extra services on Sundays from 15th July to 31st August leaving at 1100 and returning at 1150 hours and on Wednesdays leaving at 1530 and returning at 1730 hours (2005).
Tariff: Not advised.
Comments: This railway has an outstanding collection of rolling stock and whilst the journey distance is relatively short the train does travel through very attractive countryside. The 1874-built ticket office has been preserved intact. The staff members are very helpful and English is spoken.
Local Tourist Office: 4, avenue de la Gare, 33230 Guîtres. Telephone: 05 57 69 11 48. E-mail: officetourisme@cc-canton-guitres.com website: www.cc-canton-guitres.com

Chemin de fer du lac d'Artouste also known as Régie Départementale des Stations d'Altitude (RDSA)

Location: Artouste-Fabrèges, 60 km south of Pau on the road to Spain.
Department: Pyrénées-Atlantiques (64)
Getting there: By road take the autoroute A64 to Pau then the D934 to Laruns continuing on the same road towards the Spanish border. (Warning: cattle and goats roam freely on this road.) The railway can be found on the left near a large reservoir.
Route: La Sagette - Lac d'Artouste (10 kilometres).
Journey time: 50 minutes each way.
Gauge and type of traction: 500 mm; diesel.
Rolling stock: Billard and Whitcombe locotracteurs and a collection of brightly-painted open carriages.
Contact details: Regie Départementale des Stations d'Altitude, 64440 Laruns. Telephone: 05 59 05 36 99 Fax: 05 59 05 45 64.
E-mail: artouste.tourisme@wanadoo.fr
Website: www.trainartouste.com
Operating dates: From early June to early October - in June and September trains run every hour between 1000 and 1500 hours and in July and August every half hour between 0900 and 1700 hours.
Tariff: An adult return ticket is 17.30€ and for a child (4-12 years) 13€ (2005).
History: This short train journey which is said to be on the highest railway in Europe was built in 1924 for accessing the building of the dam, the Barrage d'Artouste.

Billard locomotive returning to La Sagette station. *Author*

Comments: The excursion departs from the Lac de Fabrèges (alt. 1,200 m) by a 15 minute télécabine (cable car) journey to La Sagette station (alt. 2,000 m) followed by the rail journey to the Lac d'Artouste. About 75 minutes are allowed to view the dam and the lake before returning to Fabrèges. This is definitely not one for those with a fear of heights; if the cable car challenges you then the tour on much of the edge of the valley wall definitely will. However, if you can brave the journey it offers a splendid, indeed unforgettable, scenic tour in an overall round trip of 3 hours 30 minutes. (Warning: the first part of the journey is through a low tunnel about one kilometre in length, so it is advisable to have a handkerchief ready through which to breathe.)

Local Tourist Office: Maison de la Vallée d'Ossau, 64440 Laruns. Telephone: 05 59 05 31 41 Fax: 05 59 05 35 49. E-mail: ossau.tourisme@wanadoo.fr website: www.tourisme64.com

Chemin de Fer des Landes de Gascogne
part of the Ecomusée de la Grande Lande

Location: Sabres, 92 km south of Bordeaux.

Getting there: By road take the autoroutes A10 & A63 and exit at 18 on to RN134 to Sabres.

Route: Sabres to Marquèze (4 km).

Journey time: Allow at least a half day to enjoy this superb *ecomusée* and its enjoyable train journey.

Gauge and type of traction: Standard; steam.

Rolling stock: Steam locomotive type 030 T No. 1828, classed as a *Monument Historique*, and a collection of carriages.

Contact details: Monsieur Jean Tucoo-Chala, Conservateur de l'Ecomusée de la Grande Lande, Route de Solférino, 40630 Sabres. Telephone: 05 58 08 31 31 Fax: 05 58 07 56 85. E-mail: ecomusee-marqueze@parc-landes-de-gascogne.fr

Website: www.parc-landes-de-gascogne.fr

030 T No. 1828.   *Ecomusée de la Grande Lande*

Operating dates: From the end of March to the beginning of November; 1st June to 15th September there are 10 departures per day every 40 minutes; fewer departures every day before and after the above dates.

Comments: Set in the beautiful Parc Naturel Régional des Landes de Gascogne, the train hauled by this well preserved 030 T operates as part of what is bound to be an excellent visit to the *ecomusée*. The staff members here are very helpful and some English is spoken.

Local Tourist Office: 6, place du Général Leclerc, BP 305, 40000 Mont-de-Marsan. Telephone: 05 58 05 87 37 or 3265 and say 'Mont-de-Marsan' Fax: 05 58 05 87 36. E-mail: tourisme@mont-de-marsan.org

Train Touristique de la Pointe-de-Grave – le Verdon (PGV)

Location: Soulac-sur-Mer, 91 km north-west of Bordeaux.

Department: Gironde (33).

Getting there: By road take the autoroute A10 and exit on to the RN150 to Royan then take the ferry to le Verdon-sur-Mer and then follow the RN215 to Soulac-sur-Mer.

Route: Pointe-de-Grave to Soulac-sur-Mer (7 km).

Gauge and type of traction: Standard; diesel.

Rolling stock: Draisines.

Contact details: Pointe-de-Grave – le Verdon, 33123 le Verdon-sur-Mer. Telephone: 05 56 09 61 78.

Operating dates and tariff: Contact the local Tourist Office.

Local Tourist Office: 68, rue de la plage, BP 02, 33780 Soulac-sur-Mer. *Telephone*: 05 56 09 86 61 Fax: 05 56 73 63 76.

E-mail: tourismesoulac@wanadoo.fr website: www.soulac.com or the Office de Tourisme, rue F. le Breton, 33123 Le Verdon. Telephone: 05 56 09 61 78.

Train Touristique d'Albret (TTA)

DU65 diesel locomotive and carriage.   *Train Touristique d'Albret*

Member: FACS-UNECTO
Location: Nérac, 26 km west of Agen.
Department: Lot et Garonne (47).
Getting there: By SNCF train to Agen then by bus to Nérac; by road take the autoroute A62 and leave at Agen and then follow the road to Nérac; access is also possible by the Canal du Midi and the River La Baise.
Route: Nérac to Mézin (13 km).
Gauge and type of traction: Standard; diesel.
Rolling stock: Two DU65 diesel locomotives of 1970 construction and a wagon converted to carry 90 seated passengers.
Contact details: Train Touristique d'Albret, 12 ter, avenue du 19 mars 1962, Gare de Nérac, 47600 Nérac. Telephone: 06 85 62 77 47. E-mail: tt.a@wanadoo.fr
Website: www.trains-fr.org/unecto/ttalbret/albret.htm
Operating dates: In April and October operates on Wednesdays, Saturdays, Sundays and public holidays with one departure from Nérac at 1415 and returning from Mézin at 1530 hours; May and September on Wednesdays, Saturdays, Sundays and public holidays with three departures from Nérac at 1000, 1415 and 1645 and returning from Mézin at 1115, 1530 and 1800 hours; in June, July and August services operate every day except Mondays with three departures from Nérac at 1000, 1415 and 1645 and returning from Mézin at 1115, 1530 and 1800 hours. Reservations are strongly recommended especially in the height of the season.
Tariff: An adult return ticket is 8.50€ and for a child (4-12 years) 5.50€. An adult single ticket is 6.50€ and for a child 4.50€. Dogs and cycles are charged 1€ each (2006).
Comments: A spoken commentary is given on the train journey (in French!).
Local Tourist Office: 7, avenue Mondenard, 47600 Nérac Telephone: 05 53 65 27 75 Fax: 05 53 65 97 48. E-mail: accueil@albret-tourisme.com website: www.albret-tourisme.com

Grotte Préhistorique de Rouffignac

Location: Rouffignac-St-Cernin-de-Reilhac, 36 km south-east of Périgueux.
Department: Dordogne (24).
Getting there: By road from Brive-la-Gaillarde take the RN89 and D704 to Rouffignac-St-Cernin-de-Reilhac.
Contact details: Grotte de Rouffignac, 24580 Rouffignac. Telephone: 05 53 05 41 71 Fax: 05 53 35 44 71. E-mail: grottederouffignac@wanadoo.fr
Website: www.grottederouffignac.fr
Operating dates: From mid-March to the end of June and 1st September to 1st November from 1000 to 1130 hours and 1400 to 1700 hours. In July and August the cave remains open an hour extra.
Tariff: An adult ticket is 6.10€ and for a child 3.80€ (2006).
Comments: In the interests of preserving the ancient cave paintings visitors are not permitted to walk on foot but must take an electric train, hence the railway interest. Visitors are advised to take warm clothing at any time of the year.
Local Tourist Office: place de la Mairie, 24580 Rouffignac-St-Cernin-de-Reilhac. Telephone: 05 53 05 39 03. E-mail: si.rouffignac@perigord.tm.fr

TER-SNCF – l'Autorail Espérance

Location: Sarlat-la-Canéda, 54 km north-east of Brive-la-Gaillarde.
Department: Dordogne (24).
Getting there: By SNCF train to Sarlat-la-Canéda. By road take the autoroute A20 and exit at Brive-la-Gaillarde and take the D60 to Sarlat-la-Canéda.
Route: Sarlat-la-Canéda to Bergerac (69 km).
Journey time: 1 hour 10 minutes.
Gauge and rolling stock: Standard; modern autorail.
Contact details: TER-SNCF, c/o Office de Tourisme, 97 rue Neuve d'Argenson 24100 Bergerac. Telephone: 05 53 57 03 11 or from the end of June: 05 53 59 55 39.
Website: www.trainstouristiques-ter.com/autorail.htm
Operating dates: From the beginning of July to the end of August excluding weekends and public holidays.
Tariff: An adult return is 12€ and for a child (4-12 years) is 6€ (2005).
Comments: In addition to the rail journey itself, passengers are given the opportunity to taste (*dégustation*) the flavours of the region.
Local Tourist Office: Ancien Evêché, rue Tourny, BP 114, 24203 Sarlat. Telephone: 05 53 31 45 45 Fax: 05 53 59 19 44. E-mail: info@ot-sarlat-perigord.fr website: www.ot-sarlat-perigord.fr

Auvergne

The Auvergne is in the centre of France and borders the French regions of Centre to the north-west, Bourgogne to the north-east, Limousin to the west, Rhone-Alpes to the east, Languedoc-Roussillon and Midi-Pyrénées to the south. It comprises the departments of Allier (03), Cantal (15), Haute-Loire (43) and Puy-de-Dome (63). The regional capital is Clermont Ferrand and other important cities are Le Puy, Aurillac, and Vichy. This region has four heritage/tourist railways, two TER-SNCF tourist railways, one place with preserved traction, one museum and two vélorail locations.

Railways

Chemin de Fer de Haut Forez (CFHF)

Member: FACS-UNECTO
Location: Sembadel, 39 km north of Le Puy-en-Velay.
Department: Haute-Loire (43).
Getting there: By road from Lyon (100 km) and St Etienne (40 km) on the autoroutes A47 and A72 and from Andrézieux on the D498.
Route: Sembadel to Estavireilles (36 km).
Journey time: 1 hour 25 minutes
Gauge and type of traction: Standard; autorail, diesel.
Rolling stock: Picasso autorail X 4001 and autorail carriage XR 8246, also two draisines (DU 50 and DU 65) various locotracteurs and a rail crane (grue).
Contact details: Chemin de Fer de Haut Forez, Gare d'Estivareilles 42380, Estivareilles. Telephone: 04 77 50 82 03 or 06 89 86 48 84 Fax: 04 77 50 77 23. E-mail: cfhf@wanadoo.fr or chanabol.jean-jacques@wanadoo.fr
Website: www.trains-fr.org/unecto/haut-forez
Operating dates: Because this was a new venture in 2005 it only operated for a half a season. However, in 2006 it is likely to operate from April to the end of October, but check first. In 2005, it ran services from 1st July to 8th July and 1st September to 11th September on Sundays, Tuesdays and Thursdays. From 9th July to 30th August trains ran every day except on Saturdays and Mondays. Trains leave Estavireilles at 1000, 1430 and 1800 hours and Sembadel at 1605 hours and Craponne at 1105, 1630 and 1905 hours. Some services are operated as Santa Specials in the week before Christmas and also later in the winter months, snow permitting!
Tariff: An adult return ticket is 12€ and for a child (4-12 years) 9€; reduced fares for shorter journeys (2005).
History: The line was closed to passengers in the 1970s and to goods traffic in the 1980s. However, given local enthusiasm to keep the line open it was purchased in 2001 and began tourist operations in July 2005.
Comments: The railway shares with the AGRIVAP the Sembadel railway station albeit this service stops short of the platform and passengers have to alight on to some former railway sleepers and walk along the track bed; it is not easy for people with mobility difficulties. Nonetheless a beautiful railway line on which to travel.

Local Tourist Office: place de la Mairie, 43160 La Chaise-Dieu. Telephone: 04 71 00 01 16 Fax: 04 71 00 03 45. E-mail: otcasadei@aol.com

Picasso autorail No. X 4001 *en route* to Sembadel.   *Author*

Voies Ferrées du Velay (VFV)

Locotracteur with restored teak carriages.   *Voies Ferrées du Velay*

Member: FACS-UNECTO
Location: Dunières, 26 km south of St Etienne.
Department: Haute-Loire (43) part of the railway also operates in the Rhône-Alpes region.
Getting there: By road take the autoroutes A6, A7 and the A47 with the latter eventually feeding into the RN88, exit at 31 on to the D500 and then take the D23 to Dunières.
Route: Dunières to St Agrève (33 km).
Journey time: 1 hour 15 minutes (Dunières to Tence) and 35 minutes (Tence to St Agrève).
Gauge and type of traction: Metre; steam, autorail and diesel.
Rolling stock: A Billard autorail No. 222 (re-entered service on the line in 1997) and a 1937 Billard autorail type A80D No. 313 with a De Dion-Bouton No. 1 non-powered carriage (remorque) two locotracteurs which are both 030s (180 ch) No. 62 of 1946 and No. 70 of 1948. FACS-UNECTO is storing a 1906 020+020 T Blanc-Misseron steam locomotive No. 101 with VFV at St Agrève with a view to its restoration when funds become available.
Contact details: Voies Ferrées du Velay, Gare de Dunières Vallée, 22 rue de la Croix, 43220 Dunières. Telephone: 04 71 61 94 44 Fax: 04 71 61 94 44. E-mail: message@asso-vfv.net
Website: www.asso-vfv.net
Operating dates: From June to September; in high season (mid-July to end of August) it operates on Saturdays, Sundays, Tuesdays and Thursdays in the mornings and afternoons; in low season on Sundays only both in the morning and the afternoon. It is important to check beforehand the routes and times.

Tariff: Fares vary according to distance travelled. As an example, an adult return ticket from Dunières to St Agrève would be 20€ and for a child (4-12 years) 14€. Special rates for groups (2006).

History: The railway line was originally opened to traffic in 1901 as part of the Vivarais network (*see separate CFTM entry under the Rhône-Alpes region*) but was closed to commercial traffic in 1968. Fortunately, the local communes, through whose area the railway travelled, saw the potential benefits of converting the line for tourist purposes. Consequently, an inter-commune syndicate was formed to operate the service.

Comments: The trains travel through outstandingly beautiful countryside in the high Ardèche. There is a special service on Thursdays in high season from St Agrève to Le Chambon-sur-Lignon where a colourful local market is held.

Local Tourist Office: Grand'Rue, 07320 St Agrève. Telephone: 04 75 30 15 06 Fax: 04 75 30 60 93. E-mail: ot-stagr@inforoutes-ardeche.fr or st-agreve@fnotsi.net website: www.saintagreve.com also Office de Tourisme de Tence, 43190 Tence. Telephone: 04 71 59 81 99.

Chemin de Fer de la Haute-Auvergne (CFHA) also known as the Gentiane Express

Autorail No. X 2403 on the Gentiane Express line near the village of Salsignac.   *Author*

Member: FACS-UNECTO
Location: Bort-les-Orgues, 77 km south-west of Clermont Ferrand.
Department: Cantal (15).
Getting there: The nearest SNCF station is at Bort-les-Orgues but services are limited. By road take the autoroutes A10 and A71 and exit at 15 (Clermont Ferrand) then the D216 and D922 to Bort-les-Orgues.
Route: Bort-les-Orgues to Riom-ès-Montagnes to Lugarde-Marchastel (39 km).
Gauge and type of traction: Standard; autorail.
Rolling stock: An autorail No. X 2403, one of 79 examples built in France between 1951 and 1953, which was retired from active SNCF service in 1989. It is owned by Monsieur Jean-Marie Henry and is on loan to CFHA. Also retained

is autorail remorque No. XR 7415 which is also on loan from Monsieur Henry. There are also two RGP autorails Nos. X 2725 and X 2726 both fitted with powerful V12 engines delivering 825 hp. There are also two draisines - DU 65 No. M 007 and a Billard type 2M No. 004. Finally, to complete the collection, there is autorail No. X 3900 which is in need of some restoration before it will be permitted to travel on the line.

Contact details: Chemin de Fer de la Haute-Auvergne, BP17, 15190 Condat, also by the Tourist Office at Bort-les-Orgues and the Tourist Office at Riom-ès-Montagnes. Telephones: 05 55 96 02 49 (Bort-les-Orgues) or 04 71 78 07 37 (Riom-ès-Montagnes) Fax: 04 71 78 16 87. E-mail: infocfha@gentiane-express-cfha.com

Website: http://traincezallier.free.fr/

Operating dates: From April to September on Sunday afternoons (out at 1330 and back in by 1920 hours) and in July and August on Tuesdays, Wednesdays, Thursdays, Fridays and Saturdays leaving Bort-les-Orgues at 0930 and returning by 1740 hours.

Tariff: An adult return ticket is 16€ and for a child (4-12 years) 13€. Reductions for families, groups and shorter journeys (2005).

History: The original SNCF line was closed to all traffic in 1991 but two years later a group of enthusiasts came together to save the line and thus was born l'association des Chemins de Fer de la Haute Auvergne. In 1997, tourist services began between Riom-ès-Montagnes and Lugarde followed five years later with the opening of the section between Bort-les-Orgues and Riom-ès-Montagnes.

Comments: This is probably one the best ways in which to view this beautiful part of the Auvergne between Sancy and Puy Mary. There are some outstanding examples of French railway architecture (*ouvrages d'art*) on the route including the viaducts of Salsignac, Barajol, Chassagny and Lugarde. The line climbs from an altitude of 438 metres at Bort-les-Orgues to 1,012 metres at Lugarde.

Local Tourist Office: place Marmontel, 19110 Bort-les-Orgues. Telephone: 05 55 96 02 49 Fax: 05 55 96 90 79. E-mail: contact@bort-artense.com website: www.bort-artense.com

Chemin de Fer du Livradois-Forez also known as AGRIVAP

Member: FACS-UNECTO
Location: Ambert, 83 km south-east of Clermont Ferrand.
Department: Puy de Dome (63).
Getting there: By road take the autoroutes A1, A10 and A71 then the D906 and D106 to Ambert.
Route: Sembadel – La Chaise Dieu - Ambert – Courpière (85 km).
Journey time: Varies according to the route taken. It is worth noting that this is the longest railway line dedicated to tourism in France.
Gauge and type of traction: Standard; steam, autorail and diesel.
Rolling stock: Corpet Louvet steam locomotive 030 T No. 8 *Ilena* on loan from Comité Cannes Grasse (CCG) (*see page 162*), diesel locomotive No. CC 65005,

Panoramique autorail No. X 4208 at Ambert depot.   *Author*

Picasso autorails Nos. X 3867 and X 3934 and two autorail Panoramiques Nos. X 4208 (in operating condition) and X 4203 (awaiting restoration) constructed by Renault in 1959. A selection of well-restored carriages and wagons.

Contact details: Musée Agrivap, rue l'Industrie 63600 Ambert and also at La Gare, 63600 Ambert (President - Monsieur Marc Péytavy). Telephone: 04 73 82 43 88 Fax: 04 73 82 17 14. E-mail: agrivap@wanadoo.fr

Website: www.agrivap.com

Operating dates: Operates from 1st May to 1st November. Various services run over different sections of the line. In July and August on Saturdays the steam-hauled train operates between Ambert and Olliergues. On other days one of the Picasso autorails or the Panoramique runs between Coupière and Sembadel. For precise dates and times first check by telephone (English is spoken - ask for Bridget), visit the website or call at the local tourist office.

Tariff: Varies according to journey taken.

History: The line traces its history back to 1864 when construction first began, it taking over 38 years to complete, opening in stages from Vichy to Courty in 1881, to Giroux in 1882, to Ambert in 1885, to Arlanc in 1893 and to Darsac in 1902. The line was used for the carriage of passengers, agricultural products, livestock and wood. Wood was, and to a certain extent still is, an important product of this region. Indeed, in 1920 the station at Ste Alyre on this line was the second most active in the whole of France for the movement of cut wood. In 1920 the line became part of the PLM (Paris-Lyon-Méditerranée) network and in 1938 it, in turn, was nationalised to become part of the then new SNCF company. Closure of part of the line followed 43 years later and the track bed fell into disuse with nature quickly taking over. The association AGRIVAP was created in 1979 to preserve agricultural machinery including a steam engine used at a sawmill to drive cutting implements. In 1981 AGRIVAP installed its headquarters in a former sawmill which is located to the south end of the station in Ambert. Now a museum it is well worth combining a visit to it with a trip on an autorail or a steam train. In 1986 SNCF finally closed the section of line between Arlanc and Coupière. It was in the same year that AGRIVAP purchased its first Panoramique autorail which it proceeded to restore and repaint. Flushed with this success AGRIVAP decided in 1987 to recover the line between Arlanc and Sembadel in what was named 'Operation Attila' when up to 70 volunteers cleared the line of dense weeds and fast-growing shrubs. Since then AGRIVAP has gone from strength to strength. In 1992, 21 communes through whose area the line travelled came together to form an association – SIVU. Subsequently AGRIVAP was awarded a contract by SIVU to utilise the line for the carriage of merchandise by rail and to operate a tourist train service. The main source of income today is from freight (recycled paper) carried between Giroux and Courpière where there is a large cardboard box factory and recycling station. During the course of the restoration of the line AGRIVAP have replaced 22,000 sleepers, made level 60 km of track and built 13 of the 31 level crossings. Responsibility for the line is split, with SNCF still retaining ownership of the track between Coupière and Arlanc (54 km) with the remaining section between Arlanc and Sembadel being under the direction of SIVU. Incidentally this section is the steepest part of the line with the track bed rising 494 metres over a distance of 31 km.

Comments: This is a magnificent long-distance tourist railway through outstandingly attractive countryside in the Regional Nature Park of Livradois-Forez. AGRIVAP also periodically operates excursions from Ambert on to RFF (SNCF) lines to locations elsewhere in France. This is a 'must-do' visit.
Local Tourist Office: 4, place de Hôtel de Ville, 63600 Ambert.
Telephone: 04 73 82 61 90 Fax: 04 73 82 48 36.
E-mail: ambert.tourisme@wanadoo.fr

TER-SNCF - Le Train Gorges d'Allier

Location: Langeac, 54 km east of St Flour and 97 km south of Clermont Ferrand.
Department: Haute-Loire (43).
Getting there: Regular TER-SNCF services operate to Langeac and Langogne on the Clermont Ferrand – Nîmes route. By road take the autoroute A75 and exit at 20 then take the RN102, D56 and D585 to Langeac.
Route: Langeac to Langogne in the Department of Lozère (67 km).
Journey time: 1 hour 43 minutes on the Train Touristique and 1 hour 5 minutes on the regular SNCF service.
Gauge and type of traction: Standard; electric heritage locomotives and modern autorail.
Rolling stock: Electric locomotives Nos. BB 67400 or BB 66400 with Rames Réversibles Régionales (RRR) coaches (which with two in high season carry 360 passengers and one in low season with half that number).
Contact details: Boutique Train Touristique, BP27, 43300 Langeac.
Telephone: 04 71 77 70 17 or by the website.
Website: www.trainstouristiques-ter.com/auvergne.htm or alternatively www.auvergnevacances.com

Operating dates: From May to September on selected days, most being in the months of July and August. For precise information, consult the *Calendrier des circulations* on the website or contact the tourist office (2005).

Tariff: The *Train liberté* is the standard service with either the outward or the inward journey being made on the *Train Touristique* (with commentary in French) and the other leg on a regular TER-SNCF service. For this service an adult return is 19€ and for children (4-12 years) 8€. There are reductions for groups and the handicapped. There are also other tours (*Train Coup de Coeur*) which include commentary, lunch and a local visit which for adults costs 42€ and children 27€ (2005).

History: In the mid-19th century, studies were made to explore the feasibility of building this line over particularly difficult terrain. Later, it was agreed and 6,000 men were involved in its construction, building 50 tunnels and 16 viaducts. The single-track line was opened in 1870 by the then Compagnie du PLM.

Comments: This line is described by an enthusiastic SNCF employee as 'a veritable museum of architecture under the open sky' and there is no doubt of that with over 170 bridges, viaducts and tunnels. The most notable structure is the Viaduc de Chapeauroux (22 km north of Langogne) with its 28 twelve metre-wide arches. A second interesting structure is the *grande galerie voutée* – an extended cover over the track to protect the line from snow blockages, a not infrequent event in the Auvergne winters. Also on this route from Clermont Ferrand to Nîmes is the Le Cévenole line from Alès in the Department of Gard (30) to La Bastide Puylaurent, 23 km south of Langogne (*see entry under Languedoc-et-Roussillon region*).

Local Tourist Office: place A. Briand, 43300 Langeac. Telephone: 04 71 77 05 41 Fax: 04 71 77 19 93. E-mail: ot@langeac@haut-allier.com website: www.langeac.com or 15, boulevard des Capucins, 48300 Langogne. Telephone: 04 66 69 01 38 Fax: 04 66 69 16 79. E-mail: langogne@langogne.com website: www.langogne.com

TER-SNCF – Le Cantal Garabit

Location: Aurillac, 174 km south-west of Clermont Ferrand.

Department: Cantal (15).

Getting there: By road take the autoroute A75 and exit at 28 on to RN9 to St Flour. Garabit is 15 km south of St Flour.

Route: Aurillac to Garabit (85 km each way).

Journey time: 2 hours 14 minutes each way.

Gauge and type of traction: Standard; modern autorail.

Contact details: Information can be obtained from the tourist offices at Aurillac or St Flour (Telephone: 04 71 60 22 50).

Website: www.trainstouristiques-ter.com/garabit.htm

Operating dates: On certain Tuesdays and Thursdays only in July and August leaving Aurillac at 0922 and arriving at Garabit at 1136 hours; and, leaving Garabit at 1724 and arriving back at Aurillac at 1939 hours. It is possible to join and leave the train at later stages of the journey (2005).

The Garabit viaduct built by Gustave Eiffel. *Author*

Tariff: For departures from Aurillac an adult return is 40.60€ and for a child (5-15 years) 22.60€, and from Neussargues an adult return is 34.60€ and for a child is 19.60€ and from St Flour an adult return is 28.60€ and and for a child 16.60€ (2005). *Comments:* This railway is located in the Massif Central which, with the Alps and the Pyrénées, is one of the three highest mountain ranges in France. In every direction, the scenery is outstanding with much of it being the product of long-extinct volcanic activity. This is a 'must-do' trip if only to see and appreciate Eiffel's magnificent viaduct standing high above les Gorges de la Truyère. Incidentally, there is a rest area on the south bound carriageway of the A75 autoroute where there is an large exhibition about the viaduct and a superb viewing area from which, if you are lucky, you may see a train cross. The photograph *above* shows that the author was not so lucky that day!
Local Tourist Office: place du Square, 15000 Aurillac. Telephone: 04 71 48 46 58 Fax: 04 71 48 99 39. E-mail: courrier@iaurillac.com

Preserved Locomotives and other traction

Société Civile de Conservation de la 141 R 420 (SCC141 R 420)

Location: Durtol, 4 km to the north-west of the centre of Clermont Ferrand.
Department: Puy-de-Dome (63).
Getting there: By road take the autoroutes A10 and A71 and exit at 13 then follow the D447, N9 and D2 to Durtol.

Mikado No. 141 R 420 crosses the Rouzat viaduct with the Railway Touring Company's Mediterranean Steam Express excursion in 2005.   *Francois Cottebrune*

Gauge and type of traction: Standard; steam.
Rolling stock: Mikado No. 141 R 420.
Contact details: Société Civile de Conservation de la 141 R 240, BP 7, 63830 Durtol. Telephone: 04 73 30 10 05 who will be able to advise when and where this locomotive will be operating.
Website: None identified.
Comments: This Mikado, constructed by ALCO began its career at Mezidon in August 1946 and was retired at Sarreguemines in March 1975 having completed 1,075,275 kilometres fuelled by coal. It is one of twelve 141 Rs preserved and is approved for use on RFF (SNCF) tracks.
Local Tourist Office: place de la Victoire, 63000 Clermont Ferrand. Telephone: 04 73 98 65 00 Fax: 04 73 90 04 11. E-mail: tourisme@clermont-fd.com websites: www.clermont-fd.com or www.ot-clermont-ferrand.fr

Museum

Musée de la Mine (CATME)

Location: Noyant d'Allier, 57 km east of Montluçon.
Department: Allier (03).
Getting there: By road take autoroutes A10 and A71 and exit at 11 on to the N145, then the D945 and D18 to Noyant d'Allier.

Contact details: Musée de la Mine, CATME, 31, rue de la Mine, 03210 Noyant d'Allier. Telephone/Fax: 04 70 47 31 51 or telephone M. Daniel Fournier 04 70 43 62 51. E-mail: mailto:musee.mine.noyant@netcourrier.com
Website: http://musee.mine.noyant.site.voila.fr/
Opening dates: June and September on Sundays from 1430 to 1730 hours, and in July and August on Saturdays and Sundays from 1430 to 1730 hours.
Tariff: An adult ticket is 5€ and for a child (12-15 years) 2.50€. Under 12s go free (2005).
Comments: An interesting exhibition of the rail transport used in the old mines.
Local Tourist Office: 11, rue François Péron, BP 641, 03006 Moulins. Telephone: 04 70 44 14 14 Fax: 04 70 34 00 21. E-mail: O.T.Moulins@wanadoo.fr

Vélorails

Vélorails de Cezallier

Location: Allanche, 121 km south of Clermont Ferrand.
Department: Cantal (15).
Getting there: By road take the autoroutes A10, A71 and A75 and exit at 23 on to the RN9 then follow the RN122, D21 and D9 to Allanche.
Route: Allanche – Lugarde – Neussargues (31 km).
Gauge: Standard.
Contact details: Vélorails de Cezallier, Office de Tourisme, 30, Grand'Rue de l'abbé de Pradt, 15160 Allanche. Telephone: 04 71 20 49 89 Fax: 04 71 20 48 43. E-mail: ot-allanche@wanadoo.fr
Website: www.cezallier.org
Operating dates: Contact the Tourist Office to make a reservation.
Comments: Is a member of the Fédération de Vélorails de France whose website is: www.velorailsdefrance.com/velorail/index.php?page=adh#liens
Local Tourist Office: as above.

Vélorail de Pradelles Landos

Location: Pradelles, 39 km south of le Puy-en-Velay.
Department: Haute Loire (43).
Getting there: By road take the autoroutes A10, A71 and A75 and exit at 20 on to the RN102 and then follow the RN88 to Pradelles.
Route: Pradelles (11 km).
Gauge: Standard.
Contact details: Vélorail de Pradelles Landos, Office de Tourisme, 43420 Pradelles. Telephone: 04 71 00 82 65 Fax: 04 71 00 82 65. E-mail: ot.pradelles@haut-allier.com
Operating dates and Tariff: For reservations contact the Tourist Office.
Local Tourist Office: as above.

Basse-Normandie (Lower Normandy)

Basse-Normandie is in the north-west of France and borders the regions of Bretagne to the west, Haut-Normandie to the east, Pays-de-Loire to the south and Centre to the south-east. It comprises the departments of Calvados (14), Manche (50) and Orne (61). The regional capital is Caen and other important cities are St Lô and Alençon. This region has one active tourist railway, one TER-SNCF tourist railway, one discontinued railway and one vélorail service. Also of note is PontauRail (*see page 83*) which runs to Pont de Normandie, near Honfleur, Basse-Normandie.

Railways

**Train touristique du Côtentin also known as
l'Association Tourisme et Chemin de Fer de la Manche (ATCM)**

Member: FACS-UNECTO
Location: Carteret, 36 km south of Cherbourg.
Department: Manche (50).
Getting there: SNCF stations are at Carentan, Valognes or Cherbourg then by local bus. By road take the autoroute A13 then the RN13 to Carteret.
Route: Carteret – Portbail (10 km).
Journey time: 35 minutes.
Gauge and type of traction: Standard; diesel.
Rolling stock: Diesel locomotive No. BB 63069 *La Contentine*, a Moyse 33 ton locotracteur, a Moyse 12 ton locotracteur, two draisines, various carriages and wagons.
Contact details: Association Tourisme et Chemin de Fer de la Manche, Clos St Jean, 50270 St Jean-la-Rivière (Monsieur Jacques Vermont - President du Train Touristique du Côtentin). Telephone: 02 33 04 70 08.
E-mail: ttcontentin@wanadoo.fr
Website: http://ttcotentin.monsite.wanadoo.fr
Operating dates: Sunday afternoons only from the end of June to early September and also Tuesday and Thursday mornings for a local market.
Tariff: An adult return ticket is 6€ and for a child (4-12 years) 4€ (2005).
History: The Association Tourisme et Chemins de fer de la Manche (ATCM) is a heritage railway organization and like many other such railways in France enjoys charitable status. ATCM originally started life out as l'Association pour la Sauvegarde du Chemin de fer Carentan-Carteret (ASCCC) in 1982. The objectives of the association were to safeguard the railway heritage of the Manche department by addressing tourist, cultural, historic, sporting and commercial and industrial issues. From the end of 1988 to June 1994 the Train Touristique de Cotentin operated a rail service between Carentan and Baupte, a distance of 10 kilometres, using 1950s autorails Nos. X 3825 (later sold to Quercyrail in 1998) and X 2426. In June 1990 the line was opened between Carteret and Portbail using a 1930s train comprising three Bruhat carriages hauled by BB 63069. This section of line is the one that continues to operate today.
Comments: Special theme events are also run in July and August.

No. BB 63069 *La Contentine* at Carteret station.   *Train Touristique du Côtentin*

Local Tourist Office: 26 rue Philippe Lebel, BP 3, 50580 Portbail. Telephone: 02 33 04 03 07 Fax: 02 33 04 94 66. E-mail: tourisme.portbail@wanadoo.fr website: www.portbail.org

TER-SNCF – La Desserte de la Côte Fleurie

Location: Trouville-sur-Mer - Deauville, 91 km west of Rouen.
Department: Calvados (14).
Getting there: There is an SNCF station at Trouville-Deauville. By road take autoroutes A13 and A132 and then follow the RN177 to Trouville-Deauville.
Route: Trouville/Deauville-Dives/Cabourg (23 km).
Gauge and type of traction: Standard; modern autorail.
Contact details: The tourist office at Trouville, details below.
Website: www.trainstouristiques-ter.com/cote_fleurie.htm
Operating dates: La Desserte de la Côte Fleurie operates every weekend throughout the year and every day in summer.
Tariff: Normal fares apply but reductions of 50% for the card holder and one accompanying passenger can be had by purchasing an annual *Carte Sillage Loisirs* for just 7€. Third and subsequent passengers travel for 0.15€ each, making this card ideal for family travel (2006).
Local Tourist Office: 32, quai Fernand Moureaux, 14360 Trouville. Telephone: 02 31 14 60 70 Fax: 02 31 14 60 71. E-mail: o.t.trouville@wanadoo.fr website: www.trouvillesurmer.org

Discontinued Railway

Chemin de Fer Touristique de Sélune
  later known as Chemin de Fer du Mont des Avaloirs

Location: St Hilaire-du-Harcouet and later Alençon.
Departments: Manche (50) and later Orne (61).
Comments: This railway ran an autorail service on the St Hilaire-du-Harcouet to Pontaubault line (22 km), and was operated by the Association Chemin de Fer Touristiques de l'Ouest (ACTO) from 1985 to 1990. This latter association was

No. D1 arriving at Gaston station.   *Les Vélorails de Suisse Normande*

ousted in 1990 by another association which owned a steam locomotive. As a consequence ACTO moved to Alençon and operated a tourist service between Alençon and Pré-en-Pail in the department of Mayenne. Autorails type X 2400 and Picasso X 3800 were used. In 1996, the railway was closed and the rolling stock sold. The association that had 'moved in' collapsed in 1992! (Source: FACS-UNECTO.)

Vélorail

Les Vélorails de Suisse Normande also known as Amicale pour la mise en valeur de Caen-Flers (ACF)

Member: FACS-UNECTO
Location: Berjou, 60 km south of Caen.
Department: Orne (61).
Getting there: By road take autoroute A13 and exit at 33 and then follow the RN513 and D562 to Berjou.
Route: Pont Erambourg to Berjou (5 km).
Gauge: Standard.
Contact details: Les Vélorails de Suisse Normande, La Gare de Pont Erambourg, 61790 St Pierre du Regard. Telephone: 02 31 69 39 30 or 06 16 54 23 60 Fax: 02 33 35 82 12. E-mail: contact@rails-suissenormande.fr
Website: http://www.rails-suissenormande.fr/
Operating dates: From 1st April to 1st November by making a reservation through the local tourist office.
Tariff: The hire fee is 15€ for a vélorail for about 1½ hours. A deposit of 20€ is required before departure. There is a reduced tariff for groups taking a minimum of four vélorails (2006).
Comments: A Billard draisine - *Cyclops* - has been renovated to working order and a 1955 Moyse 36 TDE locotracteur is also retained by the association.
Local Tourist Office: Hôtel d'Escoville, place St Pierre, 14000 Caen. Telephone: 3265 and say 'Caen' Fax: 02 31 27 14 18. E-mail: tourisminfo@ville-caen.fr

Bourgogne (Burgundy)

Bourgogne is to the right of the centre in France and borders the regions of Champagne-Ardenne in the north, Franche-Comté in the east, Rhône-Alpes to the south-east, Auvergne to the south-west and Centre to the west. It comprises the departments of Côte d'Or (21), Nièvre (58), Saône-et-Loire (71) and Yonne (89). The regional capital is Dijon and other cities are Mâcon, Auxerre and Nevers. This region has five active heritage/tourist railways, one TER-SNCF tourist railway, one railway where operations have been suspended, two locations where there is preserved traction, two museums and two vélorail services.

Railways

Chemin de fer de la Vallée de l'Ouche (CFVO)

Member: FACS-UNECTO
Location: Bligny-sur-Ouche, 52 km south-west of Dijon and 20 km north-west of Beaune.
Department: Côte d'Or (21).
Getting there: The nearest main SNCF stations are at Dijon and Beaune. By road take the autoroute A6 exit at Beaune and then follow the D970 and D33 to Bligny-sur-Ouche.
Route: Bligny-sur-Ouche - Pont d'Ouche (6.8 km).
Journey time: One hour.
Gauge and type of traction: 600 mm; steam and diesel.
Rolling stock: Steam traction includes a 020 Decauville 1947 built on a Henschel design, a 040 KD11 Franco-Belge, a 030 T Hainaut, a 020 vertical boiler built on the design of Chaloner, six diesel locotracteurs and various carriages and wagons.
Contact details: Chemin de Fer de la Vallée de l'Ouche, avenue de la Gare, 21360 Bligny-sur-Ouche. Telephone: 03 80 20 16 65 or 06 30 01 48 29 Fax: 03 80 20 17 92. E-mail: info@lepetittraindebligny.com
Website: www.lepetittraindebligny.com
Operating dates: From 1st May to 30th September on Sundays and public holidays with departures of steam driven trains at 1500 and 1630 hours. From 1st July to 31st August there are services every day with departures of diesel driven trains at 1530 and 1700 hours.
Tariff: An adult ticket is 7€ and for a child (2-10 years) 5€ (2005).
History: One of the earliest railway lines established in France in 1837 for the movement of coal extracted from the mines at d'Epinac. It was abandoned in the 1880s and later taken over by the PLM railway company in 1905 and the line extended to Dijon. It was finally closed in 1968. It was acquired by the local authority for Canton de Bligny-sur-Ouche and began life as a tourist line in 1978.
Comments: This railway is situated in an attractive area renowned for its high quality wine production - burgundy.
Local Tourist Office: 21, place de l'Hôtel de Ville, 21360 Bligny-sur-Ouche. Telephone: 03 80 20 16 51 Fax: 03 80 20 17 90. E-mail: ot.blignysurouche@wanadoo.fr and website: www.cc-cantondeblignysurouche.fr

Train Touristique des Lavières (TTL)

Location: Is-sur-Tille, 20 km north of Dijon.
Department: Côte d'Or (21).
Getting there: The nearest main SNCF station is at Dijon and there is a local station at Is-sur-Tille. By road take the D3 north to Is-sur-Tille.
Route: The circuit is in a pine forest at Is-sur-Tille (1.4 km).
Journey time: 15 minutes.
Gauge and type of traction: 500 mm; diesel.
Rolling stock: A locotracteur named *Pétolat* classed as a *Monument Historique*.
Contact details: Train Touristique des Lavières, 6 rue des Capucins, 21120 Is-sur-Tille. Telephone: 03 80 95 36 36.
Website: www.Côtedor-tourisme.com/index and on the page's search engine type <train touristique>
Operating dates: From mid-June to mid-September on Sundays from 1500 to 1900 hours and on the last Saturday in August at 2000 hours.
Tariff: An adult ticket is 1.50€ and for a child (less than 15 years) is 1€. Adults can purchase a carnet of 10 tickets for 12€ and under-15s for 7€ (2006).
Local Tourist Office: 1, rue du Général Charbonnel, 21120 Is-sur-Tille.
Telephone: 03 80 95 24 03 Fax: 03 80 95 28 08.
E-mail: ot.paysdestroisrivieres@wanadoo.fr website: www.is-sur-tille.com

Chemin de Fer des Combes (CFC)

Location: Parc des Combes at Le Creusot, 92 km south-west of Dijon and 40 km west of Chalon-sur-Saône.
Department: Saône-et-Loire (71).
Getting there: The nearest SNCF station is the TGV station at Le Creusot-Montchanin. By road take the autoroute A6 and exit at 26 (Chalon-sur-Saône) and then follow the RN80 to Le Creusot. Parc des Combes is on the north-west side of the town.
Route: Le Creusot - Les Combes (5.2 km).
Journey time: 45 minutes.
Gauge and type of traction: 600 mm; steam, diesel.
Rolling stock: A 040 DFB steam locomotive, six diesel locotracteurs and a selection of 15 coaches. The magnificent 1925 Schneider-built 241 P17 (Mountain) locomotive is also on display.
Contact details: Chemin de Fer des Combes, rue des Pyrénées, 71200 Le Creusot. Telephone: 03 85 55 26 23 Fax: 03 85 55 92 14. E-mail: info@parcdescombes
Website: www.parcdescombes.com
Operating dates: The theme park is open from the first weekend in March to the beginning of November at weekends and for public holidays and school holidays. Opening hours are from 1400 to 1900 hours but opening earlier in July and August at 1100 hours. Trains, however, only run from the end of April to the beginning of November but check first especially outside the main July/August holiday season. Trains depart at 1400, 1500, 1600 and 1700 hours.

An 040 DFB steam locomotive with carriage.   *Parc des Combes*

Tariff: A day park pass for a number of attractions including the train journey for an adult is 15€, for a junior (up to 16 years and taller than 1.25 m) 12€ and for a child under 1.25 m tall 8€. A ticket for the train only for an adult is 6€ and for a child 4€ (2006).

History: At the beginning of the 20th century the line was built to transport metal products from the Schneider factories – nearly 500 tonnes of scoria were moved every day. The line was taken out of service in the 1950s. In 1990 it was re-opened as a tourist line and today is very popular with visitors; for example, in a year as many as 33,000 passengers are carried.

Comments: A visit to the Parc des Combes can and should easily consume a full day. There is much to see and do for the whole family and not just for the railway enthusiasts. It is possible to enjoy a high quality meal on the train.

Local Tourist Office: Château de la Verrerie, 71200 Le Creusot. Telephone: 03 85 55 02 46 Fax: 03 85 80 11 03. E-mail: otsi.le.creusot@wanadoo.fr website: www.le-creusot.fr

Train Touristique du Pays de Puisaye-Forterre also known as Association des Autorails Touristiques de l'Yonne (AATY)

Member: FACS-UNECTO
Location: Villiers St Benoît, 25 km west of Auxerre.
Department: Yonne (89).
Getting there: By SNCF to Montargis, Gien, Briare or Cosne (Bourbonnais line) or Laroche-Migennes (Impériale line) or Auxerre stations. By road take the autoroute A6 to Auxerre then follow the D84, D158 and D965 to Villiers-St Benoît.
Route: Villiers-St Benoît to Etang-de-Moutiers via Toucy-Ville (27 km).
Journey time: 1 hour 40 minutes.

Picasso autorail No. X 3814 *Le Transpoyaudin.*
Joël Michel/Chemin de fer touristique du Pays de Puisaye-Forterre

Gauge and type of traction: Standard; autorail, diesel.
Rolling stock: Autorail Picasso No. X 3814, an RGP2 (Rame Grand Parcours) No. X 2716 renovated in 2000 and a second Picasso No. X 3871 currently out of service. There is also a 1930 Billard draisine (ex-CFTA-Clamacy) and a 1914 Crochat locotracteur (ex-ALVF) both in operational order.
Contact details: Train Touristique du Pays de Puisaye-Forterre, avenue de la Gare 89130 Toucy. Telephone: 03 86 44 05 58. E-mail: aaty@wanadoo.fr
Website: http://perso.wanadoo.fr/aaty/
Operating dates: From April to end of September with Sunday services in April and daily services thereafter.
Tariff: An adult return ticket is from 5.50€ to 9€ and for a child (5-14 years) is from 3.50€ to 5.60€ according to the distance travelled (2005).
History: The line was originally constructed between 1880 and 1885 by the PLM company. It was integrated into the south-east network of the newly formed SNCF in 1938 and at that time the line stopped carrying passengers. All commercial traffic was finally stopped on the line in 1988. The association (AATY) was created in 1985 when it acquired its first Picasso autorail and began its first tourist train service in 1987 with the approval of SNCF. Subsequent recovery of the track bed from the grip of nature by local enthusiastic volunteers now means that 27 km is available and a further extension to St Saveur may be possible in due course.
Comments: Trains operate all year round for special group bookings. The train is known locally as the *Le Transpoyaudin*. The railway also operates a vélorail facility (*see later entry*). Château Saint-Fargeau with its collection of heritage locomotives is nearby.
Local Tourist Office: 1, place de la République, 89130 Toucy. Telephone: 03 86 44 15 66 Fax: 03 86 44 15 66. E-mail: ot.toucy@wanadoo.fr

Association du Train Petite Vitesse de Massangis (ATPVM)

Location: Massangis, 48 km south-east of Auxerre.
Department: Yonne (89).
Getting there: By road take the autoroute A6 and exit at Nitry and follow the D312 to Massingis.
Route: Massingis to Civry (2.5 km)
Journey time: 50 minutes round trip.
Gauge and type of traction: 600 mm; diesel.
Rolling stock: A 1910 Campagne locotracteur with a two-cylinder Ceres diesel engine, a 1950 Calc JW15 locotracteur also with a two-cylinder Ceres diesel engine, and a 1953 Deutz FILO20 locotracteur with a 9 hp mono-cylinder diesel engine. The association has built four of its own covered carriages each capable of carrying 12 passengers.
Contact details: ATPVM, le p'tit train de l'Yonne, Gare de Massangis, 89440 Massangis (President – Monsieur Yves Machebouef).
Website: http://massangis.com
Operating dates: From mid-May to the end of August with services on Sundays with some extra days in July and August, from 1430 to 1730 hours with trains leaving every half hour. There is also a Père Noel (Santa Special) service on the Saturday immediately before Christmas.
Tariff: An adult ticket is 4.50€ and for a child (4-12 years) 3€ (2005).

Deutz No. 2 of 1953. *Pascal Fayard*

History: This metre gauge line started life in 1887 and was utilised for the transport of passengers and goods in the form of local stone. Incidentally, it was stone from Massangis that was used for the 'feet' in the construction of the Eiffel Tower in Paris. The line was closed in 1951, yet another casualty of the growth in the use of automobiles.

Comments: The railway highlights an interesting fact about the running of such operations in France; for every hour's train journey, six hours of labour in preparation, driving, repair, track maintenance and other support work is required. A passing point has been installed on this railway allowing for two train operations. A journey on this railway makes for a pleasant tour down the Serein valley.

Local Tourist Office: 1-2, quai de la République, 89000 Auxerre. Telephone: 03 86 52 06 19 Fax: 03 86 51 23 27. E-mail: info@ot-auxerre.fr

TER-SNCF – Le Vézelay

Location: Sens, 132 km south-west of Paris.

Department: Yonne (89).

Getting there: It is possible to take a train from Paris to Sens (1 hour 5 minutes). By road take the autoroutes A6, A5 and A19 direct to Sens.

Route: Sens to Avallon (138 km).

Journey time: 2 hours 10 minutes one way.

Gauge and type of traction: Standard; modern autorail.

Contact details: Through the local tourist office.

Website: www.trainstouristiques-ter.com/vezelay.htm

Operating dates: In July and August Le Vézelay departs at 1836 hours from Sens on Fridays and returns from Avallon at 1823 hours on Sundays (2005).

Tariff: The normal TER-SNCF fare structure applies.

Local Tourist Offices: place Jean Jaurès, 89100 Sens. Telephone: 03 86 65 19 49 Fax: 03 86 64 24 18. E-mail: OTSI.SENS@wanadoo.fr or 6 rue Bocquillot, 89200 Avallon. Telephone: 03 86 34 14 19 Fax: 03 86 34 28 29. E-mail: avallon.otsi@wanadoo.fr

Railway Operations Temporarily Suspended

Chemin de Fer de la Cote d'Or (ACFCO) running on the lines of the former and now defunct Petit Train de la Côte d'Or (APTCO)

Location: Plombières-Dijon, 9 km to the west of Dijon.

Department: Côte d'Or (21).

Getting there: By road, from Dijon take the D905 west in the direction of the A38 autoroute. Do not take the autoroute but keep to the D905.

Route: The original route run by APTCO was Plombières-Canal to Velars-la-Cude (15 km).

Journey time: Previously was 1 hour 15 minutes round trip.

Gauge and type of traction: Metre; not known.

Contact details: Association du Chemin de Fer de la Cote d'Or (President - Monsieur Olivier Bligny) Ancienne Gare de Velars-la-Cude, place Osburg 21370 Velars-sur-Ouche. Telephone: 03 84 82 39 77 (secretariat) E-mail: mail@acfco.com

Website: www.acfco.com

Operating dates and Tariff: Visit the website or contact the railway at Gare de Velars-la-Cude to ascertain when services will resume.

History: This railway line has a long history, the section Epinac to Pont d'Ouche having been originally approved for construction by King Charles X in 1830. From the outset its prime function was to transport coal from Epinac to Dijon especially in winter when the other main means of transport, the Canal de Bourgogne, became frozen. The line was taken over by the PLM at the end of the 19th century and was also used for transporting passengers with up to three services per day using 030 Bourbonnais locomotives. At this time it also became popular with anglers and their families on day trips from Dijon to the countryside. In the mid-1930s autorails (ABJ, ABH, Billard and Picassos) were introduced for the increased passenger traffic. World War II saw the start of closures on various sections of the line with their requisition for military use by the German forces. After the war concluded the closures continued and in 1988 SNCF terminated all operations. Towards the end of SNCF involvement, the Association (APTCO) was formed and began to develop the line for tourist purposes. It was a successful venture and much was achieved in restoring the track, improving the buildings and acquiring rolling stock. However, in 1995 the local authority (Mairie) of Plombières decided that it wanted to re-possess the station and its surrounding grounds for a building project. The Mairie required APTCO to move the platform at the railway's own cost, a request which was refused by the founding president, a retired railwayman. There followed some difficulty within the association and the president, said to be the principal financier, decided to withdraw. The association went into a decline and finally went into liquidation in 2003. By the end of 2004 most of the rolling stock, much of it not having been maintained for a long time and some badly vandalised, was sold on. Notwithstanding this sad end, a group of former APTCO members have since come together to form the new association, ACFCO. The railway infrastructure fortunately is in the care of ACFCO and it is hoped one day soon that tourist railway services will run again.

Comments: This little train ran alongside the Canal de Bourgogne at a speed of no more than 16 kph passing Notre-Dame-de-Velars, Mont Afrique and Rochet du Crucifix. However, it has had other difficulties operating, other than that with the local Mairie, due to finding the cost of making repairs to the line.

Local Tourist Office: 34 rue des Forges, BP 82296, 21000 Dijon. Telephone: 08 92 70 05 58 Fax: 03 80 30 90 02. E-mail: info@dijon-tourism.com   website: www.dijon-tourism.com

Preserved locomotives and other traction

Autorails Bourgogne Franche-Comté (ABFC)

Picasso autorail No. X 4039 standing at Dijon-Perrigny.   *Alain and Thomas Gallé*

Member: FACS-UNECTO
Location: Dijon, 151 km south-east of Auxerre.
Department: Côte d'Or (21).
Getting there: By road take the autoroutes A6 and A38 and then follow the RN5 to Dijon.
Gauge and type of traction: Standard; autorail.
Rolling stock: A Picasso autorail No. X 4039, autorail No. X 3943, which is the property of l'association Les Amis de la ligne Bourg–Oyonnax (address: La Marcelliere, rue de la Gare, 01250 Ceyzériat), autorail No. X 3886 belonging to ARE (Autorail à Récupération d'Energie) is kept at Nancy and operates from this station. There is also the autorail No. X 2719 ('le Lézard vert') awaiting a new engine.
Contact details: Association X 4039, 11d rue de Bellevue, 21000 Dijon. Telephone: 03 88 36 57 46.
Website: http://x4039.free.fr/trains.htm
History: The association ABFC was founded in 1983 by a small number of enthusiasts who wished to combine heritage with tourism in a railway project. They managed to acquire initially two Picassos, Nos. X 4025 and X 4039, and a little later the last in the series X 4051. In 1994 an RGP autorail was obtained but it did not and still does not have authorisation to operate on RFF (SNCF) tracks. Of the Picassos, only one is now in full working order, X 4039. Of the other two, X 4025 stands in reserve and X 4051 has gone to CFTA (*see entry under Île de France region*). No. X 4039 soldiers on performing all of ABFC's excursion

activity but it is hoped that one day, when funds become available, it will be supported by other autorails.

Comments: This association maintains a collection of preserved autorails of its own or on behalf of others some of which are approved for use on RFF (SNCF) tracks. In 2005, ABFC undertook eight excursions, one of three days duration to Brive-la-Gaillard and Sarlat-la-Canéda, one of two days to Versailles and the remainder were one-day tours.

Local Tourist Office: 34 rue des Forges - BP. 82296, 21000 Dijon. Telephone: 08 92 70 05 58 Fax: 03 80 30 90 02. E-mail: info@dijon-tourism.com   website: www.dijon-tourism.com

L'Amicale des Anciens et Amis de la Traction à Vapeur section Centre & Val de Loire (AAATV Centre)

Location: Cosne-Cours-sur-Loire, 76 km east of Vierzon.

Department: Nièvre (58).

Getting there: By SNCF train to Cosne-Cours-sur-Loire. By road take the autoroutes A6 and A77 and exit at 22 on to D114 to Cosne-Cours-sur-Loire.

Rolling stock: The Mikado No. 141 R 840.

Contact details: AAATV-Centre, Dépôt des Locomotives, rue Eugène Perreau, 58200 Cosne-Cours-sur-Loire. Telephone: 03 86 28 58 31 or 03 86 26 95 29 and also AAATV Centre/Val de Loire, Secrétariat, 7 allée des Brigamilles, 18570 Touy. Telephone: 02 48 64 74 58. E-mail: mail@141r840.com

Website: www.141r840.com

History: AAATV-Centre was formed in 1973 with the sole objective of preserving the Mikado 141 R 840. This was one the 1,340 imported into France from the USA at the end of World War II as part of the Marshal Aid Plan aimed at assisting Europe in reconstruction. This Mikado was built by Baldwin and

Mikado 141 R 840 at Paray le Monial.   *Pascal Bouché*

began its career at Avignon in April 1947 and was retired at Vierzon in December 1975 having competed 1,655,314 kilometres during its career. It was one of a number of Mikados that was converted from coal to heavy oil-fired. No. 141 R 840 came to the association in May 1978 and whilst it had avoided the blow torch it certainly had not missed out on the adverse affects of the weather. Initially, in 1979, the locomotive was kept in the open at the old railway workshops at Vierzon. However, a shelter was needed which did not materialise until 1985 when one was found at Cosne-Cours-sur-Loire. Restoration work then began in earnest and in July 1992 the locomotive was started up again for the first time. However, it was not until more renovation work had been finally completed that No. 141 R 840 returned to full operation. On 19th September, 1997, almost 20 years after the project began, it first ventured back on to the rails for a short trip. Since then the locomotive has completed more than 20,000 kilometres hauling special excursions, all in France, to such places as Bourges, Dijon, Epernay, Laroche Migennes, Le Creusot, Montluçon, Paris (Gare de Lyon) Paris (Gare de l'Est) Tournon Saint Martin, Tours, Vierzon, Lyon, Le Havre, Loches, Amiens and the Baie de Somme. AAATV Centre/Val de Loire has 215 members providing a strong, experienced and professional team who deliver a first class heritage locomotive for the enjoyment of all. A journey on a train hauled by 141 R 840, as with any of the other four Mikados preserved in working order, is a 'must-do'.

Comments: Holds and maintains the preserved Mikado 141 R 840 approved for use on RFF (SNCF) tracks.

Local Tourist Office: Communauté de Communes Loire et Nohain, place de l'Hôtel de Ville, BP 111, 58205 Cosne-Cours-sur-Loire. Telephone: 03 86 28 11 85 Fax: 03 86 28 11 85. E-mail: otcosne@club-internet.fr or contact@otcosnesurloire.fr website: www.ot-cosnesurloire.fr

Museums

Château de Saint-Fargeau

Location: Saint-Fargeau, Puisaye-Forterre, 31 km north of Cosne-Cours-sur-Loire and 76 km east of Vierzon.

Department: Yonne (89).

Getting there: By road take the autoroute A77 and leave at exit 21 and take the D965 in the direction of Toucy and then follow the signs to the château at Saint-Fargeau. From Cosne-Cours-sur-Loire take the D114, D220 and D18 to Saint-Fargeau.

Exhibits: A collection of steam locomotives and other rolling stock which are classed as *Monuments Historiques*.

Contact details: Château de Saint-Fargeau, 89170 Saint-Fargeau. Telephone 03 86 74 05 67.

Website: www.chateau-de-st-fargeau.com/locos.html

Operating dates: From the end of March to Armistice Day (11th November) every day from 1000 to 1200 and from 1400 to 1800 hours. NB: dogs are not allowed in the château grounds.

Tariff: Entry for an adult is 15€ and for a child (under 15 years) is 8€ (2006). *Comments*: The exhibition of locomotives is only part what is on offer here. There is, of course, the 1,000 year-old château itself to see as well take a ride in a 19th century horse-drawn post carriage, see a local history exhibition and experience the château's working French farm. This is a worthwhile day out for all the family. *Local Tourist Office*: 1, place de la République, 89130 Toucy. Telephone: 03 86 44 15 66 Fax: 03 86 44 15 66. E-mail: ot.toucy@wanadoo.fr

Le Hameau du Vin

Location: Romaneche Thorins, 17 km south of Mâcon and 13 km north of Belleville.
Department: Saône-et-Loire (71).
Getting there: By road from Mâcon take the RN6 to Romaneche Thorins.
Exhibits: A 040 (ex-PLM) steam locomotive and an Impériale Napoléon III coach.
Contact details: Le Hameau du Vin et Musée, La Gare, 71570 Romaneche Thorins. Telephone: 03 85 35 22 22.
Website: http://membres.lycos.fr/emailpassion/adresses/duboeuf.html
Comments: Created in 1993 by Georges Duboeuf, le Hameau du Vin is a centre of attraction unique in France. Whilst wine is the main promotion, there is an interesting museum of early 19th century artefacts supporting all aspects of the wine business of that time including its transport. Whilst railway transport forms only a tiny part of this museum it does not necessarily deserve a special trip but if you are in the immediate area it is well worth the visit; allow about two hours to enjoy all of the site. *Local Tourist Office*: Hôtel Dieu Bureau d'Accueil, 68 rue de la République, 69220 Belleville. Telephone: 04 74 66 44 67 Fax: 04 74 06 43 56. E-mail: ot.beaujolaisvaldesaone@wanadoo.fr

Vélorails

Le Cyclorail de Puisaye

Location: Villiers-St Benoît, 34 km west of Auxerre.
Department: Yonne (89).
Getting there: By road from Auxerre take the D965 and then the D950 to Villiers St Benoît.
Route: Villiers-St Benoît to St Martin-sur-Ouanne (7.8 km).
Gauge: Standard.
Contact details: Cyclorail de Puisaye, La Gare, 89130 Villiers-St Benoît. Telephone: 03 86 45 70 05 Fax 03 86 45 70 05. E-mail: via the website.
Website: www.cyclorail.com
Operating dates: By reservation with the cyclorail organizers at Villiers-St Benoît.
Tariff: Vélorail hire for 1 hour is 15€, 1 hour 30 minutes is 19€, 2 hours is 22€, 2 hours 30 minutes is 27€, 3 hours is 30€, half a day is 42€ and a full day is 54€. There are reductions for groups (2006).

History: The line was originally opened in 1884 carrying passengers until 1939 and goods traffic until 1980. The line was neglected for 10 years and quickly became overgrown. A decision eventually was made to recover the line from the ravages of nature. This huge task was undertaken by just one man with a strimmer! It took another year to repair the signals and construct picnic areas. In June 2002 the cyclorail was opened to the public.

Comments: This cyclorail is linked to Le Cyclorail du Sancerrois (*see next entry*).

Local Tourist Office: Syndicat d'Initiative de la Puisaye Nivernaise, square de Castellamonte, 58310 Saint-Amand-en-Puisaye. Telephone: 03 86 39 63 15 Fax: 03 8 39 63 15 E-Mail: si-saint-amand-en-puisaye@wanadoo.fr website www.ot-puisaye-nivernaise.fr/puisayenivernaise_contact_liens.htm

Le Cyclorail du Sancerrois

Location: Port Aubry near to Cosne-Cours-sur-Loire, 76 km east of Vierzon and 75 km south-west of Auxerre.

Department: Nièvre (58).

Getting there: By road take the autoroute A77 south to its end and then follow the RN7 to Cosne-Cours-sur-Loire.

Route: Cosne-Cours-sur-Loire to Sancerre (10.6 km)

Gauge: Standard.

Contact details: Cyclorail du Sancerrois, Port Aubry 58200 Cosne-Cours-sur-Loire. Reservations through Cyclorail de Puisaye, La Gare, 89130 Villiers-St Benoît. Telephone: 03 86 45 70 05 Fax 03 86 45 70 05. E-mail: via the website.

Operating dates: Timings are fixed by reservation with Cyclorail de Puisaye at Villiers-St Benoît (*see previous entry*).

Tariff: Vélorail hire for 1 hour is 15€, 1 hour 30 minutes is 19€, 2 hours is 22€, 2 hours 30 minutes is 27€, 3 hours is 30€, half a day is 42€ and a full day is 54€. There are reductions for groups (2006).

History: The line was originally opened in 1893 to both passenger and goods traffic. However, the line was closed to passengers in the 1960s and to goods traffic in 2000. It was in that year that the cyclorail project began, the idea of Monsieur Patrick Bertrand, but it was until July 2004 that the facility was opened from Port Aubry to a point 3.5 km after Bannay. In 2005, the line was extended to St Satur (Sancerre).

Comments: This cyclorail is linked with Le Cyclorail de Puisaye.

Local Tourist Office: Communauté de Communes Loire et Nohain, place de l'Hôtel de Ville, BP 111, 58205 Cosne-Cours-sur-Loire. Telephone: 03 86 28 11 85 Fax: 03 86 28 11 85. E-mail: otcosne@club-internet.fr contact@otcosnesurloire.fr website: www.ot-cosnesurloire.fr

Bretagne (Brittany)

Bretagne is in the north-west corner of France and borders the regions of Pays-de-Loire to the south-east and Basse-Normandie to the north-east. It comprises the departments of Côtes d'Armor (22), Finistère (29), Ille-et-Villaine (35) and Morbihan (56). The regional capital is located at Rennes and other important centres are Vannes, Brest and Saint-Brieuc. This region has three railways, two TER-SNCF tourist railways, one railway project, one discontinued railway, and one vélorail service.

Railways

Association des Chemin de Fer des Côtes-du-Nord (ACFCdN)

An 030 T Orenstein & Koppel with the LKM locotracteur.   *Patrick Voisine*

Member: FACS-UNECTO
Location: Langueux, 85 km west of St Malo and 100 km north-west of Rennes.
Department: Côtes d'Armor (22).
Getting there: The nearest SNCF station is at Saint-Brieuc. The depot of the Association is situated at Boutdeville a few kilometres from Saint-Brieuc. From the RN12 dual carriageway to the east of Saint-Brieuc take the exit for Langueux or Yffiniac and follow the signs for Les Grèves or Parc de Boutdeville – La Briqueterie.
Route: Langueux (4 km with more to follow in 2006).
Gauge and type of traction: Metre; steam, autorail and diesel.
Rolling stock: A 1926-built 030 T Orenstein and Koppel steam locomotive formerly of the Chemin de Fer des Asturies (Spain) and awaiting restoration, two De Dion-Bouton autorails i.e. OC1 of 1937 construction which has been classified of historical interest and on which restoration work will soon begin and OC2 of 1946 which is in the course of restoration, one Billard draisine fully operational, a Brimont-Latil locotracteur, a 1950s LKM locotracteur which is

fully operational, a 1931 Renault draisine and many wagons, some fully operational, others awaiting restoration.

Contact details: Association des Chemin de Fer des Côtes-du-Nord (ACFCdN) Parc de Boutdeville, 1 promenade Harel de la Noë 22630 Langueux. Telephone: 02 96 72 75 88. E-mail: acfcdn@wanadoo.fr

Website: www.trains-fr.org/cdn/ or www.trains-fr.org/cdn/index.html

Operating dates and tariff: Excursions began in 2005 and subject to permissions being granted will continue over an extended length of track in 2006. Contact Monsieur Fabien Bonic on the e-mail address above for more detail about operations - he can speak English.

History: The Association was formed in December 1986 exactly 30 years after the closing of the local railway network. The objective of the Association was to preserve as much as they could of the artefacts of the old railway before they disappeared. Several years later, a suggestion arose that they should re-create a line. After several months of research a route from Boutdeville to Langueux was identified. Since 2003, the first stage of the line has been completed and track-laying work is continuing.

Comments: This is an excellent railway to visit both for its attractive route following the Bay of Saint Brieuc as well as viewing its interesting rolling stock. When fully completed the excursions will be even better. Members of the association are very enthusiastic and helpful and welcome encouragement from visitors.

Local Tourist Office: 7 rue Saint-Gouéno, BP 4435, 22044 Saint-Brieuc. Telephone: 08 25 00 22 22 Fax: 02 96 61 42 16. E-mail: info@baiedesaintbrieuc.com website: www.baiedesaintbrieuc.com

La Vapeur de Trieux

Member: FACS-UNECTO

Location: Pontrieux, 130 km west of St Malo and 140 km north-west of Rennes.

Department: Côtes d'Armor (22).

Getting there: The nearest SNCF station is at Pontrieux. By road take the autoroutes A10, A11 & A81, the latter becoming the RN157 then follow the RN136, RN12 and D6 to Pontrieux.

Route: Pontrieux to Paimpol (18 km).

Journey time: 30 minutes.

Rolling stock: A superb 1912 Henschel-built Pacific No. 231 K 8.

Gauge and type of traction: Standard; steam.

Contact details: La Vapeur de Trieux, Connex-Bretagne, Gare de Paimpol, 22500 Paimpol. Telephone: 02 96 20 52 06 or 08 92 39 14 27. E-mail: contact via the website.

Website: http://www.vapeurdutrieux.com/index_trieux.asp www.cfta.fr

Operating dates: Last week in May to the third week in September and operating on Wednesdays to Sundays and some Tuesdays. However it is important to check first as 231 K 8 undertake charters elsewhere on RFF (SNCF) tracks throughout France.

Tariff: An adult return ticket with a stop is 21€ and without a stop is 13€ and for a child (4-11 years) with a stop is 10.50€ and without a stop is 8€. An adult single ticket with a stop is 18€ and for a child with a stop is 8€. A family ticket (two adults and two children) with stops is 59€ (2005).

No. 231 K 8 approaching Tournon-sur-Rhône on the Railway Touring Company's Mediterranean Express in 2005. *Author*

Comments: Preserved 231 K 8 which is approved for use on RFF (SNCF) tracks is owned by Matériels Ferroviaires et Patrimoine National (MFPN). (*See entry under Île de France Region*.) This railway is one of the Connex-Tradition operated services. *Local Tourist Office*: Maison de la Tour Eiffel, place de Trocquer, 22260 Pontrieux. Telephone: 02 96 95 14 03 Fax: 02 96 95 14 03. E-mail: tourisme.pontrieux@wanadoo.fr website: www.pontrieux.com

Chemin de Fer Touristique Auray–Pontivy also known as Espace Rail des pays d'Auray, Rohan, Blavet (Parb'er)

Member: FACS-UNECTO
Location: Auray, 127 km south-west of Rennes.
Department: Morbihan (56).
Getting there: The nearest SNCF station (TGV or TER) is at Gare d'Auray. By road from Rennes take the RN24, RN166 and RN165 to Auray.
Route: Auray to Pontivy (53 km).
Journey time: 1 hour 35 minutes.
Gauge and type of traction: Standard; autorail.
Rolling stock: Autorail type X 4500 and other autorails chartered from SNCF.
Contact details: Chemin de Fer Touristique Auray–Pontivy (Parb'er) place Raoul Daultry, 56400 Auray. Telephone: 06 86 58 33 44.
E-mail: assoc.parber@wanadoo.fr
Website: www.train-blavet-ocean.com
Operating dates: From May to September on some Sundays only – check operations in advance.
Tariff: Return tickets for adults cost 15€ and for children (6-12 years) 8€. Special excursions cost adults 20€ and children 10€ (2005).
History: The controlling association is called the Association de Defense des Usagers de la gare d'Auray (ADUGA) and was formed in 1989 to maintain the

TER-Bretagne autorail No. 2141 at Camors station. *Chemin de Fer Touristique Auray-Pontivy*

local railways and the station given the possible threat from the coming of the extended TGV services. Whilst retaining the same acronym the association changed its name in 2002 to Association de Developpement Urbain de la Gare du Pays d'Auray to reflect more the heritage objectives of the association rather than just its rail user representation.

Comments: A number of special events are held from June to September on the local RFF (SNCF) tracks hence the Sunday-only operations. In 2003, they undertook four tours carrying 800 passengers, in 2004, nine tours with 2,100 passengers and in 2005, eight tours, the number carried not being available at the time of writing. In 2006, the association is proposing to have a greater programme of events, hopefully with a wider appeal.

Local Tourist Office: 20, rue du Lait - Chapelle de la Congrégation, 56400 Auray. Telephone: 02 97 24 09 75 Fax: 02 97 50 80 75. E-mail: infos@auray-tourisme.com website: www.auray-tourisme.com

TER-SNCF – Le Tire Bouchon

Location: Auray, 125 km south-west of Rennes and 20 km west of Vannes.
Department: Morbihan (56).
Getting there: The nearest SNCF station is at Auray. By road from Rennes take the RN24, RN166 and RN166 via Vannes to Auray.
Route: Auray to Quiberon (30 km).
Journey time: 36 minutes.
Gauge and type of traction: Standard; modern autorail.
Contact details: Call the Tourist Office or visit the website.
Website: www.trainstouristiques-ter.com/tire_bouchon.htm
Operating dates: Every day from the beginning of July to the end of August. Ten departures per day from Auray, the first being at 0814 hours and the last being at 2048 hours; from Quiberon also 10 departures per day, the first being at 0906 hours and the last being at 2140 hours.

Tariff: At the station an adult single ticket is 2.80€ and a return 5€. On the train the single ticket is 3€ from the conductor. A book of 10 single tickets is 20€. Cycles travel free (2006).

Comments: An enjoyable journey to spend a superb day on La presqu'île de Quiberon off the attractive coast of Brittany.

Local Tourist Office: Office de Tourisme de Quiberon, 14, rue de Verdun 56174 Quiberon. Telephone: 02 97 50 07 84 Fax: 02 97 30 58 22. E-mail: quiberon@quiberon.com website: www.quiberon.com

TER-SNCF – Le Léon à Fer et à Flots

Location: Morlaix, 59 km east of Brest and 180 km west of St Malo.

Department: Finistère (29).

Getting there: There are SNCF stations at Morlaix and Roscoff. By road from St Malo take the RN137, RN176 and RN12 to Morlaix. By channel ferry from Plymouth to Roscoff.

Route: Morlaix to Roscoff (26 km).

Journey time: Rail journey takes 30 minutes but allow the whole day for the organized tour.

Gauge and type of traction: Standard, modern autorail.

Contact details: Information and bookings can be made by telephoning 02 98 62 07 52 or by e-mail afer.aflots@laposte.net

Website: www.afer.aflots.org

Operating dates: From the beginning of May to the last week in September mainly on Saturdays or Sundays and also on Tuesdays and Thursdays in July and August – the full programme can be found on the website www.aferaflots.org/programme.pdf or by contacting the local tourist office.

Tariff: An adult return ticket is 20€ and for a child (4-12 years) 10€ (2005).

Comments: This enjoyable excursion will allow the visitor on foot, by autorail and on a small cruise boat (*vedette*) to discover the beautiful Léon countryside and the Bay of Morlaix. There are two tours. The first tour starts at 1000 hours at the Tourist Office in Morlaix with a short visit to the town before going to the railway station. An autorail then takes the visitors on a 30 minute journey to Roscoff. There passengers embark on the boat and travel to the Île de Batz where they arrive at 1315 hours and lunch can be taken. The remainder of the afternoon is free time until 1800 hours before embarking again on the boat and sailing to the locks at Morlaix where the tour ends. The second tour starts at Roscoff at the Tourist Office at 1100 hours. A short visit to the town of Roscoff follows before taking the autorail to Morlaix arriving there at midday to see the viaduct followed by free time for lunch. At 1600 hours there is a tour of the town before meeting at the locks and embarking on the boat for the return journey to Roscoff arriving there at 1900 hours. The hours sometimes can vary and can be affected by weather conditions so check first with the respective tourist office.

Local Tourist Office: Office de Tourisme de Morlaix, place des Otages, 29600 Morlaix. Telephone: 02 98 62 14 94 Fax: 02 98 63 84 87. E-mail : officetourisme.morlaix@wanadoo.fr website: www.morlaix.fr or

Office de Tourisme de Roscoff, 46, rue Gambetta, BP 58, 29681 Roscoff. Telephone: 02 98 61 12 13 Fax: 02 98 69 75 75.
E-mail: tourisme.roscoff@wanadoo.fr website: www.roscoff-tourisme.com

Railway Project

L'Association des Chemins de Fer du Centre Bretagne (CFCB)

Location: Loudèac, 88 kilometres west of Rennes.
Department: Côtes d'Armor (22).
Getting there: By road, take the D164 from Rennes to Loudèac.
Route: Pontivy to St Rivalain (proposed).
Journey time: Not as yet known.
Gauge and type of traction: Standard; autorail.
Rolling stock: An ABDP autorail No. X 2423 one of a class built between 1951 and 1955 by Renault with a 300CV diesel engine and capable of 120 km/h. A loan agreement has been signed between CFCB and l'association ART for use of the Picasso autorail No. X 3890 named *Ville de Loudéac* also built by Renault in 1953 with similar characteristics to the X 2423.
Contact details: CFCB, La Commanderie Brélévenez, 22300 Lanion. Telephone: 02 96 48 44 36 Fax: 02 96 48 41 71. E-mail: mi.joindot@wanadoo.fr
Website: www.cfcb-asso.org
Operating dates and Tariff: To be advised on opening.
History: In 1982 a group of enthusiastic amateurs of the Guingamp area of the Côtes d'Armor department came together to safeguard the future of the *Picasso* autorail No. X. 3890 which in its 30 year career had travelled over 3.8 million kilometres. An agreement was struck with SNCF to park the autorail at Guingamp. In 1990, CFCB was formed to continue the restoration project. Owing to the deterioration of the autorail caused by successive winters as well as local vandalism, after lengthy negotiations with SNCF, it was eventually agreed in 1995 to house the autorail under cover at Loudèac. Restoration then began in earnest. The next stage of development for CFCB after completing the restoration was to set about introducing a tourist train service between Pontivy and St Rivallain, linking to another tourist train service between Pontivy and Auray operated by Parb'er (*see page 57*). This project is ongoing so to follow progress visit the website.
Comments: This is an exciting project soon, hopefully, to come to fruition. Early indications are that it will be a success especially after the weekend of 28th/29th May, 2005 when CFCB operated their two autorails at Saint Brieuc and Le Légué over a short length of track – 3 kilometres. Notwithstanding the shortness of the journey, over that weekend the two autorails undertook 110 round trips, completed 400 kilometres and carried over 1,700 people without any problems.
Local Tourist Office: Pays du Centre Bretagne, 1 rue St Joseph, BP 315, 22600 Loudèac. Telephone: 02 96 28 25 17. E-mail: tourisme@centrebretagne.com or info-tourisme.loudeac@wanadoo.fr

Discontinued Railway

Chemin de Fer de Guerlédan

Location: Mur-de-Bretagne.
Department: Cotes d'Armor (22).
Comments: An unusual network between Mur-de-Bretagne and Caurel based on 310 mm gauge and built by an Englishman in 1978. After two years' operation the railway closed and the rolling stock and other material 'emigrated' to Great Britain. (Source: FACS-UNECTO.)

Vélorails

Vélorail de Médréac

Location: Médréac, 37 km north-west of Rennes.
Department: Ille-et-Villaine (35).
Getting there: The nearest main line SNCF station is at Rennes and Lamballe (both TGV). By road take autoroutes A10, A11, & A81 on to the RN157, RN136 and RN12 to Médréac.
Route: Médréac to Becherel (6 km) and Médréac in the direction of la Brohinière (14 km).
Gauge: Standard
Contact details: Vélorail de Médréac, Gare de Médréac, 35360 Médréac Telephone: 02 99 07 30 48.
Website: www.trains-fr.org/unecto/medreac
Operating dates: Operating every day in June, July, August and September from 1000 to 1800 hours. In April, May and October the service operates on Sundays and public holidays between 1400 and 1800 hours. The Vélorail can also be operated at any time in the year subject to making a prior reservation and there being sufficient numbers.
Tariff: Vélorail hire for the 6 km return journey is 8€ plus 2€ for each child less than eight years and for the 14 km return journey is 12.59€ plus 3.50€ each for children under eight.
Comments: This vélorail service has been operating since 1994. It offers the riders a *binôme* for a maximum two persons alongside each other. There are smaller machines (*les nacelles*) available for children under eight and other machines slightly bigger for juniors. There also two motorised draisines which are also used on the line.
Local Tourist Office: Activités Touristiques Intercommunales, La Gare, 35360 Médréac. Telephone and Fax 02 99 07 30 48 and E-mail: lagaredemedreac@wanadoo.fr

Centre

Centre, as its title would suggest, is in the centre of France bordering the regions of Haute-Normandie to the north, Île-de-France to the north-east, Bourgogne and Pays-de-Loire to the east, Auvergne to the south-east, Limousin and Poitou-Charentes to the south-west, and Basse-Normandie to the north-west. It comprises the departments of Cher (18), Eure-et-Loir (28), Indre (36), Indre-et-Loire (37), Loir-et-Cher (41) and Loiret (45). The regional capital is at Orléans and other cities include Blois, Tours, Châteauroux, Chartres and Bourges. This region has four railways, one TER-SNCF tourist railway, one railway where operations have been temporarily suspended, one museum and one vélorail service.

Railways

Train Touristique de la Vallée du Loir (TTVL)

Autorail No. X 2419.   *Collection TTVL*

Location: Thoré-la-Rochette, 41 km north-west of Blois and 10 km west of Vendôme.
Department: Loir et Cher (41).
Getting there: By road take the autoroutes A10 and A11 then follow the RN10 and D917 to Thoré-la-Rochette.

Route: Thoré-la-Rochette – Trôo (18 km).
Journey time: 2 hours 50 minutes round trip.
Gauge and type of traction: Standard; autorail.
Rolling stock: 1952-built autorail No. X 2419 which was taken out of SNCF service after 37 years. Initially this autorail spent time with the Train à Vapeur de Touraine (TVT) before coming to this line. In 1992, it was given its distinctive livery by Monsieur Claude Bayle, the task taking him over 300 hours to paint the carriages with scenes depicting the beautiful locations in the valley of the river Loir.
Contact details: Train Touristique de la Vallée du Loir (President - Monsieur Claude Germain), c/o Mairie, 41100 Thoré-la-Rochette. Telephone: 02 54 72 80 82 Fax: 02 54 72 73 38. E-mail: thoremairie@wanadoo.fr
Website: www.tourisme.fr/train-touristique
Operating dates: From 1st June to 15th September on Saturdays, Sundays and public holidays with trains leaving Thoré-la-Rochette at 1425 and returning by 1715 hours. Two extra services (morning and evening) operate in July and August. The autorail can be hired at any time of the year by groups for special excursions on the line and at 460€ is not expensive.
Tariff: An adult ticket is 10€ and for a child (5-16 years) 7.50€ (2005).
History: This railway line traces its history back to 1873 when the compagnie du PO made a proposal to build a connection between Blois-Vendôme-Montoire-Pont de Braye but it was not until eight years later that it was completed. Its role was to convey passengers and local merchandise. During World War I operations were severely limited owing to the military authorities requisitioning the line and rolling stock. After the war services resumed but during the 1930s there was a decline owing to passengers increasingly choosing to use automobile transport. In 1938, with the formation of the nationalised railway industry in the form of SNCF, a decision was taken on economic grounds to close the line to passenger traffic. However, goods traffic continued between Vendôme and Pont de Braye. World War II came and again the railway was requisitioned by the military authorities but this time, however, with a difference - it was by the Germans. This line, incidentally, witnessed an historic event when on 24th October, 1940 the station at Montoire-sur-le-Loir hosted the meeting of Marshal Pétain and Chancellor Hitler, the outcome of which established collaboration between the German and French Governments. In 1943 and 1944 the railway suffered heavy bombardment from which some of the line never recovered. After the war ended, some sections of the line were dismantled and the decline continued. Happily, the tourist line began business in the 1990s and restoration included not only the rolling stock but also the stations themselves.
Comments: This railway is an outstandingly beautiful area of France and there is no better way to view it than to take a tour on this train. The Mairie at Thoré-la-Rochette is particularly helpful.
Local Tourist Office: c/o the Mairie, 41800 Trôo. Telephone: 06 88 53 52 69 Fax: 02 54 72 61 38. E-mail: troo-st-jacques-de-guerets@fnotsi.net

Chemin de fer Touristique de Pithiviers (AMTP)

040 T Henschel type DFB No. 4.   *Alain and Thomas Gallé*

Member: FACS-UNECTO
Location: Pithiviers, 44 km north-west of Orléans and 80 km south of Paris.
Department: Loiret (45).
Getting there: By SNCF train to Etampes then local bus to Pithiviers. By road take the RN20 to Etampes then follow the RN921 Pithiviers.
Route: Pithiviers – Bois-de-Bellébat (4 km).
Gauge and type of traction: 600 mm; steam, diesel.
Rolling stock: Five steam locomotives, a 020 T Schneider, a 030 T Blanc-Misseron (ex-Parame-Rotheneuf), a 031 T Decauville, a 040 T Henschel type DFB, and a 130 T Meuse. All are in working order and classed as being of historical interest (*Monuments Historiques*). There are also two diesel locotracteurs, a Crochat petro-electric autorail, 20 carriages and other wagons. There are a number of other non-operational locomotives and other transport items which are on view in the museum or may be viewed in the depot yard on request.
Contact details: Chemin de Fer Touristique de Pithiviers Musée et Ateliers, rue Carnot 45300 Pithiviers (President – Monsieur Alain Elambert). Telephone: 02 38 30 50 02 Fax: 02 38 30 55 00. E-mail: amtp45@wanadoo.fr
Website: http://assoc.wanadoo.fr/amtp45/welcome.html
Operating dates: Services run from 1st May to mid-October on Sunday afternoons and in June, July, August and September extra services on Saturday afternoons.

Tariff: An adult ticket for the train journey and museum is 7€ and for a child (4-14 years) 5€ (2006).

History: Pithiviers, in former times, was the departure point for a 35 km tramway called the le Tramway de Pithiviers à Toury (TPT). The line was constructed by Ets. Décauville and opened to passenger and freight traffic in 1892. Passenger traffic was stopped exactly 60 years later but freight, the carriage of *betteraves* (sugar beet), continued until the end of 1964. In 1966, for the first time in France, a railway about to be closed and disappear forever was saved by a group of amateur enthusiasts.

Comments: The museum is an important part of this preserved railway and a visit is included in the train tour.

Local Tourist Office: 'Les Remparts', 45300 Pithiviers. Telephone: 02 38 30 50 02 Fax: 02 38 30 55 00. E-mail: pithiviers-tourisme@wanadoo.fr website: www.ville-pithiviers.fr

Train Touristique du Lac de Rillé (AECFM)

Member: FACS-UNECTO

Location: Lac de Rillé, 56 km west of Tours.

Department: Indre-et-Loire (37).

Getting there: Lac de Rillé is situated 35 km from Tours and a similar distance from Saumur, both can be accessed by train TER-SNCF and then local transport. By road take autoroutes A10 & A28 and exit on to the D766 then follow the D69, D68, D3 and D49 to Rillé.

Route: Lac de Rillé (2.5 km).

Journey time: 20 minutes.

Gauge and type of traction: 600 mm; steam and diesel.

Rolling stock: Kept at Rillé: a steam locomotive 040 with tender Henschel No. 15937 of 1918, formerly operating in Poland until 1981 on the Chemin de Fer Forestier de Biatystok (this was the last DFB to operate an industrial service in Europe), a steam locomotive 040 No. 764.203 of 1949 formerly of Romania (the only one in France), a 020 Decauville type of 1949, a steam locomotive 020 T Orenstein and Koppel of 1913 No. 5829, a Comessa locotracteur (10 tonnes) for hauling local slate transport at Anjou, a CACL locotracteur, and three locotracteurs of the type Decauville TMB 15 formerly of the uranium mines in the Vendée. Kept at Marcilly: a Billard locotracteur, a Ruston locotracteur, a Berry locotracteur, a Decauville TMB 15 locotracteur, and a Comessa locotracteur 15 hp. A variety of carriages and wagons of the region are also preserved as well as a carriage constructed by the students of the college at Noyant. The rails and points are in the main of SNCF origin. The line is equipped with preserved SNCF signalling.

Contact details: AEFCM, 37330 Marcilly-sur-Maulne. Telephone: 02 47 96 42 91 or 02 47 24 07 95 or 02 37 21 97 35.

Website: www.trains-fr.org/aecfm/

Operating dates: From late April to end of September on Sundays and public holidays steam trains operate every 45 minutes from 1430 to 1800 hours. In July and

August diesel trains also operate on Saturdays every 45 minutes from 1530 to 1730 hours. Special trains can be pre-booked for Fridays and Saturdays all the year round. *Tariff*: An adult ticket is 3.80€ and for a child (4-12 years) 3.20€ (2005). *History*: This railway has been operated by volunteers since 1977 and its aim is to preserve and restore narrow gauge rolling stock. From 1981 to 1989 it utilised a railway route at Marcilly but a new line was created at Lac de Rillé in 1990. *Comments*: Steam locomotive experience courses – *Conduite, chauffe, maintenance et sécurité* – are available on prior application. There is a local hotel as well as a camping site close to the Lac de Rillé leisure park. *Local Tourist Office*: place de la Bilange, BP 241, 49418 Saumur. Telephone: 02 41 40 20 60 Fax: 02 41 40 20 69. E-mail: infos@ot-saumur.fr website: www.saumur-tourisme.com

Chemin de Fer Touristique du Bas-Berry (CFBB)
operated by Société pour l'Animation du Blanc-Argent (SABA)

Member: FACS-UNECTO
Location: Luçay-le-Mâle, 67 km west of Vierzon.
Department: Indre (36).
Getting there: The nearest SNCF station is at Salbris. By road take the autoroutes A10 & A71 and exit at Lamotte-Beuvron then follow the D923, D922, D924, D128, D4, D956 and D960 to Luçay-le-Mâle.
Route: Luçay-le-Mâle – Argy (7 km).
Gauge and type of traction: Metre; diesel.
Rolling stock: An interesting collection of traction and other rolling stock including some diesel locotracteurs such as Deutz Nos. 56116 and 56117, a Brookville and a 1935 Comessa. There are two draisines - a 1930 construction ex-PO in the course of restoration and a 1954 model of Decauville design. There are also some 1917-built 30-seat carriages formerly of the Swiss Oberaargau-Jura-Bahn awaiting restoration.
Contact details: SABA, Chemin de Fer Touristique du Bas-Berry, Mairie 36180 Heugnes. Telephone: 02 54 39 03 29.
Website: http://perso.wanadoo.fr/denis.huron/sabaF/saba.htm or http://perso.wanadoo.fr/gite.vernusset/AccueilBA.html
Operating dates: Sundays from 5th June to 25th September plus Wednesday afternoons in July and August (2005).
Local Tourist Office: c/o the Mairie, 36180 Pellevoison. Telephone: 02 54 38 00 68 Fax: 02 54 39 00 66. E-mail: pellevoisin@wanadoo.fr

TER-SNCF – Le Petit Train Blanc-Argent

Location: Salbris, 27 km north of Vierzon and 65 km south of Orléans.
Department: Loir-et-Cher (41).
Getting there: The nearest SNCF station is at Salbris. By road take the autoroutes A10 and A71 and leave at exit 4 to Salbris.

Route: Salbris – Luçay-le-Mâle (67 km).
Journey time: 1 hour 20 minutes.
Gauge and type of traction: Metre, autorail.
Rolling stock: Recent (2003) X 74500 autorails, and two 1980s X 240 type autorails.
Contact details: Chemin de Fer du Blanc et Argent, Gare de Romarantin, 41200 Romorantin. Telephone: 02 54 76 06 51.
Website: www.trainstouristiques-ter.com/blanc_argent.htm
Operating dates: All year with up to four return services per day from Salbris to Romorantin and two to Valençay and two to Luçay-le-Mâle.
Tariff: An adult single ticket from Salbris to Luçay-le-Mâle is 9.50€, to Valençay is 8.20€, and to Romorantin is 4.90€ (2005).
History: In 1882 the idea of building this railway was mooted and in 1893 a concession was given to la Compagnie du Paris-Orléans (PO) to construct the line. Work commenced in 1899 and was completed three years later. In 1906 the then Compagnie du Chemin de Fer du Blanc à Argent (BA) was created and services were operated using steam trains. In 1921 the first diesel locomotives were deployed as well as some Tartary-constructed automotrices and later some De Dion-Bouton type autorails. After the end of World War II the line abandoned steam in favour of Billard and Verney autorails. The X 240 autorails arrived in the 1980s and at the same time four Verney autorails were renovated at the SNCF workshops in Bordeaux. In 1991, BA was integrated into the TER-Centre network.
Comments: A worthwhile train journey through the wild forests and woodlands of Boischaut Nord du Berry. A visit to this railway usefully links to a trip on the Chemin de Fer Touristique du Bas-Berry (*see previous entry*).
Local Tourist Office: 1 rue du Général Giraud, 41300 Salbris. Telephone: 02 54 97 22 27 Fax: 02 54 97 22 27. E-mail: otsi.salbris@wanadoo.fr website: www.salbris-developpement.com/tourisme

Railway Operations Temporarily Suspended

Trains à Vapeur de Touraine (TVT)

Member: FACS-UNECTO
Location: Richelieu, 20 km south of Chinon.
Department: Indre-et-Loire (37).
Getting there: The nearest SNCF station is at Chinon. By road take autoroutes A10 and A85 and leave at the first exit on to the RN152 then follow the D749 to Chinon.
Route: Chinon – Ligre Rivière – Richelieu (16 km).
Gauge and type of traction: Standard; steam, diesel.
Rolling stock: Steam locomotives 030 T Fives-Lille, 141 C 100, 040 TA 137 and 230 G 352, diesel-electrics A1A-A1A Nos. 62032 and 62036, locotracteur No.1 Ateliers de Construction Argent ex-French Army, autorail No. X 902 ex-CFD and various carriages, postal cars and other wagons.
Contact details: Trains à Vapeur de Touraine, Gare de Richelieu, BP66, 37120 Richelieu. Telephone: 02 47 58 12 97 Fax: 02 47 58 28 72. E-mail: train-vapeur-touraine@wanadoo.fr

Website: www.train-vapeur-touraine.com
Operating dates: Check with operator for re-opening dates.
History: The line was first put into service in 1884 and after World War II became a departmental line until it was finally abandoned in 1971. An agreement was later made with AJECTA (*see entry under Île-de-France region*) leading to the first tourist service operating in June 1974. An agreement followed in 1978 with SNCF allowing for an extension of the line to Chinon. A year later the association - Trains à Vapeur de Touraine - was formed. In 1995 another four km of track bed was purchased from SNCF.
Comments: The railway did not operate in 2005 so check with the operator for future operations. When it re-opens the rolling stock at this railway, at the very least, will make a visit worthwhile. Seeing the Châteaux of the Loire also adds to the pleasure of visiting this interesting railway.
Local Tourist Office: 7. Place Louis XIII, BP 3, 37120 Richelieu. Telephone: 02 47 58 13 62 Fax: 02 47 58 29 86. E-mail: otsi.richelieu@wanadoo.fr   website: www.cc-pays-de-richelieu.fr

Museum

Musée Laumônier de la Locomotive à Vapeur

Location: Vierzon, 87 km south of Orléans.
Department: Cher (18).
Getting there: By SNCF to Vierzon. By road take the autoroute A71 and exit at Vierzon.
Contact details: 15, rue de la Société Française, 18100 Vierzon. Telephone: 02 48 71 10 94 Fax: 02 48 71 98 06. E-mail: locovapeur@wanadoo.fr   or patrimoine@ville-vierzon.fr
Website: www.ville-vierzon.fr/Pages/decouvrir/pages/visites/visite-f.html and select from the menu <Musée Laumônier>
Operating dates: From the beginning of March to the week before Christmas, with services from Wednesday to Sunday each week from 1400 to 1800 hours. Ample parking is nearby and there are facilities for the handicapped. Special group visits (minimum of 20 persons) may be arranged for any time in the year (2006).
Tariff: An adult ticket is 3€, for a child (5-13 years) 1€ and for students, unemployed and handicapped 2€ (2005).
History: The town of Vierzon, in the very early days of railway development in France, opened its first station on 1st May, 1843 for the PO (Paris-Orléans) line and by 1847 had become an important railway crossroads. The engine shed (roundhouse) located there in those days originally accommodated 12 locomotives and had a turntable diameter of 4.5 metres. The story of Vierzon, however, is very much the story of the development of the railway network in France. More and better facilities were installed over the second half of the 19th century as traffic grew. For example, by 1904 Vierzon had 60 locomotives based there, 25 for passenger duties and 35 for goods traffic. Every day 70 trains

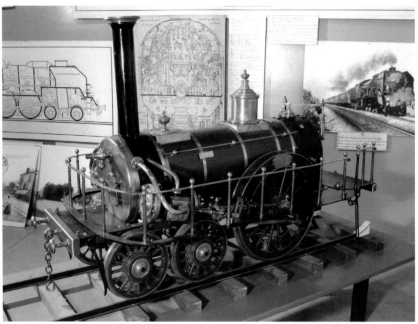

Model of an early French steam locomotive in the Laumonier Museum.

Musée Laumônier

regularly passed through the station. In 1907 the new powerful Pacific locomotives arrived. More locomotives meant more coal so in 1910 a huge coal storage depot was built. By 1919, with the installation of much heavy equipment Vierzon had developed into an important centre for the maintenance and repair of locomotives and rolling stock. From 1925 to 1935 between 80 and 90 locomotives were regularly based there. Electrification came to the Paris-Vierzon line at the end of 1926. World War II led to much bombardment particularly in 1944 and the depot suffered considerable damage which was not fully repaired until 1950. After World War II, coal supplies increasingly became scarce so decisions were made to change some locomotives over from being powered by coal (*charbon*) to heavy oil (*fuel lourd*). Notable amongst the classes of locomotive which underwent such modification was the Mikado 141 Rs. Vierzon had 83 of this class of which 69 were converted from coal to oil-fired. Vierzon, as elsewhere in France, indeed the world, saw the end of steam in the 1970s with the last at Vierzon being subject to *radiation* (struck off the active list prior to scrapping) in 1973. With its long railway history it is not surprising that there came the idea of developing a museum, and so it was that Monsieur Raymond Laumonier, the Depot Chief at Vierzon, having retired from his post at the end of October 1976, decided to develop the project. However, before he retired he organized an open day in 1975 on the theme of steam locomotives at the Vierzon depot. On his retirement he was made

Honorary Chef de Dépôt and was able in this capacity to organize another open day in 1977. Both open days were a great success convincing him that a railway museum was needed. Over the following 25 years he amassed an important collection of material of the 'Steam Era'. In 2002 at the age of 83 years, he handed over his collection to the Town Council of Vierzon which opened the museum dedicating it to him and the age of the steam locomotive, thus ensuring that his life's work was safeguarded for posterity.

Comments: Given the importance of Vierzon in railway history this museum is well worth a visit especially for those interested in a detailed account of the industry and its impact on the development of a French town. A visit here can be usefully combined with a trip on the TER-SNCF tourist service – Le Petit Train Blanc-Argent – operating from Salbris, 27 km to the north of Vierzon and Luçay le Mâle (*see page 66*).

Local Tourist Office: 26, place Vaillant Couturier, 18100 Vierzon. Telephone: 02 48 53 06 14 Fax: 02 48 53 09 30. E-mail: office-tourisme@ville-vierzon.fr

Vélorail

Cyclo-draisine d'Aubigny

Location: Aubigny-sur-Nère, 48 km north-east of Vierzon.

Department: Cher (18).

Getting there: By road take autoroutes A6 and A77 and exit at 19 on to the D940 to Aubigny-sur-Nère.

Route: Aubigny-sur-Nère – Etang de Puits (14 km).

Gauge: Standard.

Contact details: Cyclo-draisine d'Aubigny, Mairie, 18700 Aubigny-sur-Nère. Telephone: 02 48 81 50 07 or 02 48 58 35 81 (weekends and public holidays) Fax: 02 48 81 50 98.

Website: www.aubigny-sur-nere.fr/sortir/cyclo_draisine.htm

Operating dates: From the beginning of May to the end of September at weekends and on public holidays from 0900 to 1900 hours.

Tariff: Vélorail hire for 1 hour is 8€, half a day is 19€ and a full day is 30€ (2005).

Local Tourist Office: 1, rue de l'Eglise, BP 87, 18700 Aubigny-sur-Nère. Telephone: 02 48 58 40 20 Fax: 02 48 58 40 20. E-mail: tourisme@aubigny.org Website: www.aubigny.org

Champagne-Ardenne

Champagne-Ardenne is in the north-east of France and borders Belgium and the regions of Picardie to the north-west, Île-de-France to the west, Bourgogne to the south, Franche-Comté to the south-east and Lorraine to the east. It comprises the departments of the Ardennes (08), Aube (10), Marne (51) and Haute-Marne (52). Its regional capital is Reims and other cities are Troyes, Charleville-Mézières and Chaumont. This region has four heritage/tourist railways, one railway project and two vélorail services.

Railways

Chemin de Fer Touristique de la Traconne (CFTT)

Location: Esternay, 58 km south-west of Épernay.
Department: Marne (51).
Getting there: By road take the autoroute A4 and leave at exit 13 then follow the D231 and RN4 to Esternay.
Route: Esternay – Sézanne (16 km).
Journey time: 30 minutes.
Gauge and type of traction: Standard; autorail.
Rolling stock: A 1951-built Picasso autorail No. X 3818.
Contact details: Chemin de Fer Touristique de la Traconne, 15 avenue Victor Hugo, 51310 Esternay. Telephone: 03 26 42 67 01 or 03 26 81 50 13 Fax: 03 26 42 67 01. E-mail: chemin.fer.traconne@wanadoo.fr
Website: www.traconne.org
Operating dates: Runs on Sundays only from the beginning of July to the last weekend in September – afternoon services leaving from Esternay at 1245, 1530 and 1715 hours and returning from Sézanne at 1430, 1615 and 1800 hours (2005).
Tariff: An adult return ticket from Esternay to Sézanne is 7€, or from Esternay to Le Meix is 4€ and for a child (4-11 years) a return ticket from Esternay to Sézanne is 4€, or from Esternay to Le Meix is 2.50€. A ticket for a special Sunday tour for an adult is 12€ and for a child 7€ (2005).
History: The railway line, known as ligne 21, from Gretz to Vitry-le-François was opened in November 1885 and offered an alternative route from Paris to Strasbourg which was by then already congested. A number of other lines were introduced locally notably those from Metz to Romilly and Provins to Neuvy. The towns of Esternay and Sézanne quickly established themselves as important railway centres; for example, at the beginning of the 19th century Sézanne housed 40 steam locomotives and employed more than 200 people on railway duties. Sadly, the decline began early on in World War II, July 1940, when the bridges over the Aube at Anglure and the Seine at Conflans were destroyed; they were not subsequently rebuilt. Passenger traffic consequently stopped between Romilly and Anglure and between Romilly and Conflans. After the war, in 1952, the route Provins to Esternay lost its passenger services and as did the Metz to Esternay route a year later. More closures followed so that by 1991 all rail traffic had ceased except for the routes Connantre to

Esternay and Sézanne to Anglure on which SNCF allowed the newly-created CFTT to run freight trains carrying cereals. In August 1993, CFTT expanded its operations by providing tourist services using a Picasso autorail. In the summer of 2001 a vélorail service was introduced.

Comments: CFTT offer every Sunday in July, August and September a special Sunday tour - *Les Balades du Dimanche* - where a journey is taken on the autorail coupled with a visit by bus (a Saviem S45) to a local place of interest. CFTT also offers a vélorail facility - Vélorail du Grand Morin - see entry later.

Local Tourist Office: place des Droits de l'Homme, 51310 Esternay. Telephone: 03 26 80 27 07 Fax: 03 26 80 27 07. E-mail: si.esternay@wanadoo.fr website: www.esternay.com

Chemin de Fer Touristique du Sud des Ardennes (CFTSA)

Picasso autorail No. X 3838.   *Yves Cointe*

Member: FACS-UNECTO
Location: Attigny, 56 km north-east of Reims.
Department: Ardennes (08).
Getting there: By road take the autoroute A4 to Reims then follow the D980 and D25 to Attigny.
Routes: (a) Attigny to Vouziers to Challerange (30.8 km) and (b) Attigny to Amagne-Lucquy (9.5 km).
Journey time: (a) 1 hour 5 minutes, and (b) 20 minutes.
Gauge and type of traction: Standard; autorail.
Rolling stock: Four autorails. A Picasso autorail No. X 3838 which first entered service in 1952 at Nancy and ended its days there in June 1987. It was first acquired by Train à Vapeur des Cévennes (CITEV) (*see entry under Languedoc*

and Roussillon region) and then came to this line in 1991. Autorail No. X 3850 came into service in January 1953 at Vesoul and retired at Mohon in May 1987. Autorail No. X 3898 began life in 1954 at Vitry and was retired into the hands of the Chemin de Fer Touristique du Rhin (CFTR) (*see entry under Alsace region*) later Chemin de Fer Touristique des Trois Vallées Dinant - Givet (Belgium) before coming to this line in April 2000. Autorail No. X 2468 is believed to have started service at Rennes in 1955 before going to Limoges where it was retired into the hands of Chemin de Fer Touristique Midi-Pyrénées (not now operating) before coming to this line in February 1992 - it is currently up for sale (2005).

Contact details: Chemin de Fer Touristique du Sud des Ardennes, Cour de la Gare, 08130 Attigny. Telephone: 03 24 71 47 60 Telephone and Fax: 03 24 38 26 79. E-mail: cftsa-attigny@wanadoo.fr

Website: http://cftsa.free.fr

Operating dates: Services run on Sundays from late June to early September with departures from Attigny to Challerange at 1000 and 1515 hours and returning from Challerange at 1120 and 1645 hours; departures from Attigny to Amagne-Lucquy are at 1415 and 1755 hours returning from Amagne-Lucquy at 1435 and 1820 hours.

Tariff: For journey (a) an adult return ticket is 12€ and for a child (4-12 years) a return ticket is 7€. A single journey ticket is 8€ for an adult and 5€ for a child. For journey (b) an adult return ticket is 8€ and for a child 5€. A single journey ticket is 6€ for an adult and 4€ for a child (2005).

History: The railway line is part of the association Amis de la Traction Vapeur en Ardennes (ATVA) which was founded in 1979 and whose prime objective is to put back into service a steam locomotive.

Local Tourist Office: 17, rue Chanzy, 08400 Vouziers. Telephone: 03 24 71 97 57 Fax: 03 24 71 34 87. E-mail: otav@wanadoo.fr website: www.ville-vouziers.fr

Chemin de Fer de Blaise et Der (CFTBD)

Location: Wassy, 85 km south-east of Épernay.

Department: Haute-Marne (52).

Getting there: By road take the autoroute A5 and exit at 20 then the RN6, RN19, D960, D400 and D4 to Wassy.

Routes: a) Wassy to Eclaron; and, b) Wassy to Dommartin-le-Franc and on to Doulevant-le-Château (Total for both journeys is 40 km).

Gauge and type of traction: Standard; autorail, diesel.

Rolling stock: Autorails.

Contact details: Chemin de fer de Blaise et Der, 1 rue de Cdt. Hugeney, 52130 Chaumont or La Gare, 52130 Wassy. Telephone: 03 25 32 88 88 or 06 07 50 55 72 (mobile).

Website: www.mairie-saintdizier.fr/decouvrir/I_2_2.htm

Operating dates: Autorails leave the 19th century station at Wassy at 1500 hours on Sundays in July and from 15th to 31st August. Two routes are possible, Wassy to Eclaron or Wassy to Dommartin-le-Franc to Doulevant (2005).

Local Tourist Office: 7 rue du Général Gresley, 52130 Wassy. Telephone: 03 25 07 64 47 Fax: 03 25 07 64 47. E-mail: syndicat.initiative-wassy@wanadoo.fr.

Autorail Touristique Vallée de la Meuse

Location: Mouzon, 110 km north-east of Reims.
Department: Ardennes (08).
Getting there: By road take autoroutes A4, A34 & A203 and then on to D964 to Mouzon.
Route: Mouzon to Stenay (21 km plus 3 km on a bus-navette).
Gauge and type of traction: Standard; autorail.
Rolling stock: Autorails Nos. X 4608 and X 4611.
Contact details: via the Tourist Office, details below.
Operating dates: Every Sunday between the beginning of June to the beginning of September (2005). Hours of operating and tariff not known.
Comments: It would not be difficult to combine a visit to this railway with one to Chemin de Fer Touristique du Sud des Ardennes, 47 km to the west (*see page 72*).
Local Tourist Office: Le Paquis de Frappant, 08110 Mogues.
Telephone: 03 24 29 79 91 Fax: 03 24 29 79 45.
E-mail: officedetourismedes3cantons@wanadoo.fr website: www.3cantons.com

Railway Project

Association Chemin de Fer Touristique Aubois (ACTA)

Location: Troyes, 75 km north east of Auxerre.
Department: Aube (10).
Getting there: By road, take the autoroute A5 or A26 and exit at Troyes.
Proposed route: Troyes to St Florentin in the department of Yonne (89)
Gauge and type of traction: Standard; autorail.
Rolling stock: Picasso autorail No. X 3897.
Contact details: ACTA, BP 174, 10005 Troyes. Telephone: 03 25 24 99 11. E-mail: g.capet@wanadoo.fr
Operating dates and tariff: To be announced.
Comments: The project was begun in January 2000. The association acquired its Picasso autorail in the summer of 2002 from Chemin de Fer Touristique du Sud des Ardennes (*see CFTSA entry earlier*). It will be worth seeing how this project develops for when it comes into operation it will be an interesting journey to enjoy.
Local Tourist Office: 16, boulevard Carnot, BP 4082, 10000 Troyes. Telephone: 03 25 82 62 70 or 03 25 73 36 88 Fax: 03 25 73 06 81. E-mail: contact@ot-troyes.fr or troyes@club-internet.fr

Vélorails

Cyclo-rail des Trois Vallées

Location: Andelot-Blancheville, 23 km north-east of Chaumont.
Department: Haute-Marne (52).
Getting there: By road take the autoroute A5 and exit at 24 then follow the D10 and RN74 to Andelot-Blancheville.
Route: Andelot-Blancheville - Chanteraine – Briaucourt (9 km).
Gauge: Standard.
Contact details: Cyclo-rail des Trois Vallées, Communauté de Communes de la Région d'Andelot, BP9, 52700 Andelot-Blancheville. Telephone: 03 25 32 33 18.
Operating dates: In May, June and September on Saturday and Sundays between 1400 and 1800 hours. In July and August, it operates every day between 1000 and 1900 hours.
Local Tourist Office: place Cantarel, 52700 Andelot-Blancheville. Telephone: 03 25 03 78 60. E-mail: si3vallees@wanadoo.fr website: http://perso.wanadoo.fr/si.troisvallees/

Vélorail du Grand Morin

Location: Esternay, 58 km south-west of Épernay.
Department: Marne (51).
Getting there: By road, take the autoroute A4 and leave at exit 13 then follow the D231 and RN4 to Esternay.
Route: Esternay to Neuvy (4 km).
Gauge: Standard.
Contact details: Vélorail du Grand Morin, c/o Chemin de Fer Touristique de la Traconne, 15 avenue Victor Hugo, 51310 Esternay. Telephone: 03 26 42 67 01 or 03 26 81 50 13 Fax: 03 26 42 67 01. E-mail: chemin.fer.traconne@wanadoo.fr
Website: www.traconne.org or http://perso.wanadoo.fr/chemin.fer.traconne/velora_f.htm
Operating dates: Vélorails are available every Sunday from the end of March to the end of October. Each cyclo-draisine, as they are called here, takes four adults or two adults and three children.
Tariff: The cost for an hour's hire of the unit is 10€ or 14€ for 1½ hours (2005).
Comments: This vélorail service is operated by Chemin de Fer Touristique de la Traconne (CFTT) (*see earlier entry*).
Local Tourist Office: place des Droits de l'Homme, 51310 Esternay. Telephone: 03 26 80 27 07 Fax: 03 26 80 27 07. E-mail: si.esternay@wanadoo.fr website: www.esternay.com

Corse (Corsica)

The island comprises the departments of Corse-du-Sud (2A) and Haute-Corse (2B). Its capital is Ajaccio with Bastia being the second city. This region has one TER-SNCF tourist railway service.

Railway

TER-SNCF - Chemin de Fer de la Corse (CFC)

Autorails of various vintages including railcar No. 106 and trailer No. 113 at Calvi station.
Luc Beaumadier

Location: Island of Corsica.
Department: Corse-du-Sud (2A) and Haute-Corse (2B)
Getting there: By air or by ferry from Marseille, Nice or Toulon.
Route: Bastia to Ajaccio (158 km), Ponte-Leccia to Calvi (74 km). Ponte-Leccia is the junction for Calvi in the north-west and Bastia in the north-east.
Journey time: Bastia to Ajaccio 3 hours 50 minutes, Ajaccio to Calvi 4 hours and Ajaccio to Ponte-Leccia 1 hour 5 minutes.
Gauge and type of traction: Metre; autorails.
Rolling stock: A total of 16 autorails, seven of which are of the type Soulé X 97500 built between 1989 and 1997 each offering 44 seats, five autorails type CFD X 2000 built 1975/76 each offering 48 seats, two autorails type CFD X 5000 built 1982/83 each offering 48 seats, and two autorails type Renault ABH 8 built in 1949 each offering 40 seats. There are 12 trailer carriages (remorques) of various types and vintage, two of which are Billard baggage trailers without seats. The older rolling stock is of particular interest given that most others of this vintage on the mainland of France have long since been retired.
Contact details: Chemin de Fer de la Corse, BP170, 20294 Bastia. Telephone: 04 95 32 60 06.

Website: www.trainstouristiques-ter.com/corse.htm or www.sncf.fr

Operating dates: All year round with four return journeys per day to and from Ajaccio and Bastia throughout the week but only two on Sundays and public holidays. There are also two returns daily to and from Bastia and Calvi.

History: The railway traces its origins back to the mid-19th century when a decision was made to build the island's network. Metre gauge was chosen owing to the difficulties of the terrain, a common decision elsewhere in France where the mountainous characteristics precluded the use of standard gauge, such as in the Alps, the Cévennes, the Cerdagne and the Ardèche. Between 1855 and 1894, the line between Bastia and Ajaccio was built and which for a long time had been considered impossible given the geographical problems. During that period lines were built between Bastia, Corte, Ajaccio and Bocognano (1888), Bocognano and Vizzavona (1889), Vizzavona – Vivario (1892), Ponte Leccia and Calvi (1890) and Corte and Vivario (1894). By the beginning of World War I the Corsican railway network totalled 295 km. By the beginning of World War II the network had been extended to Porto-Vecchio. Unfortunately the war stopped any further expansion. Thereafter, like many other railways in mainland France, the decline began with closures leaving the network as it is today with a total 232 km. The responsibility of the network passed to the local regional government in Corsica in 1983. TER-SNCF now has the contract to provide the rail services. There are plans in 2006 to invest more than 110 million euros in improving the rolling stock and the lines themselves which hopefully will reduce the travelling time from Ajaccio to Bastia to 2 hours 30 minutes.

Comments: Corsica is a beautiful island and the route of the railway allows the traveller to enjoy that beauty from a different, indeed, often exciting perspective. The railway itself is a work of art with over 800 different structures to admire. There are 76 bridges, one of which – the Viaduc du Vecchio - has been declared a *Monument Historique*. It is a 100 metres high and 140 metres long and was built by Gustave Eiffel, builder of the Eiffel Tower in Paris and the Viaduc de Garabit south of Clermont Ferrand. There are 45 tunnels, the notable ones being the Vizzavona at 3,916 metres long and the Bastia at 1,485 metres long. There are 83 level crossings. Travelling on this railway is a 'must-do'.

Local Tourist Office: 3 boulevard du Roi Jérôme, BP 21, 20181 Ajaccio. Telephone: 04 95 51 53 03 Fax: 04 95 51 53 01.
E-mail: ajaccio.tourisme@wanadoo.fr website: www.ajaccio-tourisme.com

Franche-Comté

Franche-Comté is in the eastern part of France and borders Switzerland and the French regions of Bourgogne to the west, Champagne-Ardenne to the north-west, Lorraine to the north, Alsace to the north-east and Rhône-Alpes to the south. It comprises the departments of Doubs (25), Jura (39), Haute-Saône (70) and Belfort (90). Its regional capital is Besançon and other cities are Vesoul, Belfort and Lons le Saunier. This region has one heritage/tourist railway, one TER-SNCF tourist railway, one museum and one vélorail service.

Railways

Chemin de Fer Touristique de Pontarlier-Vallorbe (CFTPV) also known as Coni'fer

Member: FACS-UNECTO
Location: Les Hôpitaux-Vieux, 75 km south of Besançon.
Department: Doubs (25).
Getting there: By SNCF train to Pontarlier, Frasne or Vallorbe-CFF then by local bus or taxi. By road take the RN57 from Besançon towards Lausanne; the railway is located between Pontarlier (12 km) and Vallorbe (6 km from the Swiss border).
Route: Les Hôpitaux-Neufs to Fontaine Ronde to Le Touillon (7.5 km).
Journey time: 75 to 90 minutes return.
Gauge and type of traction: Standard; steam, diesel.
Rolling stock: Tigerli 030 T steam locomotive, three A1A-A1A 62000's, one locotracteur No. Y 51232, two other diesel locotracteurs and various coaches and wagons including five La Poste wagons.
Contact details: Chemin de Fer Touristique de Pontarlier-Vallorbe, Office de Tourisme de Metabief-Mont d'Or, 2 rue de la Seigne, 25370 Les Hôpitaux-Vieux. Telephone-Fax: 03 81 49 10 10 (direct to Coni'Fer).
E-mail: information@coni-fer.org
Website: www.coni-fer.org
Operating dates: From early June to late September; in June and September on Sunday afternoons; from the beginning of July to mid-July on Wednesday and Saturday evenings and Sunday afternoons; from mid-July to the end of July on Wednesday, Thursday, Friday and Saturday evenings and Sunday afternoons; in August operating every day in the evening or some afternoons (2005).
Tariff: An adult ticket is 7€, for a child (6-16 years) 3.50€ and children under six go free (2006).
History: The line Pontarlier to Vallorbe was opened in July 1875 and operated passenger and freight services until its closure in 1969. It was in 1857 that a concession was granted to the railway company PLM (Paris-Lyon–Méditerranée) with its Swiss counterpart to build the railway line which traversed the frontier between the two countries. Given the nature of the terrain, the weather and the fact two countries were involved, its construction proved long and arduous. The line, once completed, was also difficult to operate given the absence of regular crossover points. Between the two World Wars, PLM did

its best to close operations in the interests of economy but thankfully the line survived. In 1940, the line was cut by the French Army at the Jougne tunnel in order to stop the advancement of the German Army. One claim to fame for the line was that in April 1945 Marshal Pétain, head of the French Government which collaborated with the Germans, took the train at Les Hôpitaux-Neufs for his return to Paris. It was in the 1990s that Coni'Fer began the project to reconstruct the railway for tourist services. It has run successfully ever since.
Comments: Fortunately the original 23 km of the line is still intact and whilst only 7.5 km have been in operation since 1993 there are plans to extend the line in due course.
Local Tourist Office: 1, place de la Mairie, 25370 Les Hôpitaux-Neufs.
Telephone: 03 81 49 13 81 Fax: 03 81 49 09 27. E-mail: infos@montdor-2lacs.com website: www.montdor-2lacs.com

TER-SNCF – Les Hirondelles

Location: Dole, 51 km south-east of Dijon and St Claude is 58 km north-west of Geneva.
Department: Jura (39).
Getting there: By road take the autoroute A39 and exit at 6 then follow the D973 to Dole. To St Claude from Geneva take the RN5 and the D436.
Route: Dole – St Claude – Dole on Wednesdays and St Claude – Dole - St Claude on Thursdays (Dole to St-Claude is a total of 123 km).
Journey time: 2 hours 36 minutes each way but allow a full day for the excursion.
Gauge and type of traction: Standard; modern autorail.
Rolling stock: Latest autorails, Alsthom-built type X 73500 with panoramic windows which replaced the ageing X 2800s some of which can be seen elsewhere on heritage lines throughout France.
Contact details: Reservations can be made at the Tourist Offices at Dole or St Claude. A 30 per cent deposit must be paid before 1200 hours the day before departure.
Website: www.trainstouristiques-ter.com/franche_comte.htm
Operating dates: From 1st June to 30th September leaving Dole on Wednesdays at 0929 and returning the same day at 1633 hours. Leaving St Claude on Thursdays at 0805 and returning the same day at 1730 hours.
Tariff: An adult return ticket is 50€, for a child (4-12 years) 26€ and children under four 5€. NB the price includes the ticket, commentaries on the train in French, the midday meal including wine and coffee, a visit to the old town and entrance to the Pasteur Museum so it does represent good value for money (2005).
Comments: This is another example of French railway engineering overcoming the challenges of crossing a difficult mountainous region. The line, of which 107 km was built over the 50 years between 1862 and 1912, includes 36 tunnels, the highest being the Tunnel de la Savine at an altitude of 948 metres. There are 18 viaducts.
Local Tourist Offices: Office de Tourisme du Jura Dolois, 6, place Jules Grévy, 39100 Dole. Telephone: 03 84 72 11 22 Fax: 03 84 82 49 27. E-mail: ot.juradolois@wanadoo.fr or Office de Tourisme de St Claude, 1 avenue de Belfort, 39200 St Claude. Telephone: 03 84 45 34 24 Fax: 03 84 41 02 72. E-mail: contact@haut-jura.fr

Museum

Musée du Tacot

Location: Cléron, 29 km south of Besançon.
Department: Doubs (25).
Getting there: By road take the D9 south from Besançon.
Contact details: Musée du Tacot, 25330 Cléron. Telephone: 03 81 62 13 31.
Website: http://membres.lycos.fr/METRIQUE70/newpage4.htm
Operating dates: Musée du Tacot is open during school holidays and on public holidays in April, May to mid-June; then from mid-June to the end of September it is open every day except on Tuesdays. Opening hours are from 1430 to 1800 hours.
Tariff: Adults and children 3€ each (2005).
Comments: A small, but nevertheless, interesting museum, managed by Monsieur Lornet the son of a former employee of the Chemin de Fer de Doubs (CFD). The exhibition retraces the local history of the railway which was finally closed to all traffic in 1953. The museum is situated in the *zone artisanale* outside the village near to an attractive railway viaduct. On the first Sunday in August each year Monsieur Lornet organizes a walk to discover the viaducts of Cléron. Whilst the museum alone may not be worth a detour to visit, it may be beneficial if combined with a trip on the Chemin de Fer Touristique de Pontarlier-Vallorbe (CFTPV) also known as Coni'fer located at Les Hôpitaux-Neufs, 60 km to the south-west or travel on the TER-SNCF Tourist service – Les Hirondelles - from Dole 70 km to the west (*see the two previous entries*).
Local Tourist Office: c/o the Mairie, 25330 Cléron. Telephone: 03 81 62 14 29 Fax: 03 81 62 07 15 (NB: The Mairie is open Monday and Wednesday from 1600 to 1800 hours and on Saturdays from 1000 to 1200 hours).

Vélorail

Les Vélorails de Pays de Vesoul

Location: Vesoul, 112 km west of Mulhouse and 48 km north of Besançon.
Department: Haute-Saône (70).
Getting there: The nearest SNCF station is at Vesoul. By road take the autoroutes A5 and A31 and exit at 7 and then follow the RN19 to Vesoul.
Route: Sortie-de-Vaivre to Mont-le-Vernois (4 km).
Gauge: Standard.
Contact details: Les Vélorails de Pays de Vesoul, 45 rue Gérôme, 70000 Vesoul. Telephone: 03 84 96 07 52.
Operating dates: Contact the tourist office to make a reservation.
Local Tourist Office: Rue Gevrey B.P. 117, 70002 Vesoul. Telephone: 03 84 97 10 85 Fax: 03 84 97 10 84. E-mail: otvesoul@club-internet.fr website: www.vesoul.fr

Haute-Normandie (Higher Normandy)

Haute-Normandie is in the north of France with regional borders to Basse-Normandie in the west, Picardie in the east, Île-de-France to the south-east and Centre to the south. It comprises the departments of Eure (27) and Seine-Maritime (76). Its regional capital is Rouen and other important cities are Evereux and Dreux. This region has three heritage / tourist railways and one location where there is preserved traction.

Railways

Train touristique Etretat - Pays de Caux (TTEPAC)

Member: FACS-UNECTO
Location: Les Loges, 52 km south of Chaumont.
Department: Seine Maritime (76).
Getting there: By SNCF train to Fécamp then by bus to Les Loges. By road take autoroutes A16, A28 and A29 then follow D910 and D72; from Paris take the autoroutes A13 and A131.
Route: Les Ifs – Les Loges – Etretat (5 km).
Gauge and type of traction: Standard; diesel, autorail.
Rolling stock: Autorail No. X 3907 (ANF-SAURER of 1954 construction) formerly operated by SNCF at Sotteville and autorail carriages Nos. XR 7559 and XR 8238. There is a diesel locomotive Y 2296, one Moyse BN28 locotracteur No. 1005 and three draisines.
Contact details: Train Touristique Etretat - Pays de Caux, BP 14, Gare de Loges, 76790 Les Loges. Telephone: 02 35 29 49 61 Fax: 02 35 27 60 58. E-mail: ttepac76@free.fr
Website: www.trains-fr.org/unecto/ttepac/
Operating dates: From late March to the end of October. In April, May, and June on Wednesdays, Saturdays and Sundays; in July and August every day; and, in September and October on Saturdays and Sundays. Check beforehand for the exact operating hours.
Tariff: An adult ticket is 4€ and for a child (4-14 years) 2€ (2005).
Comments: A vélorail service (or cyclo-draisine as it is referred to on this railway) is also operated in conjunction with the train services. It is possible to take the cyclo-draisine out from Les Loges station and return on the train. The tariff for this service is 18€ for 2 persons, 20€ for 3, 22€ for 4 and 24€ for 5 (2006).
Local Tourist Office: place Maurice Guillard, BP 3, 76790 Etretat. Telephone: 02 35 27 05 21 Fax: 02 35 28 87 20. E-mail: ot.etretat@wanadoo.fr
website: www.etretat.net

ABJ4 autorail No. X 3601 and diesel locotracteur No. Y 2005 standing at Pacy-sur-Eure station.

Chemin de Fer de la Vallée de l'Eure (CFVE)

Member: FACS-UNECTO
Location: Pacy-sur-Eure, 88 km west of Paris.
Department: Eure (27).
Getting there: By SNCF train to Vernon, Bueil or Evreux then by taxi. By road take the autoroute A16 exit at 16 then follow the RN13 to Pacy.
Route: Pacy-sur-Eure to Breuilpont and Pacy-sur-Eure to Cocherel to Chambray (15 km).
Gauge and type of traction: Standard; autorail, diesel.
Rolling stock: A 1948 Renault Autorail ABJ4 No. X 3601, another ABJ4 No. X 3623 is on loan to the Chemin de Fer du Vermandois (*see entry under Picardie region*), two locotracteurs (a Fauvet-Girel and a Deutz) and a 1946 Whitcombe diesel BB 8082. There is also a comprehensive and interesting collection of other locotracteurs, autorails, carriages, wagons and other rail artefacts in various states of operational order, restoration or storage. Each year CFVE achieves a programme of renovation.
Contact details: Chemin de Fer de la Vallée de l'Eure, BP 6, Gare de Pacy-sur-Eure, avenue de Poilus, 27120 Pacy-sur-Eure. Telephone: 02 32 36 04 63 Fax: 02 32 26 40 43. E-mail: contact@cfve.org
Website: www.cfve.org
Operating dates: Various dates all the year round but consult the railway by telephone or visit the internet site. In July and August a service operates every Wednesday and Sunday afternoons.
Tariff: An adult ticket is between 8€ and 15€ and a child (5 years+) between 6€ and 10€ depending on which of the two routes is taken (2005).
History: The original public railway line from Rouen to Orléans was opened to traffic in 1873. In 1951 passenger traffic was halted followed by all freight traffic

in 1989. The line was de-classified by SNCF in 1996. In 1997 the tourist line was opened and was subsequently extended in 1998 and 2005. In 2003 the station at Pacy was completely restored by the local municipality.

Comments: The railway operates a comprehensive programme of special events throughout the year. The route of the line is perhaps uninspiring but Pacy is well worth a visit for railway enthusiasts not least of all to see its interesting collection of rolling stock and attractive station.

Local Tourist Office: place Dufay, 27120 Pacy-sur-Eure. Telephone: 02 32 26 18 21 Fax: 02 32 36 96 67.

PontauRail

Location: Pont Audemer, 54 km west of Rouen.

Departments: Eure (27) and Calvados (14) in the Basse-Normandie region.

Getting there: The nearest SNCF station is at Pont Audemer. By road take the autoroute A13 and exit at 26 on to D89, then follow the RN 175 & D810 to Pont Audemer.

Route: Pont Audemer to Pont de Normandie, near Honfleur (28 km).

Journey time: 55 minutes on the train and 10 minutes on the connecting bus service to Honfleur.

Gauge and type of traction: Standard; autorail.

Rolling stock: Autorail No. X 4555 was acquired by PontauRail in July 2004. It was first brought into service at Lyon in November 1965 and over time worked from depots at Nevers, Marseille and Longueau from where it was retired in September 2003. It has a six-cylinder plat Saurer engine producing 425 hp delivering traction through a De Dietrich automatic gearbox. Autorail No. X 2426 is Unifié type 600, constructed in 1952 by Établissements Décauville, it has two Renault engines each producing 300 hp and delivering traction through a manual transmission. In its heyday it could achieve 120 km/h and pull up to three non-powered carriages.

Contact details: PontauRail, c/o Office de Tourisme, place Maubert, 27500 Pont Audemer. Telephone: 02 32 41 08 21 or 06 08 42 90 81 Fax: 02 32 57 11 12 or 02 32 41 22 58. E-mail: tourisme@ville-pont-audemer.fr website: www.ville-pont-audemer.fr PontauRail's direct e-mail is info@pontaurail.com

Website: www.pontaurail.com

Operating dates: The association may vary the operating dates for each year so check beforehand but they usually operate on Sundays and French public holidays from the last weekend of June to the first weekend in September. Departures from Pont Audemer are at 0930, 1400 and 1635 hours and from Honfleur town bus station at 1015, 1515 and 1730 hours.

Tariff: An adult return ticket is 10€ and for a child (3-12 years) 5€ (2005).

History: The association, PontauRail, was formed in 1995 with the prime objective of preserving a tourist train service between Pont Audemer and Honfleur. The association has a membership of 50, all volunteers, 30 of whom are active in running the railway.

Comments: A bus service connects Pont de Normandie rail terminus with Honfleur town centre. A vélorail service also operates between Pont Audemer

Autorail No. X 4555 with Pont Normandie in the background. *Jean-Francois Fessard*

and the Pont de Normandie. The number of places is limited so reservations are necessary. Special events take place during the year and group bookings can be made.
Local Tourist Office: As above.

Preserved Locomotives and Other Traction

Pacific Vapeur Club (PVC)

Member: FACS-UNECTO
Location: Rouen, 136 km north-west of Paris.
Department: Seine-Maritime (76).
Getting there: By SNCF rail to Rouen. By road from Paris take the autoroute A13 and exit at 22 to Rouen. Sotteville-les-Rouen and its huge marshalling yards are near to the Zone Industrielle de Jonquay.
Gauge and type of traction: Standard; steam.
Rolling stock: Pacific No. 231 G 558 (Etat).
Contact details: Pacific Vapeur Club, BP 115, 76302 Sotteville-les-Rouen. Telephone: 02 35 72 30 55 Fax: 02 35 03 06 69. E-mail: pacificvapeurclub@free.fr
Website: http://pacificvapeurclub.free.fr
History: Pacific 231 G 558 was built in Nantes in 1922 by Batignolles-Chatillon company and was one of 283 built. It is classed as a *Monument Historique*. The proud owners, the Pacific Vapeur Club, say the locomotive is unlike any other! As one of the last prestigious steam locomotives of France it is kept near to Rouen. Working on the l'Etat and the la Région de l'Ouest networks between 1922 and 1968 it regularly hauled six passenger carriages (five 2nd and one 1st class) a postal carriage and a restaurant car and was capable of taking almost 500 passengers at speeds of up to 100 km per hour.
Comments: This preserved Pacific, which is approved for use on RFF (SNCF) tracks, makes four or five excursions per year which are often over-subscribed, so advanced booking is essential (*see photograph on title page*).
Local Tourist Office: 25, place de la Cathédrale, BP 666, 76000 Rouen. Telephone: 02 32 08 32 40 Fax: 02 32 08 32 44.
E-mail: accueil@rouentourisme.com website: www.rouentourisme.com

Île de France

Île de France is the capital heart of France and comprises the departments of the Ville de Paris (75), Seine-et-Marne (77), Yvelines (78), Essonne (91), Hauts-de-Seine (92), Seine-Saint-Denis (93), Val-de-Marne (94) and Val-d'Oise (95). Paris, of course, is the regional capital but other important centres are Pontoise, Créteil, Bobigny, Nanterre, Evry, Melun and Versailles. The main Paris Tourist Office is located at 25 rue des Pyramides, 75001 Paris and can be contacted by telephone on 08 92 68 31 12 or 08 92 68 30 00 or by fax 01 49 52 53 00 or 01 49 52 53 10 or by visiting the website www.parisinfo.com This region has three heritage/tourist railways, six locations where preserved traction can be found, four museums, one temporarily closed museum and one discontinued railway.

Railways

Chemin de Fer des Chanteraines (CFC)

A 1920-built Decauville 030 T No. 1770 double-heading with *La Bouillote* a 1914-built Decauville 020 T No. 869 type Le Progrès.   *Chemin de Fer des Chanteraines*

Location: Villeneuve-la-Garenne, 12 km north of the centre of Paris.
Department: Hauts de Seine (92).
Getting there: By RER rail service to Gennevilliers. By road consult the Paris map.
Route: Pont d'Epinay to Pompidou (5.5 km within the Parc des Chanteraines).
Journey time: 48 minutes.
Gauge and type of traction: 600 mm; steam, diesel.
Rolling stock: Seven steam locomotives (four in service which are a 020 T Decauville, 030 T Decauville, an Orenstein & Koppel and a 020 T saddle tank

85

constructed in the 1970s by Alan Keef of Bala Lake in North Wales), 13 diesel locotracteurs, eight of which are in operational service, 13 passenger carriages and 20 goods wagons.

Contact details: Chemin de Fer des Chanteraines, 46 avenue G. Pompidou, 92390 Villeneuve-la-Garenne. Telephone: 01 40 85 86 20 Fax: 01 40 85 86 20. E-mail: marc-andre.dubout@wanadoo.fr

Website: http://perso.wanadoo.fr/cf-chanteraines/

Operating dates: From March to October on Wednesdays, Saturdays, Sundays and public holidays with afternoon services between 1500 and 1800 hours.

Tariff: An adult ticket is 4€ and for a child (3-12 years) 2.90€ (2005).

History: The tourist line was created in 1981 and its association in 1984. The following year the first steam locomotive arrived and a restoration project began. The service quickly became popular, for example, by 1989 a total of 30,000 passengers had been carried. In 1991 the line was extended to its present length and a second depot built. It has enjoyed a number of shared events with the Festiniog Railway of North Wales.

Comments: Said to be the only steam railway operating in sight of the Eiffel Tower the line passes through a beautiful park with some of the track running alongside the River Seine. It is possible to hire trains for special events.

Local Tourist Office: 58 rue Pierre Timbaud, 92230 Gennevilliers. Telephone: 01 41 47 92 10 Fax: 01 41 47 90 29. E-mail: otsi.gennevilliers@wanadoo.fr website: www.ville-gennevilliers.fr

Tacot des Lacs

Member: FACS-UNECTO

Location: Montcourt-Fromonville, 85 km south of the centre of Paris.

Department: Seine-et-Marne (77).

Getting there: By SNCF train to the stations at Fontainebleau or Bourron-Marlotte. By road take the RN7 from Fontainebleau then the D40 to Montcourt-Fromonville. The departure point for trains is alongside the canal 100 metres before reaching the village.

Route: Moncourt to Grez-sur-Loing (2.5 km).

Journey time: 1 hour round trip.

Gauge and type of traction: 600 mm; steam, diesel.

Rolling stock: There are 10 steam locomotives including examples of Baldwin (notably the 1917 Baldwin 131 T named *Felin Hen*) Arnold-Jung, Koppel, Henschel, Borsig, Decauville, Krauss and Maffëi manufacture, the oldest being a 1905 020 T Koppel No. 1329. There are 62 (yes 62!) diesel locotracteurs with examples of Baldwin, Billard, British Westinghouse, Citroen, Comessa, Deutz, Dick Kerr, Gmeinder, Koppel, Diema, Whitcomb and Patry manufacture, the oldest being two British-built Dick Kerr units going back to 1916. There are 83 wagons of various descriptions, an autorail, three draisines and a tram.

Contact details: Association du Tacot des Sablières de Bourron, 77880 Grez-sur-Loing. Telephone: 01 64 28 67 67 Fax: 01 64 78 30 78.

E-mail: tacotdeslacs@wanadoo.fr

Maffëi 020 No. 3921 crossing the Pont de Tacot.   *Tacot des Lacs*

Website: www.tacot-des-lacs.com

Operating dates: In April, October and November on Sunday and public holiday afternoons; from May to September on Saturday afternoons and daily in July and August. Special events are also held at Easter, May Day, Mothers' Day, Whitsun, Fathers' Day, Bastille Day (14th July) 15th August and 16th September.

Tariff: An adult ticket is 7.50€ and for a child (3-12 years) 5€ (2005).

History: This project was the dream of a young railway enthusiast Patrick Mourot, who, in 1980, with a handful of friends began to create this important collection and has since developed an extraordinary leisure park which was first opened to the public in 1985.

Comments: A short but nevertheless picturesque tour with interesting preserved railway artefacts. There are ambitious plans to construct a huge building to house and protect this vast quantity of material and where, in comfort, visitors can see this important historical collection. The association publishes in French a quarterly review, *Tortillard,* which is helpful to keep abreast of what is happening on the industrial heritage scene in France. A visit to Paris must take in a visit to Tacot des Lacs if at all possible.

Local Tourist Office: 116, rue Wilson, 77880 Grez-sur-Loing. Telephone: 01 64 45 69 12 Fax: 01 64 45 69 12. E-mail : si.grez@club-internet.fr website: www.ot-grezsurloing.fr

Petit Train du Port-aux-Cerises (PTPC)

Member: FACS-UNECTO
Location: Draveil, 25 km south of the centre of Paris.
Department: Essonne (91).
Getting there: By SNCF Transilien RER services (lines C or D) to Juvisy and then 10 minutes on foot, or by line D to Vigneux and 15 minutes on foot. By road take the autoroute A6 in the direction of Orly then the RN7 to Juvisy, or by the RN6 and exit at Draveil or Vigneux.
Route: Port-aux-Cerises to Draveil (3 km).
Journey time: 25 minutes.
Gauge and type of traction: 600 mm; steam, diesel.
Rolling stock: A steam locomotive Decauville 030 T No. 1583 classed as a *Monument Historique*, a Comessa locotracteur and six open carriages, three of which are of army origin.
Contact details: Base Régional de Plein Air et de Loisirs, rue du Port-aux-Cerises, 91210 Draveil. Telephone: 01 69 83 46 10 Fax: 01 69 83 46 11. E-mail: info@portauxcerises.fr
Website: www.portauxcerises.asso.fr
Operating dates: From February to November during the afternoon on Wednesdays, school holidays, weekends and public holidays. In July and August services operate every weekday from 1030 hours and at weekends and on public holidays from 1400 hours.
Tariff: An adult return ticket is 3.80€ and for a child (4-12 years) 2.30€. A day ticket for an adult is 4.50€ and for a child 3€ (2006).
Comments: This line is incorporated within the Leisure Park. The park offers something for all the family. It is wise to allow at least half a day to get the best out of the visit.
Local Tourist Office: place de la République, BP 7, 91211 Draveil. Telephone: 01 69 03 09 39 Fax: 01 69 42 50 02. E-mail: office-tourisme-draveil@wanadoo.fr website: www.mairie-draveil.fr

Discontinued Railway

Chemin de Fer de St Eutrope

Location: Evry.
Department: Essonne (91).
Comments: This railway operated on an old 600 mm track close to Evry's former race track. After closing down all the rolling stock was sold on to other tourist railways. (Source - FACS-UNECTO.)

Preserved Locomotives and Other Traction

FACS-UNECTO

Voiture à bogies No. 89 formerly of the Réseau Breton classed as *Monument Historique*, and kept by Chemin de Fer du Vivarais (CFV).   *Author*

Member: FACS-UNECTO
Location: Paris.
Department: Paris (75).
Getting there: By metro or train to Gare de l'Est located on the boulevard de Strasbourg.
Gauge and type of traction: All; steam, diesel and electric.
Rolling stock: FACS-UNECTO has been highly successful in saving heritage (*patrimoine*) traction and rolling stock from the cutter's torch. At present it has the following in safe-keeping in various locations in France: 231 K 8 with Matériel Ferroviaire et Patrimoine National, No. 230 G 352 and autorail Billard No. 902 with Trains à Vapeur de Touraine, No. 140 C 314 with Chemin de Fer Touristique du Vermandois, 020 T Corpet-Louvet ex-Et FROT, 030 T ex-Chemin de Fer du Morbihan and voiture à essieux ex-VFIL with Chemin de Fer de la Baie de Somme, 030 T Corpet-Louvet with Musée des Tramways à Vapeur et des Secondaires Français, 040 T 22 Corpet-Louvet ex-Et FROT and 020+020T 101 ex-POC (awaiting restoration) with Association Voies Ferrées du Velay, 040 T 24 Corpet-Louvet ex-Et FROT, three voitures à bogies Nos. 39, 40 and 41 ex-Tramways de la Sarthe, two voiture à bogies Nos. 89 and 107 ex-Réseau Breton and a fourgon No. 225 ex-Réseau Breton with Chemin de Fer du Vivarais, 130 T 77 and voiture salon Ex-POC with Chemin de Fer Touristique de Pithiviers, 230 E 327 ex-Réseau Breton with GECP - Trains des Pignes and, finally, 2D2 5525 in conjunction with the associations AFAC and COPEF at Gare de l'Est in Paris.
Contact details: FACS-UNECTO, Gare de l'Est, 75475 Paris. Telephone: 01 40 38 39 07 Fax: 01 40 38 41 39.

Website: www.trains-fr.org/materiel/spem.htm and to see a photograph of this locomotive visit www.trains.asso.fr/galerie/spe/img0271.jpg
Comments: This is the organization in France looking after the interests of heritage and tourist railways as well as the safeguarding of its own material.
Local Tourist Office: see main Paris Tourist Office details in the introduction to this Region.

Matériels Ferroviaires et Patrimoine National (MFPN)

No. 231 K 8 standing at Tournan-sur-Rhône station.   *Author*

Member: FACS-UNECTO
Location: Gare de Paris-Nord, central Paris.
Department: Paris (75).
Gauge and type of traction: Standard; steam, electric.
Rolling stock: Pacific steam locomotive No. 231 K 8 and electric locomotive No. CC 40110.
Contact details: Matériels Ferroviaires et Patrimoine National, 1 rue du TGV, 94190 Villeneuve-St-Georges. Telephone: 01 43 89 48 60 Fax: 01 43 89 48 70.
E-mail: mfpn@ifrance.com
Website: http://mfpn.free.fr
Comments: Both these preserved locomotives are approved for use on SNCF lines. Pacific 231 K 8 and its tender 38 A 1 are the property of FACS (Fédération des amis des Chemins de fer Secondaires) which bought the locomotive from SNCF in 1975 after it had been retired from service earlier in 1971. Built in 1912 at Cassel in Germany by Henschel & Sohn, she was one of a series of locomotives of the Pacific

type 231 (or whose wheel formation would be described in the UK as 4-6-2) ordered by the PLM company (Paris-Lyon-Méditerranée). In its career 231 K 8 worked from various depots with PLM before entering service with the newly-formed SNCF in 1938 in its Sud-Est region and later in 1950 in the Nord region. It is currently the only working example of this class in France. It is designated as a *Monument Historique* and is based at Pontrieux with La Vapeur de Trieux line. *(See entry under the Bretagne Region.)* CC 40110 was built by Alsthom and brought into service in April 1970 and was used for hauling the TEE (Trans Europ Express) between France and the Benelux countries. It was retired from service in April 1998 at which time it was purchased by MFPN.

Local Tourist Office: see main Paris Tourist Office details in the introduction to this Region.

Association Française de Conservation de Locomotives (AFCL)

Location: Paris
Department: Paris (75).
Gauge and type of traction: Standard; electric.
Rolling stock: The electric locomotive 2D2 9135 is in the process of being restored and when completed will become one of only two preserved 2D2s authorised for running on RFF (SNCF) lines.

No. 2D2 9135 in the course of restoration at Paris Gare de Lyon. *Alain and Thomas Gallé*

Contact details: Association Française de Conservation de Locomotives, AFCL, Dépôt de Paris Sud-Est, 21 rue de Charolais, 75012 Paris.
Website: www.trains-fr.org/materiel/spem.htm and for photograph go to www.trains.asso.fr/galerie/spe/img1039.jpg
Local Tourist Office: see main Paris Tourist Office details in the introduction to this Region.

AJECTA

Member: FACS-UNECTO
Location: Longueville, 93 km south-east of Paris.
Department: Seine-et-Marne (77).
Getting there: By road take the autoroute A4 and exit at 13 on to D231 to Longueville. It is possible to take a suburban train from Paris-Est station (one hour journey time).
Gauge and type of traction: Standard; steam, diesel and autorails.
Rolling stock: Steam locomotive 140 C 231 ex-Etat (Consolidation) built by North British in Glasgow. Other steam locomotives retained by AJECTA are 141 TB 407 ex-Est (ANF - Blanc-Misseron), 141 TC 19 ex-Etat (Fives-Lille), 140 C 231 ex-Etat (Consolidation), 030 No. 3032 *Rimaucourt* (Batignolles), 040 No. 4.853 ex-Nord (Cail), 030 No. 3467 (Schneider), 020 No. 105 (Corpet), 020 No. 2 (Cockerill), 040 TA 137 (ANF - Blanc-Misseron), 030 TU 22 (Davenport), 130 B 348 and 476 (Cie. Est – Ateliers d'Epernay). These are all kept at Longueville as are locotracteurs T104 (Schneider), T106 (BDR) and 931 (CAFL/CEM). AJECTA

Nos. 141 TB 407 and 140 C 231 at AJECTA's depot at Longueville.
G. Rouvelet/Collection AJECTA

also has two autorails which are ABJ4 No. X 3601 and 150cv No. X 5506 (both located with the CFVE at Pacy-sur-Eure) and a huge collection of vintage carriages and wagons which is probably the most important in France.
Contact details: AJECTA, BP 1, 77650 Longueville. Telephone: 01 64 60 26 26.
Website: www.ajecta.org
Comments: The depot and the Musée de Longueville keeps preserved locomotives approved for use on SNCF railway lines. The Depot at Longueville is normally open for visits on Saturdays and Sundays between 0930 and 1730 hours except when the volunteers are engaged in preparing for special train excursions.
Local Tourist Office: Chemin de Villecran, BP 44, 77160 Provins.
Telephone: 01 64 60 26 26 Fax: 01 64 60 11 97. E-mail: info@provins.net
website: www.provins.net

CFTA

A Thury electric (368kw) locomotive standing at La Mure station in the Isère department with passenger carriages, some of which have been renovated by CFTA.   *Author*

Location: Nanterre, 13 km west of the centre of Paris.
Department: Hauts-de-Seine (92).
Getting there: By train RER to Nanterre.
Gauge and type of traction: Standard; autorail.
Rolling stock: CFTA owns autorail No. X 3876 named *Le Furet du Morvan* but also has been responsible for the revision for SNCF of 22 of the type BB 63000s and the renovation and/or maintenance of many other items such as steam

locomotive 230 G 353, Henschell Mallet 020+020 T, Picasso No. X 4039 (formerly of ABFC) and 230 G 558.
Contact details: CFTA, Parc des Fontaines, 169 avenue Georges Clemenceau, 92735 Nanterre. Telephone: 01 46 69 30 00. E-mail: off the website.
Website: www.cfta.fr
Comments: CFTA assists in the preservation of locomotives approved for use on SNCF and other railway lines. CFTA is also linked with Connex-Tradition (www.connex-tradition.com) which operates Le Petit Train de La Rhune in Aquitaine (www.rhune.com), La Vapeur du Trieux in Bretagne (www.vapeurdutrieux.com), Le Chemin de Fer de La Mure in the Rhône-Alpes (www.trainlamure.com) and Les Chemins de Fer de Provence (www.trainprovence.com) in Provence-Alpes-Côte-d'Azur.
Local Tourist Office: 4, rue du Marché, 92000 Nanterre. Telephone: 01 47 21 58 02 Fax: 01 47 25 99 02. E-mail: info@ot-nanterre.fr website: www.ot-nanterre.fr

Cercle Ouest Parisien d'Études des Ferroviaires (COPEF)

Location: Paris.
Department: Paris (75)
Rolling stock: COPEF owns a number of railway items such as a postal carriage and an automotrice from the tramway of Vienne which is kept under cover at the workshops of Tramway du Val de Seine at Issy-Les Moulineaux. This automotrice has been adapted for use on the RATP network which occasionally it does on the T2 line (Tramway du Val de Seine). As a member of the Association E525 with two others - FACS and Association Française des Amis des Chemins de fer (AFAC) - it co-owns the electric locomotive 2D2 5525, the only one of the 2D2 class at the moment preserved in working order.
Contact details: Cercle Ouest Parisien d'Études des Ferroviaires (COPEF) 9 rue du Château-Landon 75010 Paris. Telephone: 01 45 81 11 06 Fax : 01 45 81 11 05. NB: the office is manned only on Wednesdays between 1430 and 1745 hours but not at all in July and August. E-mail: copef.copef@voila.fr
Website: www.copef.org
Comments: The association COPEF was formed at the beginning of 1973 and is run by employees of SNCF albeit the association is independent. Its prime objective is to promote knowledge about railways of the past, present and the future both in France and abroad. Its first event was actually before the association was formed, when, in 1972, a special electric train was run from Paris St Lazare station to Argenteuil. The main activity is the organization of special train excursions not only on the RFF (SNCF) network but also on RATP, urban and industrial networks, as well as outside France to countries in Europe. Other activities include the safeguarding of railway material of historical interest to be kept in working order; restoration of historical wagons; visits to railway installations and factories; the giving of film and slide shows; and, the running of conferences. Membership is drawn from all walks of life not just *cheminots*, and, in the most part, members are resident in the Île de France.
Local Tourist Office: see main Paris Tourist Office details in the introduction to this Region.

No. 2D2 5255 at Gare d'Austerlitz, Paris. *Alain and Thomas Gallé*

Museums

Musée des Tramways à Vapeurs et Secondaires Français (MTVS)

Member: FACS-UNECTO
Location: Butry-sur-Oise, 37 km north of Paris.
Department: Val d'Oise (95).
Getting there: By road from Paris take the autoroute A115 and then the D928 to Butry-sur-Oise.
Route: Butry-sur-Oise to Valmondois (1 km).
Gauge and type of traction: Metre and 800 mm; steam, diesel and electric.
Rolling stock and Exhibits: Ten steam locomotives comprising two 030 T bicabine ex-Sarthe Nos. 60 and 16, a 030 T No. 75 ex-Ille-&-Vilaine, a 030 T No. 36 ex-Côtes-du-Nord, a 130 T No. E96 ex-Portugal Railways, a 030 T No. 16 ex-Drôme, a 130 T No. 13 ex-VFIL Oise, a 020 T Corpet ex-Paul Frot Industries, a 020 T Corpet-Louvet, a 020 T (vertical boiler) Cockerill. Also kept are an autorail De Dion-Bouton (ex CFD), six locotracteurs both diesel and electric, and about 50 other items characteristic of French secondary network material.
Contact details: Mairie de Butry-sur-Oise, 95430 Butry-sur-Oise. Telephone: 01 34 73 04 40. E-mail: mtvs@voila.fr
Website: http://www.trains-fr.org/mtvs

An historic train hauled by 1925 Corpet-Louvet locomotive 030 T No. 36 ex-Chemin de Fer des Côtes-du-Nord.   *MTVS*

Operating dates: From April to All Saints Day (1st November) on Sundays and public holidays and in July and August on Saturdays as well. Operating hours are from 1400 to 1800 hours.

Tariff: An adult ticket is 5€ and for a child (6-12 years) 2€ (2006).

Comments: Situated close to the station at Valmondois and alongside the banks of the River l'Oise the museum exhibits a vast collection of metric and sub-metric rolling stock some of which is in operational order or in the process of restoration. Since 1989 a short metric railway line has been laid by members of the de l'association de l'ancienne ligne Valmondois - Marines des Chemins de fer Economiques. This museum should not be confused with the Chemin de Fer du Vermandois, 170 km to the north at St Quentin in Picardie.

Local Tourist Office: Office de Tourisme, l'Oise et de la Vallée du Sausseron (OTOS) 95620 Parmain. Telephone: 01 34 08 95 00 Fax: 01 34 69 61 27. E-mail: contact@ot-otos.fr

L'Association pour la Reconstruction et la Préservation du Patrimoine Industriel (ARPPI)

Location: Paris

Department: Paris (75).

Display: A dynamic reconstruction of the tubular boiler locomotive invented by Marc Seguin.

Contact details: ARPPI, 4 rue Carolus Duran, 75019 Paris.

Telephone: 01 64 08 60 62. E-mail: webmaster@art-et-histoire.com

Website: www.art-et-histoire.com/laseguin.htm This website is well worth visiting especially for those wish to know about Seguin's important pioneering engineering work in France.

Reconstruction of Seguin's locomotive on display in Paris in the Champs Elysées for the 'Le Train Capitale' exhibition on 25th May, 2003.   *Alain and Thomas Gallé*

Comments: The Association, created in 1980, in part commemorates the life and work of Marc Seguin who lived between 1786 and 1875, the French inventor credited with the design of the first tubular boiler and the first suspension bridge at Tournon-sur-Rhône close to the departure point for Chemin de Fer du Vivarais (*see entry under Rhône-Alpes region*). A replica of this locomotive has been built by Professor of Mechanics Monsieur Gaston Monnier of the Technical College at Ledru-Rollin in Paris. As did the original, this replica locomotive comprises a chassis, four wooden rimmed wheels, a tubular boiler made of copper and a two-cylinder (vertical) steam engine. Contact ARPPI for the viewing arrangements.
Local Tourist Office: see main Paris Tourist Office details in the introduction to this Region.

Musée de Chemin de Fer (Rosny-Rail)

Member: FACS-UNECTO
Location: Rosny-sous-Bois, 13 km east of the centre of Paris.
Department: Seine-St-Denis (93).
Getting there: By the RER-A line or RER-E line services to Rosny-sous-Bois station.
Exhibits: This is a museum which, with its wide variety of artefacts, both inside and outside, traces the history of railways in France and whilst it does not have any locomotives, it does have a draisine on which visitors may ride.
Contact details: Musée de Chemin de Fer (l'association Rosny-Rail), Gare de Rosny-sous-Bois, 1 place des Martyrs de la Résistance, 93110 Rosny-sous-Bois. Telephone: 01 43 00 58 05 or 01 40 18 64 74.
Website: http://www.mairie-rosny-sous-bois.fr/article.php3?id_article=86

Operating dates: Throughout the year on Saturdays from 1400 to 1800 hours and on Sundays from 1000 to 1800 hours.
Tariff: No charge on Saturday afternoons between 1400 and 1600 hours. At other times an individual entry is 5€ and for individual members of groups 3€, however, children under 12 years go free (2006).
Comments: The museum also has a simulator of a driver's cab in which visitors can experience driving a train.
Local Tourist Office: see main Paris Tourist Office details in the introduction to this Region.

Musée Decauville (CEMNAD)

An example of a draisine designed and built by Paul Decauville. This example stands at St Georges-de-Commiers on the Chemin de Fer de la Mure.   *Author*

Location: Evry, 33 km south of central Paris.
Department: Essonne (91).
Getting there: By train take the RER-D line service to Evry. By road take the autoroute A6 and exit at the RN449 for Evry.
Contact details: Musée Decauville, le Comité Evyren pour la Création du Musée National Decauville (CEMNAD), 13 place Gauvain, 91000 Evry. Telephone: 01 60 78 53 88 Fax: 01 60 78 29 36.
E-mail : marc-andre.dubout@wanadoo.fr
Website: http://musee-Decauville.ifrance.com/
Operating dates: Visits to the centre at Chemin de la Grange Feu Louis in Evry have to be arranged beforehand. They can take place on Mondays and Thursdays between 1400 and 1700 hours.

Tariff: Not known but it is understood that the association is seeking funds to preserve an automotrice Z 600 from St Gervais-Chamonix-Vallorcine as well as other material so a donation may be appropriate in the absence of a charge.
Comments: CEMNAD was formed as an association with charitable status to safeguard the history of Paul Decauville, a French railway engineer of some considerable distinction. There are almost 150 members drawn from France and abroad. A bulletin, *Les Amis du Musée Decauville*, is produced three times per year and there are also three or four open days held annually. The association has a number of objectives including the promoting and assisting research on Paul Decauville and his works, the safeguarding of documents, the preservation of material, e.g. a Z 600 automotrice, locotracteurs, etc., and to create a library with multimedia centre.
Local Tourist Office: see main Paris Tourist Office details in the introduction to this Region.

Museum Operation Temporarily Suspended

Musée des Transports Urbains, Interurbains et Ruraux (AMTUIR)

Member: FACS-UNECTO
Location: Colombes, 12 km from the centre of Paris.
Department: Hauts-de-Seine (92).
Getting there: By RER train to Colombes.
Gauge and type of traction: All gauges; trams.
Rolling stock: Over 100 vehicles are stored including former metro (underground) traction, (omni)buses, hippomobiles (horse-drawn carriages), steam trams, a Mékarski compressed air tram from Nantes (the only one preserved in the world), electric trams, trolley-buses, autocars and steam locomotives from the former secondary rail network. Also retained is the (re-constructed) first Parisian autobus of 1905.
Contact details: Musée des Transports Urbains, Interurbains et Ruraux, 163 boulevard Charles de Gaulle, 92700 Colombes. Telephone: 01 43 28 37 12 or 01 42 42 43 96 Fax: 01 46 52 16 18. E-mail: amtuir@amtuir.org
Website: www.amtuir.org/
Operating dates: The museum is presently closed but it may be viewed by arrangement. Yearly heritage open days are sometimes held - contact the museum for more details.
Comments: This museum, with its outstanding collection of historical transport material, was created on the initiative of Monsieur Jean Robert in 1957. Sadly for those who are interested in visiting this interesting collection there is no indication at present of when it will be re-opened to the public. However the information is included here to identify what exists coupled with the hope that the financial and other problems will one day be resolved thus allowing public access to this important historical material.
Local Tourist Office: see main Paris Tourist Office details in the introduction to this Region.

Languedoc-Roussillon

Languedoc-Roussillon is in the south of France and has a frontier with Spain in the south and regional borders with Midi-Pyrénées to the west, Auvergne to the north, Rhone-Alpes to the north-east and Provence-Alpes-Côte-d'Azur to the east. It comprises the departments of Aude (11), Gard (30), Hérault (34), Lozère (48) and Pyrénées Orientales (66). Its regional capital is Montpellier and other cities include Nîmes, Perpignan, Mende, and Carcassonne. This region has three heritage/tourist railways, two TER-SNCF tourist railways, and one location where preserved traction is stored and which also happens to be an active railway development project.

Railways

Train à Vapeur des Cévennes (CITEV)

SACM-built 030 T No. 8158 and Renault VH24 autorail at St Jean-du-Gard station.   *Author*

Member: FACS-UNECTO
Location: Anduze, 47 km north-west of Nîmes.
Department: Gard (30).
Getting there: By SNCF train to Alès then by bus or taxi. By road take the autoroutes A7 and A9 to Nimes then the RN106 towards Alès for 22 km then follow the D982 and D907 to Anduze.
Route: Anduze to St Jean-du-Gard (13 km).
Journey time: 40 minutes each way.
Gauge and type of traction: Standard; steam, diesel and autorail.

Rolling stock: Steam locomotives comprising a 030 T No. 8158 built by SACM, a Krupp-built 040 T No. 1751 and 140 C 27 steam locomotive which is presently for sale, a Renault VH24 autorail (Iroquois), a Renault autorail Panoramique, two Schneider diesels, Nos. 902 and 906, and a d'Hermoult type diesel No. 61005. The Panoramique No. X 4206 was awaiting restoration but has now been sold (January 2006). There is a varied collection of carriages and goods wagons.
Contact details: CITEV, 36 place de la Gare, BP50, 30140 Anduze (President – Monsieur François Zielinger, brother of the founder). Telephone: 04 66 60 59 00 Fax: 04 66 60 59 09. E-mail: contact@citev.com
Website: www.citev.com
Operating dates: From 1st April to 1st November with services every day to 17th September then excluding Mondays to 31st October but CITEV does operate a service on 1st November if it is a Monday as this date is All Saints Day, a public holiday in France. Departures from Anduze are at 0930, 1130, 1500 and 1700 hours. Departures from St Jean-du-Gard are at 1030, 1400, 1600 and 1800 hours.
Tariff: An adult return ticket is 11€ and for a child (4-12 years) 7€. An adult single ticket is 8.50€ and for a child 6€. The charge for cycles and dogs is 3€ for a single or return journey (2006).
History: The line traces its origins back to 1881 when la Compagnie des Chemin de Fer Paris-Lyon-Méditerranée (PLM) opened a standard gauge railway line between Alès, then a developing coal-mining centre, and the nearby town of Anduze. In 1897 an extension of the line was planned to St Jean-du-Gard but it was not until 1903 that the construction work actually began. Such was the nature of the terrain that a number of major works had to be undertaken including the construction of four tunnels, a large metal viaduct crossing the River Gardon outside Anduze, a further five stone-constructed viaducts and many kilometres of retaining walls. A number of projects also had to be undertaken to reduce the threat of water to the line so it was not until May 1909 that the extension was finally opened for passenger and goods services. However, the full active life of the line was of limited duration. In June 1940, the passenger services were terminated. Goods services continued to operate during and after the end of hostilities, but these were eventually terminated in July 1971 and the line was abandoned. Twelve years later saw the formation of a voluntary association – Train à Vapeur des Cévennes - which established a tourist line run by volunteers. In the following three seasons nearly 30,000 passengers were carried but in spite of this success, the association ceased all activity in 1985. In 1986 Benoît Zielinger and others created the Compagnie Internationale des Trains Express à Vapeur, or CITEV as it is known for short, which recommenced tourist services and which continue today providing a highly popular tourist attraction in the region. This railway is extremely well run and with the line travelling through most beautiful countryside, it is a definite 'must-do'.
Comments: A beautiful train journey through the lower Cévennes countryside made famous by Robert Louis Stevenson in *Travels with my Donkey*.
Local Tourist Office: Plan de Brie, BP 6, 30140 Anduze. Telephone: 04 66 61 98 17 Fax: 04 66 61 79 77. E-mail: anduze@ot-anduze.fr
website: www.ot-anduze.fr

Picasso autorail standing at Bize-Minervois railway station. *Author*

Autorail Touristique du Minervois (ATM)

Member: FACS-UNECTO
Location: Narbonne, south-west France close to the Mediterranean coast and 100 km north of the Spanish border.
Department: Aude (11).
Getting there: By TGV to Narbonne. By road take the RN9 or the autoroute A9 from Béziers or Perpignan.
Route: Narbonne to Bize (20 km).
Journey time: Varies between 1 hour and 1 hour 30 minutes.
Gauge and type of traction: Standard; autorail.
Rolling stock: Three former SNCF Picasso autorails Nos. X 3846, X 3900 and X 4028 and a non-powered carriage (remorque) No. XR 7967.
Contact details: Autorail Touristique du Minervois, 53 avenue Wilson, 11200 Lézignan-Corbières. Telephone: 04 68 27 05 94 Fax: 04 68 27 24 87.
Website: http://www.atm.fr.tc or www.trains-fr.org/unecto/atm/
Operating dates: From the second Sunday in July to the second Sunday in October inclusive. In July and August on Saturday afternoons and Sunday mornings and in September and October on Sunday afternoons only.
Tariff: An adult return is 9.50€ and for a child (6-12 years) 6.50€ (2005).
History: The line was first opened in the summer of 1887 for the carriage of passengers and local merchandise including wine. The line stopped carrying passengers in the spring of 1939 and some time later the carriage of all freight was halted. In July 1983, a group of railway enthusiasts took over the operation of the line and began running tourist services using their restored and brightly painted autorails.
Comments: Departs from a platform on rue Paul Vieu in Narbonne behind the office of the Gendarmerie which is about 500 metres from the main railway station. An extra service operates on a Monday in mid-August for a local pottery fair at Sallères d'Aude. A public swimming pool is available in Bize-Minervois. The line crosses the River Aude on a girder bridge constructed by Gustave Eiffel.
Local Tourist Office: place Roger Salengro, 11100 Narbonne. Telephone: 04 68 65 15 60 Fax: 04 68 65 59 12. E-mail: office-tourisme.narbonne@wanadoo.fr

Train du Pays Cathare et du Fenouillèdes (TPCF)

Member: FACS-UNECTO
Location: Rivesaltes, 58 km south of Narbonne.
Departments: Pyrénées -Orientales (66) and Aude (11).
Getting there: By rail take the TGV to Narbonne and then a local train to Rivesaltes. By road take the RN9 or the autoroute A9 from Béziers or Perpignan and then the RN113 to Rivesaltes.
Route: Rivesaltes – Axat (60 km).
Journey time: 2 hours 15 minutes each way.
Gauge and type of traction: Standard; autorails, diesel.
Rolling stock: Picasso autorail No. X 3944, Caravelle No. X 4545 and a remorque No. XR 8601, two diesel locomotives Nos. BB 63048 and BB 63138, an ex-SNCF 5M 057 draisine, various wagons and two open carriages.
History: Although the railway was planned back in 1883 it was not until 1904 that the complete line between Rivesaltes and Quillan came into service. In 1939, like many other local lines, it was closed to passengers shortly after the creation of SNCF. After World War II, it was little used although it came into its own in 1951 when a mudslide closed the Route National road between Axat and Quillan. It was finally disposed of by SNCF at the end of 1989. With the support of local enthusiastic volunteers it became a tourist line in 2002.
Contact details: Train du Pays Cathare et du Fenouillèdes (TPCF) 7 avenue de la Gare, 66220 Caudiès-de-Fenouillèdes. Telephone: 04 68 59 99 02 Fax: 04 68 59 96 18. E-mail: info@tpcf.fr
Website: www.tpcf.fr
Operating dates: From May to September; in May, June, September and October services run on Saturdays and Sundays; and, in July and August daily except Mondays. The hours of operation are usually in the mornings and the afternoons of these days but check first for precise timings.
Tariff: An adult return is 17€ and for a child (5-12 years) 12€; cycles and pushchairs go free (2005).
Comments: Trains usually leave from the main railway station in Rivesaltes but on occasions from a separate platform (No. 101) to the west of the main SNCF station; however, do arrive early and check first. A large parking area, which is free of charge, adjoins either of the departure points. There is ample free parking at other main stations on the route. A truly beautiful line on which to travel, it rises from 50 m above sea level at Rivesaltes to 514 m at Campérié on gradients at times of 2.5 per cent (1 in 40). The railway architecture is particularly interesting with numerous viaducts, bridges and tunnels. There are stopping stations at Cases de Péne, Estagel, Maury, St Paul-de-Fenouillèdes, Caudiès and La Pradelle-Puilaurens. The journey from Rivesaltes to Caudiès (49 km) and return is completed in a Caravelle autorail. On reaching Caudiès passengers transfer to the diesel-hauled train comprising open carriages and travel on up to Axat. In the summer months ensure protective headwear is worn to prevent sunburn. There is a superb open-air swimming pool next to the railway station at Axat which is open to the public on payment of a small charge.

Local Tourist Office: Office d'Animation et du Tourisme, avenue Ledru-Rolin, 66600 Rivesaltes. Telephone: 04 68 64 04 04 Fax: 04 68 64 56 17. E-mail: office.tourisme.rivesaltes@wanadoo.fr

Diesel No. BB 63138 with two open carriages leaving La Pradelle station and passing below the famous Cathars fort of Chateau Puilaurens. *Author*

TER-SNCF - Le Petit Train Jaune de Cerdagne

The 'little yellow train' crossing the Cerdagne plain. *Author*

Location: Villefranche-de-Conflent, 53 km west of Perpignan.
Department: Pyrénées-Orientales (66).
Getting there: By rail take the TGV to Perpignan, then TER-SNCF to Villefranche-de-Conflent. By road take the autoroute A9 and then exit at 42 on to the RN116 to Villefranche-de-Conflent.
Route: Villefranche-Vernet-les-Bains to Latour-de-Carol–Enveitg (66 km).
Journey time: 2 hours in summer and 2 hours 30 minutes in winter.
Gauge and type of traction: Metre; electric (850W) delivered by a third rail.
Rolling stock: Renovated Z100s and also recently introduced Z152s.
Contact details: SNCF, Gare de Villefranche-de-Conflent – Vernet-les-Bains, 66820 Villefranche-de-Conflent. Telephone: 04 68 96 56 62 or 08 92 35 35 35. E-mail: via the website.
Website: www.trainstouristiques-ter.com / train_jaune.htm
Operating dates: All year but services can be subject to adverse weather conditions in winter. In summer ensure suitable headwear is worn. Ten services operate per day in the summer months but fewer in winter.
Tariff: Obtainable on request by telephoning 08 92 35 35 35 or via the website. An example of a fare for an adult return ticket for the full route from Villefranche-Vernet-les-Bains to Latour-de-Carol–Enveitg is 34€ (2006).
History: The approval for the building of the line was given in 1883 but construction did not begin until 20 years later. It was seven years before the first and most difficult section of just over 27 km was opened to Mont-Louis. A year later another 28 km of line was opened to Bourg-Madame. However, owing to the intervention of World War I, the final section of eight kilometres to the Franco-Spanish border at Latour-de-Carol–Enveitg was not completed until 1925.
Comments: Operated by TER-SNCF, it is often referred to as Le Canari (canary) by virtue of its distinctive yellow-coloured carriages. The train links at Latour-de-Carol–Enveitg with Spanish rail services (RENFE) from Barcelona. There are

A Z152 and a Z100 standing at Villefranche station.   *Author*

many spectacular views to be enjoyed on the journey as well as appreciating the outstanding feats of engineering, for example, the stone-constructed Pont Séjourné and the Pont Gisclard suspension bridge.
Local Tourist Office: place de l'Eglise, 66500 Villefranche-de-Conflent. Telephone: 04 68 96 22 96 Fax: 04 68 96 07 66.
E-mail: otsi-villefranchedeconflent@voila.fr.

TER-SNCF – Le Cévenole

Location: Alès, 41 km north-west of Nîmes.
Department: Gard (30).
Getting there: By TGV services to Nîmes and then TER-SNCF services to Alès. By road take the autoroute A9 and exit at 25 on to the RN106 to Alès.
Route: Alès to La Bastide Puylaurent (79 km) where there may be a change of trains to go on either to Langogne connecting with the les Gorges de l'Allier service (*see entry under the Auvergne region*) or to Mende (127 km) and Marvejols (150 km).
Journey time: 1 hour 7 minutes to La Bastide Puylaurent and a further 25 minutes to Langogne or a further 2 hours 30 minutes to Marvejols.
Gauge and type of traction: Standard; modern autorail.
Contact details: TER-SNCF, La Gare, 31000 Alès.
Website: www.ter-sncf.com/languedoc/Default.htm
Operating dates: All year with seven services per day.
Tariff: Consult TER-SNCF.

Autorail No. X 73805 near Barjac in the Cevennes.   *Author*

Comments: Another outstandingly beautiful railway as the train traces its route through the Cévennes National Park via Génolhac and Villefort. This is a 'must-do' journey.
Local Tourist Office: place de la Mairie, 30100 Alès-en-Cévennes. Telephone: 04 66 52 32 15 Fax : 04 66 52 57 09. E-mail: tourisme@ville-ales.net

Preserved Locomotives, Other Traction and a Railway Project

Association pour l'Entretien, la Préservation et l'Evaison Touristique (l'APEPETE)

Location: Nîmes, 50 km south-west of Avignon and 123 km north-west of Marseille.
Department: Gard (30).
Getting there: By rail take TGV to Nîmes. By road take the RN7 and RN113 or the autoroutes, A7 and A9 from Lyon.
Gauge and type of traction: Standard; steam and autorail.
Rolling stock: a 030 T No. 8157 *Ilène*, an autorail Renault 150 hp No. X 5845 owned by Monsieur Jean-Marc Chelly, a 030 T 8 *Léonie*, autorails Nos. X 3824, X 2403 and remorque XR 7415 all three owned by Monsieur J-M Henry, and X 3824 owned by Monsieur J-P Isnard.
Contact details: Association pour l'Entretien, la Préservation et l'Evaison Touristique, 16 rue Melchior Doze, 30000 Nîmes.
Telephone: 04 66 23 00 58. E-mail: lapepete@wanadoo.fr
Website: http://monsite.wanadoo.fr/lapepete/
Comments: This is a tourist railway project in the Nîmes area with many of the locomotives which are stored approved for use on RFF (SNCF) tracks. This is a project is in its early stages, but the intention is to establish a tourist railway service from Nîmes down to the coast at Le Grau du Roi via the fortified town of Aigues-Mortes, a total distance of about 50 km.
Local Tourist Office: 6, rue Auguste, 30020 Nîmes. Telephone: 04 66 58 38 00 Fax: 04 66 58 38 01. E-mail: info@ot-nimes.fr website: www.ot-nimes.fr

Limousin

Limousin is left of centre in France with regional borders to Centre to the north, Auvergne to the east, Midi-Pyrénées to the south, Poitou-Charentes to the north-west and Aquitaine to the south-west. It comprises the departments of Corrèze (19), Creuse (23) and Haute-Vienne (87). The regional capital is at Limoges and other important centres include Guéret and Brive-la-Gaillarde. This region has one heritage/tourist railway, one railway project, one museum and one vélorail service.

Railway

Train Touristique Vapeur en Limousin also known as the Chemin de fer Touristique Limousin-Perigord (CFTLP) in conjunction with the Association Vienne Vézère Vapeur (VVV)

No. 141 TD 740 standing at Limoges station. *Collection CFTLP*

Location: Limoges, 100 km east of Angoulême.
Department: Haute-Vienne (87).
Getting there: By SNCF to Limoges-Bénédictins. By road take the autoroute A20 and exit at 33 which is nearest link to Limoges-Bénédictins railway station.

Routes: Limoges to Eymoutiers (for La Haute Vallée de la Vienne), Limoges to Meymac (for Le Plateau de Millevaches), Eymoutiers to Châteauneuf-Bujaleuf (for Les Gorges de la Vienne) and Meymac to Ussel (for La Cité des Ventadour). Total distance on the SNCF line from Limoges to Ussel is 110 km.

Journey time: Limoges to Eymoutiers – 2 hours 5 minutes; Limoges to Meymac – 4 hours; Eymoutiers to Châteauneuf-Bujaleuf – 20 minutes; Meymac to Ussel – 20 minutes.

Gauge and type of traction: Standard; steam, diesel.

Rolling stock: Steam locomotives Nos. 141 TD 740 built in 1932 and retired from service at Paris in 1967 and is classed as a *Monument Historique*, 140 C 38 built in 1919 and retired in 1975 and is present undergoing restoration with the hope that it will be operational again in the spring of 2006, a Moyse locotracteur built in 1934 and retired from service with France Telecom in 1997 and a collection of passenger carriages, some of which are undergoing restoration.

Contact details: Association CFTLP, Secretariat, 9 rue Martin Freminet, 87100, Limoges. E-mail: cftlp@wanadoo.fr   For information and reservations on this railway contact Association Vienne Vézère Vapeur (VVV) Syndicat Monts et Barrages, Le Château, BP 5, 87460 Châteauneuf-Bujaleuf.

E-mail: vienne.vezere.vapeur@wanadoo.fr No telephone numbers are provided but the Tourist Offices at Limoges, St Leonard de Noblat (05 55 56 25 06), Eymoutiers (05 55 69 27 81), Meymac (05 55 95 18 43), Ussel (05 55 72 11 50), Châteauneuf-Bujaleuf (05 55 69 63 69) and Maison du Limousin in Paris (01 40 07 04 67) can help and do take reservations. English is spoken.

Website: www.trainvapeur.com

Operating dates: The excursions operate on currently active SNCF lines and therefore their frequency is limited. Each year about 14 trips are made during the months of June to September and usually on Sundays and Thursdays. However, the 2006's ambitious programme has 19 including one excursion with three nights away in the Bordeaux and Perigueux area. Consult the website to view the current programme of tours.

Tariff: An adult return ticket for Limoges to Eymoutiers is 25€ and for a child (6-12 years) 14€; Limoges to Meymac for an adult return is 35€ and children 18€; Eymoutiers to Châteauneuf-Bujaleuf for an adult return is 12€ and a child 7€; Meymac to Ussel for an adult return is 8€ and for a child 5€. All children under six years go free but they must be carried on a knee! (2005).

History: CFTLP was founded in May 1981 and which at that time was called the Chemin de Fer Touristique Périgord-Quercy. The objectives of the association were and still are to bring together persons interested in railways, to safeguard the historic material, to create a tourist train service local to Limoges and, finally, to send preserved locomotives and carriages to other regions of France as working exhibits. To date all the objectives have been achieved and in respect of the latter their locomotive 141 TD 740 has to date visited 28 departments in France and in so doing has travelled over 45,000 km. Originally, the association's was located at the Du Buisson depot but in 1991 they moved to Limoges-Puy Imbert and it was at this time that the name change took place. In 1993, the Association Vienne Vézère Vapeur was formed with 100 members drawn from volunteers, local communes, local tourist offices and organizations offering tourist services. VVV has become the commercial working arm of the heritage railway operations. Since the formation of VVV the number of excursions has tripled in the past five years.

Comments: This is an enthusiastic and energetic operation in the heart of France. The excursions, utilising superbly restored preserved locomotives and carriages, travel through outstandingly beautiful countryside. This is a 'must-do' trip appealing not only to railway enthusiasts but to those who just love to see the beautiful French countryside.

Local Tourist Office: 12, boulevard de Fleurus, 87000 Limoges. Telephone: 05 55 34 46 87 Fax: 05 55 34 19 12. E-mail: info@tourismelimoges.com website: http://www.tourismelimoges.com

Railway Project

Association pour la Sauvegarde du Viaduc et le Chemin de Fer de la Luzège (ASTTRE-19)

Location: Soursac, 120 km south-west of Clermont Ferrand.
Department: Corrèze (19).
Getting there: By road, take the autoroute A89 and leave on to the RN89 and then follow the D216 and D941 to Soursac.
Route: Lapleau to Soursac.
Gauge and type of traction: Metre; steam, autorail.
Rolling stock: Steam locomotive Piguet 030 T and also De Dion-Bouton and Billard autorails.
Contact details: ASTTRE-19, c/o Mairie de Soursac, 19550 Soursac. Telephone: 05 55 27 52 61. E-mail: viaduc.sur.luzege@libertysurf.fr or senexter@netcourrier.com
Websites: http://transcorrezien.free.fr
Operating dates and tariff: To be announced.
History: Built in 1913 this line, known as *Le Transcorrezien*, ran between Ussel and Tulle but was finally closed to traffic at the end of 1959. A beautiful section, which is the focus of the restoration project, is between Lapleau and Soursac where deep in woodland the line travels in a horseshoe crossing the River Corrèze on the suspension bridge Viaduc des Rochers-Noirs built by the engineer Gisclard famous for a similar designed bridge in the Pyrénées (*see TER-SNCF - Le Petit Train Jaune de Cerdagne*).
Comments: An exciting project to restore a short stretch of line with a magnificent viaduct. If in the area, the project is well worth visiting, walking the track, seeing the viaduct and the rolling stock and, of course, giving some encouragement.
Local Tourist Office: Mairie, Pointe du Bourg, 19550 Soursac. Telephone: 05 55 27 52 61 Fax: 05 55 27 67 31.

Museum

Historail also known as Musée Limousin des Chemins de Fer

Location: St Leonard-de-Noblat, 22 km east of Limoges.
Department: Haute-Vienne (87).
Getting there: By SNCF to St Leonard-de-Noblat. By road on autoroutes A10, A71 and A20 and take exit 27 on to RN141 to St Leonard-de-Noblat.
Contact details: Historail - Musée Limousin des Chemins de Fer, 18 rue de Beaufort, 87400 St Leonard-de-Noblat. Telephone: 05 55 56 11 12 Fax: 05 55 56 36 97. E-mail : jacques.ragon@wanadoo.fr
Website: www.trains-fr.org/historail/
Operating dates: In July and August operating every day from 1400 to 1800 hours. In April to June and from September to October operating every day except Mondays from 1430 to 1800 hours. Group bookings for other times throughout the year are possible.
Comments: Whilst this museum comprises mainly model trains, full size equipment is also exhibited and from time to time there are visits by rolling stock from other preserved railways.
Local Tourist Office: Place du Champ de Mars, 87400 St Leonard-de Noblat. Telephone: 05 55 56 25 06 Fax: 05 55 56 36 97. E-mail: otsi.stleo@wanadoo.fr website: www.ville-saint-leonard.fr

Vélorail

Omnibuss

Member: FACS-UNECTO
Location: Bussière-Galant, 35 km south-west of Limoges.
Department: Haute-Vienne (87).
Getting there: From Limoges take the RN21, D11a, D465 and the D20 to Bussière-Galant.
Route: Bussière-Galant to Châlus (6 km).
Gauge: Standard.
Contact details: OMNIBUSS, c/o Mairie, 87230 Bussière-Galant. Telephone: 05 55 78 84 41 or 05 55 78 86 47 Fax 05 55 78 16 75. E-mail omnibuss@wanadoo.fr
Website: http://www.velorail.net
Operating dates: In May, June, September and October on Saturdays from 1400 to 2000 hours and on Sundays 1000 to 1900 hours. In July and August operating every day from 1000 to 1900 hours.
Tariff: Vélorail hire for 2 hours 30 minutes maximum is 22€. Groups taking at least five vélorails enjoy a reduced charge of 18€ for 2 hours 30 minutes (2006).
Comments: The original line was closed to rail traffic in 1987. The association OMNIBUSS was formed in 1994 and soon after set to work with the help of the local commune to clear the line of overgrowth. The vélorail service began in

1995 and since then has been most successful carrying more than 130,000 passengers to date.

Local Tourist Office: Office de Tourisme de Châlus, 87230 Châlus. Telephone: 05 55 78 51 13.

A vélorail.   *Omnibuss*

Lorraine

Lorraine is in the north-east of France and has a frontier with Belgium and regional borders with Alsace to the east, Champagne-Ardenne to the west and Franche-Comté to the south. It comprises the departments of Meurthe-et-Moselle (54), Meuse (55), Moselle (57) and Vosges (88). Its regional capital is Metz and other important centres are Epinal, Bar-le-Duc and Nancy. This region has six heritage/tourist railways, one museum and one vélorail service.

Railways

Chemin de Fer de la Vallée de la Canner (ALEMF)

Member: FACS-UNECTO
Location: Vigy, 18 km north-west of Metz.
Department: Moselle (57).
Getting there: By rail to Metz and then local transport. By road from Metz to Vigy via the D2 and D52 or by the autoroute A4 and exit at Ennery-Argancy.
Route: Vigy – Hombourg–Budange (12 km).
Journey time: The round trip takes one and a half hours.
Gauge and type of traction: Standard; steam, diesel and autorail.
Rolling stock: 1931 Krupp 030 T steam locomotive, a Picasso No. X 3837 autorail, a Y6000 type locotracteur, a BDR 020 locotracteur and several carriages and wagons. Awaiting restoration is a 1900 Hohenzoller 020 T.
Contact details: Chemin de Fer Touristique de la Vallée de la Canner, Gare de Vigy, 57640 Vigy. Telephone: 03 87 77 97 50 (M. Henry Leroy)
Fax: 03 87 77 97 50. E-mail: gilzol@wanadoo.fr
Website: http://alemftrain.monsite.wanadoo.fr/index.jhtml
Operating dates: From May to September (Sundays and public holidays only) departing Vigy at 1430 and 1650 and from Hombourg at 1540 and 1800 hours. There are extra autorail departures in July and August from Vigy at 1400 and 1630 and from Hombourg at 1450 and 1740 hours. Special reservations are possible for any day of year.
Tariff: An adult return ticket is 8.20€ and for a child (4-12 years) 5.20€. An adult single ticket is 5.20€ and for a child 4.20€ (2005).
History: L'Association Lorraine d'Exploitation et de Modelisme Ferroviaire (ALEMF) was created in 1966 and by the end of 1973 had saved much of the track bed. The association had also started on the restoration of a 1927 locomotive which, from 1975, had operated on a line in the Vosges from d'Etival to Senones, at that time called the Chemin de Fer du Rabodeau. In 1985, the Association left this line and installed itself at its present location in the Vallée de la Canner. This railway originally was of strategic importance in the connection of two routes - Metz to Anzeling via Vigy in 1908 and Bettelainville to Merzig via Waldwisse in 1917. These lines fell victim to the hostilities notably with the destruction of the Failly viaduct between Vigy and Metz. The viaduct was never reconstructed. The lines were eventually taken out of service by

The 1931-built Krupp 030 T.   *ALEMF*

SNCF in 1976. Aware of the tourist interest in this area the local authorities of Moselle acquired the line in 1978 and entrusted it to the association in 1985. It was ceded completely to them in 1991. It has operated a successful tourist service ever since.

Comments: A vélorail service, Vigy-Vélorail, is also operated on this 12 km line. Contact Vigy-Vélorail, Mairie de Vigy, 57640 Vigy or telephone: 03 87 58 75 68 for more information.

Local Tourist Office: 1 rue de la Gare, 57470 Hombourg-Haut. Telephone: 03 87 90 53 53 Fax: 03 87 81 46 23. E-mail: infoshh@freyming-merlebach.fr website: www.cc-freyming-merlebach.fr

Chemin de Fer Forestier d'Abreschviller (ACFA)

Member: FACS-UNECTO
Location: Abreschviller, 50 km west of Strasbourg.
Department: Moselle (57).
Getting there: By SNCF train to Sarrebourg then bus or taxi to Abreschviller. By road take the autoroute A4 and exit at Phalsbourg then the RN4 dual carriageway in direction of Nancy and exit at Abreschviller-Donon.
Route: Abreschviller to Grand Soldat, near to Sarrebourg (6 km).
Journey time: One and a half hours round trip including a 20 minute stop at an original sawmill at Haut-Fer which is now a Museum of Wood.

Jung and Decauville locomotives at the workshops.   *Nicolas Cecotti*

Gauge and type of traction: 700 mm; steam, diesel.
Rolling stock: Four steam locomotives comprising a 1944 Jung 030 Jungenthall No. 10120 with separate tender formerly of the Steiermärkische Landesbahnen in Austria, a remarkable 020+020 T Mallet built in 1906 by Maschienenfabrik Heilbron now classed as of historical interest having been fully restored and brought back into service in 2002, a 1928 Decauville construction No. 1935 and an Orenstein & Koppel 020 T. There are three locotracteurs, a 1953-built 030 Coferna, a 020 Gmeinder and a 020 Deutz. There also 16 carriages and 12 wagons. Two draisines, originally Renault automobiles and adapted for rail use in 1925, are now used for track inspection.
Contact details: Chemin de fer Forestier d'Abreschviller, 2 place Prévôt, 57560 Abreschviller. Telephone: 03 87 03 71 45 and Telephone-Fax: 03 87 07 79 12. E-mail: for reservations train.abreschviller@wanadoo.fr
Website: http://train-abreschviller.fr
Operating dates: In April and October on Sundays and public holidays at 1500 hours; in May and September on Saturdays at 1500 hours and on Sundays and public holidays at 1500 and 1630 hours; in June on Saturdays at 1500 hours and Sundays and public holidays at 1400, 1500 and 1600; in July and August on weekdays at 1500 and 1630 hours, on Saturdays at 1500 and 1630, and on Sundays and public holidays at 1030, 1400, 1500, 1600 and 1700 hours. In addition, special events take place in the months of May to October.
Tariff: An adult return ticket is 8€ and for a child (4-12 years) 6€. An adult single ticket is 6€ and for a child 4€. There are discounts for groups (2005).
History: At the end of the 19th century the area of the forests of Donon in the Vosges, one of the largest forests in France, benefited from development of the

railways by the building of a huge rail network to transport wood. Given the beauty of the area, the line was also used for tourism. The development of other forms of transport, however, eventually led to its closure. In 1957, FACS formed a committee to safeguard the Abreschviller to Grand Soldat line. In 1967, the Association du Chemin de Fer Forestier d'Abreschviller was founded and an accord was signed for the development of a tourist service.

Comments: A railway well worth visiting where there are helpful staff and some English is spoken.

Local Tourist Office: 78 rue Jordy, 57560 Abreschviller. Telephone: 03 87 03 77 26 Fax: 03 87 03 77 26. E-mail: odt-abreschviller@wanadoo.fr website: www.officedetourisme@wanadoo.fr

Chemin de Fer du Val de Passey (CFVP)

Location: Choloy-Menillot, 32 km west of Nancy.

Department: Meurthe et Moselle (54).

Getting there: From Nancy take the autoroute A31 and exit at Toul on to the RN4 and then exit at Foug and on to Choloy-Menillot. From the village follow the road in the direction of Val de Passey.

Route: Malzeville (1 km).

Gauge and type of traction: 600 mm; steam.

Rolling stock: Two steam locomotives comprising a 030 Decauville and a 020 Belgian Bagnall saddle tank named *Charles*.

Contact details: Chemin de Fer du Val de Passey, 12 rue de Chazeau, 54220 Malzéville. Telephone: 03 83 29 21 22 Fax: 03 29 41 54 69. E-mail: cfvp@wanadoo.fr

Website: http://cfvp.monsite.wanadoo.fr

Operating dates: Trains run on the following days in 2006: Sunday 14th May, Thursday 25th May (Ascension Day), Monday 5th June (Pentecost), Sunday 18th June, Friday 14th July (Bastille Day) and Sunday 10th September.

Tariff: Not known.

History: The line was the dream of the late Monsieur Jacques Maginot who, from 1966 and until his death in 1998, turned it into reality. The line continues operations in his memory today with the enthusiastic commitment of the CFVP team.

Comments: Usually has a special open day in early September.

Local Tourist Office: place Stanislas - BP 810, 54000 Nancy Telephone: 03 83 35 22 41 Fax: 03 83 35 90 10. E-mail: tourisme@ot-nancy.fr   website: www.ot-nancy.fr

Minièresbunn Doihl-Rodange known in French as Chemin de Fer Doihl-Rodange

Location: Saulnes, 39 km north-east of Thionville in the north-east corner of France adjoining the Luxembourg and Belgian (Walloon) borders.

Department: Meurthe et Moselle (54).

Getting there: By road take the autoroute A4 in the direction of Metz and exit at junction 32 and follow the D908, RN3, RN18 and D18 to Saulnes on the border with the Grand Duchy of Luxembourg.
Route: Fond-de-Gras in Luxembourg to Saulnes in France via Lasauvage (4 km).
Journey time: Not known.
Gauge and type of traction: 700 mm; electric 500V dc.
Rolling stock: Electric (AEG and ARBED) diesel and steam locomotives.
Contact details: Minièresbunn Doihl-Rodange asbl, BP 60, 4701 Pétange, Luxembourg. Telephone: calling from France 00 352 49 00 10 or 00 352 50 47 07 (Saturdays only).
Website: No official website found but the following is useful www.jhemp.lu/indarch/main/main.shtml
Comments: This narrow gauge railway was built to carry iron ore from the Doihl mine in Rodange. The journey starts by leaving Fond-de-Gras in Luxembourg hauled by an 1897-built Krauss steam locomotive originating from the mine. The second section is by electric traction for the 1,400 metre journey underground emerging at the former mining village of Lasauvage. The final section is over the border into France to Saulnes an area also known for its mining history and its steel production. The line and its mining train is the responsibility of the association Minieresbunn Doihl-Rodange asbl which was formed in 1990. Whilst this line has only a very small section in France its arrival point in Luxembourg is in very close proximity to a most interesting heritage-tourist railway, Train 1900 (*see next entry*).
Local Tourist Office: 16, rue du Vieux Collège, 57100 Thionville. Telephone: 03 82 53 33 18 Fax: 03 82 53 15 55. E-mail: tourisme@thionville.net

Train 1900 run by Association des Musée et Tourisme Ferroviaires (AMTF)

Location: Pétange in the Grand Duchy of Luxembourg
Getting there: By road take the autoroute A4 in the direction of Metz and exit at junction 32 and follow the, RN 18 and D18 and cross over the border into Luxembourg and using the N5 follow the signs to Pétange.
Route: Pétange-Train 1900 station to Bois-de-Rodange via Fond-de-Gras (7 km)
Journey time: A single journey train hauled by steam locomotive takes about one hour and by autorail 48 minutes.
Gauge and type of traction: Standard; steam, autorail and diesel.
Rolling stock: Eleven steam locomotives with three in service as follows, a 1912 Orenstein and Koppel 030 T No. 5, a 1900 Hanomag 020 T No. 8 and a 1920 Cockerill 020 Tv No. 503. Four are at various stages of restoration which are a 1891 Graffenstaden AL-T3 No. 6114, a 1908 Hohenzollern 030 T No. 9, a 1946 Energie Marcinelle 030 T No. 507 and a 1910 Hohenzollern 020 T No. 3. Four are stored awaiting restoration and they are a 1903 Hanomag 030 T No. 12, a 1942 Meuse 040 T No. 107, a 1910 Hohenzollern 030 T No. 5, and a 1910 Cockerill 020 Tv No. 504 (presently up for sale). There are three autorails comprising railcar No. 551 669 which came from Chemin de Fer des 3 Vallées and was formerly DB VT95 669, an Uerdingen autorail Z 151 and its trailer carriage RZ 1061 built in

Train 1900 service made up of steam locomotive No. 5, ex-ARBED, Esch and ex-Ph carriages waiting to depart from Longwy station for Longuyon on the special event 'l'occasion des Journées du Patrimoine en France' (Heritage days in France) on 17th September, 2005.   *François Wagner/AMTF/Train 1900*

1951 and, finally, a Westwaggon double No. 206-216. Two steam cranes, one by Cockerill, and four diesel locotracteurs almost complete the collection. The latest acquisition, however, in 2005, was a magnificent diesel locomotive No. 7309.

Contact details: AMTF, 12, rue de Lasauvage, 4829 Rodange, Grand Duchy of Luxembourg. Telephone: calling from France 00 352 580 581 (Gare de Fond-de-Gras) Fax: 00 352 26 50 17 67 (Gare de Fond-de-Gras) Fax: 00 352 50 94 85 (President AMTF - Monsieur Albert Wolter). E-mail: train1900@pt.lu (AMTF)

Website: www.train1900.lu and to know more about the area of Fond-de-Gras visit an excellent website www.fond-de-gras.lu

Operating dates: Trains operate in the afternoon on Sundays and public holidays from 1st May until the last Sunday in September.

Tariff: An adult first class ticket is 10€ and for a child (5-11 years) 7€. An adult second class ticket is 7€ and for child 4€. Dogs may only travel second class at a cost of 3€. Tickets are for travel the whole day including stops. There is a 10 per cent reduction for groups of 10 or more (2006).

History: This area of Luxembourg, Belgium and France, during the 19th century and early 20th century, became an important centre of the mining industry and brought much prosperity to the local communities. An important need for the effective operation of the mines was the ability to transport efficiently the iron ore extracted. So it was in 1874 that the Ligne des Minières was built by the la

Compagnie de Chemins de Fer et Minières Prince Henri, PH for short. The railway worked well for almost 90 years but with the closure of the mines in 1963 so disappeared the railway. Ten years later, happily, a team of volunteers came together to form what is now Train 1900. With some financial help from the Luxembourg Government's *Service des Sites et Monuments Nationaux*, much has been achieved in restoring the railway line, stations, other buildings and, of course its rolling stock. Most of the steam locomotives lovingly restored and preserved are the originals that worked the local mining and steel industries. *Comments*: This railway whilst not in France is so close to the border and, given its superb offerings, it is well worthwhile making a visit perhaps in combination with a trip on the Minièresbunn Doihl-Rodange. Train 1900 is a 'must-do' visit.

The Maginot Line (Ligne Maginot)

Location: Longuyon, Fort de Fermont, 140 km east of Reims.
Department: Meurthe et Moselle (54).
Getting there: By road take the autoroute A4 and exit at 32 then take the D908 and RN18 to Longuyon.
Route: Fermont and Hackenburg (1 km).
Gauge: 600 mm.
Contact details: AAOFLM, 9 rue Albert Lebrun 54260 Longuyon. Telephone: 03 82 39 35 34 Fax: 03 82 39 26 46.
E-mail: ligne.maginot.fort.de.fermont@wanadoo.fr
Website: www.perso.wanadoo.fr/ligne-maginot-fort-de-fermont.asso.fr
Operating dates: It is open from the beginning of April to end of October. In April on Saturdays, Sundays and public holidays guided visits take place at 1400 and 1530 hours; in May and June on weekdays at 1500 hours and Saturdays, Sundays and public holidays guided visits are at 1400 and 1530 hours; in July and August guided tours are every day at 1400 and 1630 hours; in September and October guided visits are at 1400 and 1530 hours.
Tariff: An adult entry is 6€ and a child (7-12 years) 4€ (2006).
Comments: The Maginot Line was a powerful line of defence built in the 1930s to protect France from its traditional enemy, Germany, by defending the invasion routes from across the eastern frontier. In a sense the Maginot Line was France's 'Great Wall' which, by its collection of mainly underground forts, stretched from Switzerland to the Ardennes in the North, and from the Alps to the Mediterranean in the South. Fort Fermont was one such fort which housed as many as 600 men who waited for a German attack that never came. In May 1940 Hitler's troops attacked France through the Ardennes in what was then neutral Belgium and quickly isolated the line in Alsace from the rest of France. On 22nd June, 1940, France signed an armistice with Germany thus rendering the line, its forts and its troops redundant. Part of the tour to Fort Fermont includes a trip on the underground railway which was used in 1940. Allow up to two hours for the guided visit.
Local Tourist Office: place Allende, 54260 Longuyon. Telephone: 03 82 39 21 21 Fax: 03 82 26 44 37. E-mail: office.de.tourisme.longuyon@wanadoo.fr website: www.ot-longuyon.asso.fr

Museum

La Mine Musée du Carreau Wendel formerly Musée de la Mine de Petite Rosselle

Location: Petite Rosselle, 62 km east of Metz on the German border at Saarbrücken.

Department: Moselle (57).

Getting there: Take the autoroute A4 from Paris in the direction of Metz and exit at 40 then the autoroute A320 and exit at 42 following the D31 to Petite Roselle.

Route: Petite Rosselle – Puits Simon (5 km).

Rolling stock: The museum has an important collection of railway rolling stock with more than 40 locomotives of all types both standard and narrow gauge. There is a Picasso No. X 4042 as well as more than 100 wagons of various descriptions.

Contact details: La Mine Musée du Carreau Wendel, 57540 Petite-Rosselle. Telephone: 03 87 87 08 54. E-mail: musee.carreau.wendel@wanadoo.fr

Website: www.agglo-forbach.fr/site/tourisme_musee_mine.php

Operating dates: From April to October: in April, May, June, September and October open every day except Tuesdays; in July and August every day. Opening hours are always in the afternoons between 1400 and 1800 hours.

Tariff: An adult ticket is 6€ and for a child 4€. There are reduced rates for groups (2005).

Comments: One of three important museums in France dedicated to the mining industry and which were inextricably linked with railway transport in the first half of the 20th century. Groups can visit any time of the year by prior

A 1925-built Hanomag fireless locomotive, No. 10278. *La Mine Musée du Carreau Wendel*

Picasso autorail No. X 4042 at Petite Roselle.   *La Mine Musée du Carreau Wendel*

arrangement. The museum is presently undergoing a major refurbishment but it intends to hold an official re-opening in the second quarter of 2006.
Local Tourist Office: 11, rue du Maire Massing, BP 50339, 57203 Sarreguemines. Telephone: 03 87 98 80 81 Fax: 03 87 98 25 77. E-mail: otsgs@wanadoo.fr

Vélorail

Le Vélorail du Val de Mortagne

Member: FACS-UNECTO
Location: Magnières-Deinvillers, 53 km south-east of Nancy.
Department: Meurthe-et-Moselle (54).
Getting there: By road take autoroute A4 to Metz then the A31 to Nancy, then the A33 and finally the D914 to Magnières-Deinvillers.
Route: Magnières-Deinvillers to Lamath (20 km).
Gauge: Standard.
Contact details: Gare de Magnières-Deinvillers, 54129 Magnières-Deinvillers. Telephone: 03 83 72 34 73 Fax: 03 83 72 33 11. E-mail: val.mortagne@wanadoo.fr
Website: www.trains-fr.org/unecto/valdemortagne/
Operating dates: Vélorails operate from April to October; in April and September from 1400 to 1800 hours; in May and June from 0900 to 1200 and 1400 to 1900 hours; in July and August 0900 to 1900 hours without a lunch break. From October to March vélorails can be hired by groups subject to prior arrangement and sufficient numbers.
Tariff: Vélorail hire for 1 hour is 10€. There are reductions for groups.
Comments: Vélorails have been operating on this line since 1990.
Local Tourist Office: Aile Sud du Château, 54300 Lunéville. Telephone : 03 83 74 06 55 Fax: 03 83 73 57 95. E-mail: ot.lunevillois@freesbee.fr

Midi-Pyrénées

Midi-Pyrénées is in the south-west of France and has a frontier with Spain and regional borders with Aquitaine to the west, Limousin and the Auvergne to the north and Languedoc and Roussillon to the east. It comprises the departments of Ariège (09), Aveyron (12), Haute-Garonne (31), Gers (32), Lot (46), Hautes-Pyrénées (65), Tarn (81) and Tarn-et-Garonne (82). Its regional capital is Toulouse and other cities include Cahors, Foix, Auch, Tarbes, Albi, Montauban and Rodez. This region has two heritage/tourist railways, one railway where operations have been temporarily suspended, one location where there is preserved traction, one museum and one vélorail.

Railways

Chemin de Fer Touristique du Tarn (CFTT) also known as Association pour la Conservation Occitane de Véhicules Anciens (ACOVA)

Member: FACS-UNECTO
Location: St Lieux-les-Lavaur, 37 km north-east of Toulouse.
Department: Tarn (81).
Getting there: By SNCF rail to St Sulpice on the Toulouse line and then by taxi. By road take autoroutes A62 and A68 and leave at exit 6 on to D38.
Route: St Lieux-les-Lavaur to Les Martels (5 km).
Journey time: One hour round trip.
Gauge and type of traction: 500 mm; steam, diesel and electric.
Rolling stock: Five steam locomotives are held comprising No. 1 030 T Couillet built in 1910 and three Decauville 020 T locomotives, No. 2 of 1930, No. 3 of 1947 and No. 4 of 1931. They are all of a type Progrès and are formerly of the Forges d'Audincourt. Steam locomotive No. 5 is a 1898-built Decauville 020 T type 1, 3.25 tonnes which spent all of its working life in New Caledonia. A collection of locotracteurs including Crochat, Decauville, Heim, Campagne, Patry, Raco, Ruston, Schöma, Ruston Weitz, Yvon Genty, Duro Felguera, Whitcomb and Lokomotivbau Karl Marx make up the collection of traction along with an electric pantograph locomotive built in Spain which has been restored with some original catenary preserved. There are five open and six closed passenger carriages and 30 goods wagons of various descriptions. CFTT's interesting collection includes rolling stock drawn from Germany, Switzerland, Spain, USA and Great Britain.
Contact details: Association pour la Conservation Occitane de Véhicules Anciens, ACOVA-CFTT, BP 2040, 31018 Toulouse. Telephone: 05 61 47 44 52 or 05 61 70 33 63 Fax: 05 62 14 11 80. E-mail: secretariat@cftt.org
Website: www.cftt.org
Operating dates: From 16th April to 13th July operating on every Sunday and public holiday with departures from St Lieux-les-Lavaur at 1430, 1530, 1630 and 1730 hours; from 14th July to 31st July on every Saturday, Sunday, Monday, Tuesday (but no 1730 service on the latter) and public holiday with departures from St Lieux-les-Lavaur at 1430, 1530, 1630 and 1730 hours; from 1st to 15th August on every day with departures from St Lieux-les-Lavaur at 1430, 1530,

Decauville 020 T locomotive No. 3.   *Jacques Daffis*

1630 and 1730 hours; from 16th to 31st August on every Saturday, Sunday,
Monday, Tuesday (but no 1730 service on Tuesdays) and public holiday with
departures from St Lieux-les-Lavaur at 1430, 1530, 1630 and 1730 hours; from
1st September to 31st October on every Sunday and public holiday with
departures from St Lieux-les-Lavaur at 1430, 1530, 1630 and 1730 hours (2006).

Tariff: An adult ticket is 5€ and for a child (4-10 years) 4€. A family ticket is 18€ (2006).
History: The line was originally built between 1895 and 1903 for the Tramways
à Vapeur du Tarn, a network with a 600 mm gauge, travelling between Lavaur
and Laboutarié and which was extended in 1925 with the route from La
Ramière to St Sulpice. Closure of the operations began in 1931 and eventually
all services ended in 1937. In 1975 an enterprising group of volunteers set about
re-constructing the line utilising 500 mm gauge track. (For a full account of the
history of this railway see *Tramways à Vapeur du Tarn*, by Sarah Wright and
published by the Oakwood Press, ISBN 0 85361 570.)
Comments: The staff here are very helpful and the CFTT's secretary speaks
English. The website is also very good and is presented in English and Spanish
languages as well as in French.
Local Tourist Office: parc Georges Spenale, 81370 St Sulpice. Telephone: 05 63
41 89 50 Fax: 05 63 40 23 30. E-mail: office.de.tourisme.stsulpice@wanadoo.fr or
ot.stsulpice@wanadoo.fr

Chemin de Fer Touristique du Haut Quercy

Member: FACS-UNECTO
Location: Martel, 32 km south of Brive-la-Gaillarde.
Department: Lot (46).
Getting there: By road take the autoroutes A10, A71 and A20 exit at junction 54
then RN140 to Martel.
Route: Martel to St Denis-près-Martel (7 km).
Journey time: One and a half hours round trip.
Gauge and type of traction: Standard; steam.
Rolling stock: Steam locomotive 030 T Ferrum TKh Marine originally of Poland,
a 020 T Fives-Lille *Vesta* of 1927, and diesel locotracteurs V36 Y50 111 of 1943
and Y51 125 which is awaiting a new engine.
Contact details: Chemin de Fer du Haut Quercy, Meyrangles, 46600 Martel.
Telephone: 05 65 37 35 81.
Website: www.trainduhautquercy.info
Operating dates: The railway provides steam services on Sundays and public
holidays from the Spring to end of September departing Martel at 1430 and 1600
hours. Diesel-hauled services are also operated on Tuesdays and Thursdays
from April to September. There are other diesel and steam services on other
weekdays in July and August (2006).
Tariff: A diesel excursion for an adult is 7€ and for a child (4-11 years) 4€. A
steam excursion for an adult is 9.50€ and for a child 5.50€ (2006).
Comments: The tourist rail service known locally as 'Le Truffadou' offers an
enjoyable rail journey set in beautiful countryside in a region known particularly
for its gastronomic offerings. Do not confuse this operational railway with
Quercyrail (*see next entry*) which has temporarily suspended its services.
Local Tourist Office: Palais de la Raymondie, place des Consuls, 46600 Martel.
Telephone: 05 65 37 43 44 Fax: 05 65 37 37 27. E-mail: martel2@wanadoo.fr
website: www.martel.fr/index.php

Railway Operations Temporarily Suspended

Train Touristique - Quercyrail

Member: FACS-UNECTO
Location: Cahors, 116 km north of Toulouse.
Department: Lot (46).
Getting there: By SNCF services either to Cahors and Capdenac. By road take the RN20 or the autoroute A20 or from Rodez take the RN140 to Cahors.
Route: Cahors – Capdenac (71 km).
Journey time: A half-day.
Gauge and type of traction: Standard; autorail.
Rolling stock: There are a number of autorails comprising a 1964 Caravelle No. X 4519, a remorque No. XR 8528, a 1964 Caravelle No. X 4511 with a remorque No. XR 8515, a 1952 Picasso No. X 3825 (300 hp) and a 1951 autorail No. X 2425 (600 hp).
Contact details: Quercyrail, Gare SNCF de Cahors, 46000 Cahors. Telephone: 05 63 40 11 93. E-mail: jpison@tele2.fr
Website: www.quercyrail.fr.st
Operating dates: Check with operator for the date of the resumption of operations and tariff.
History: Opened in July 1886 this 71 km line was linked with the River Lot for the movement of locally mined coal. Sadly, this alliance began to reduce in 1926 when the river was declared no longer navigable. The line lost its passenger traffic in 1980 and its goods traffic in 1989. However the line was saved for tourism and when operating travels through one of the most picturesque areas of France, the Lot valley.
Comments: Rail trip can be included as part of an excursion to other places of local interest. The railway ceased operations in 2004 but there are hopes to revive services possibly after a new management committee has been formed.
Local Tourist Office: Maison du Tourisme, place François Mitterrand, 46000 Cahors. Telephone: 05 65 53 20 65 Fax: 05 65 53 20 74. E-mail: cahors@wanadoo.fr website: www.mairie-cahors.fr www.quercy.net

Preserved Locomotives and Other Traction

ACPR 1126 - Le Train Vapeur de Toulouse

Member: FACS-UNECTO
Location: St Jean district of Toulouse.
Department: Haute-Garonne (31)
Getting there: By SNCF rail to Toulouse. By road take autoroutes A20, A62 & A61 and leave at exit 15 on to the D112 to Toulouse.
Rolling stock: Mikado No. 141 R 1126.
History: 141 R 1126 was built in 1946 in the United States by the American Locomotive Company (ALCO) and came to Nîmes in March of 1947, being one of 1,340 machines of this class built. Thereafter she worked from depots at Nice

Mikado No. 141 R 1126 stands at Tarascon-sur-Ariège   *Alain and Thomas Gallé*

in 1950, Avignon in 1966, then again at Nice for few months in 1966 before going to Narbonne from where she was retired in 1975 having completed 2,093,334 kilometres fuelled by heavy oil. No. 141 R 1126 is one of 12 machines of this class that has been preserved.

Gauge and type of traction: Standard; steam.
Contact details: ACPR 1126, 14 rue Jacques Prévert, 31240 St Jean. Telephone: 05 61 09 42 61. E-mail: contact@trainvapeur-toulouse.com
Website: www.trainvapeur-toulouse.com
Operating dates: Special excursions are made throughout the year from Toulouse on RFF (SNCF) tracks mainly in the south-west of France.
Comments: The website is well-designed and is very helpful for the planning of a trip on one of the frequent excursions this locomotive undertakes each year mainly in the south-west of France.
Local Tourist Office: Donjon du Capitole - BP 0801, 31000 Toulouse. Telephone: 05 61 11 02 22 Fax: 05 61 22 03 63. E-mail: infos@ot-toulouse.fr
website: www.ot-toulouse.fr

Museum

Association des Cheminots et Amis du Rail du Pays de Cajarc

Location: Cajarc, 48 km east of Cahors.
Department: Lot (46).
Getting there: From Cahors take the D22, D911 and D919 to Cajarc.

Exhibition: The association, shortly after it was formed, was able to act quickly and save much material which is now exhibited in the former goods shed at Cajarc station.

Contact details: Mairie de Cajarc, 46140 Cajarc. Telephone: 05 65 40 72 04.

Website: www.quercy.net/institutions/musee_du_rail/index.html

Operating dates: The museum is open every day between 1st July and 30th September from 1500 to 1800 hours.

Tariff: Free (2006).

History: The association was founded in 1988 by a number of active as well as retired railwaymen and other enthusiasts. The initial goal was to save the line between Cahors and Cajarc which carried passenger traffic until the end of September 1980 and goods traffic until the end of September 1989.

Comments: This is a small museum but well worth a visit especially if one is in the area visiting, for example, the Chemin de Fer Touristique du Tarn (*see page 122*).

Local Tourist Office: La Chapelle, 46160 Cajarc. Telephone: 05 65 40 72 89 or 05 65 34 06 25 (high season) Fax: 05 65 40 39 05. E-mail: figeac@wanadoo.fr

Vélorail

Vélorail de Larzac

Location: Ste Eulalie-de-Cernon, 21 km south of Millau.

Department: Aveyron (12).

Getting there: By road take autoroutes A10, A71 and A75 exit on to RN9 then follow the D277, D77 and D23 to Ste Eulalie-de-Cernon.

Route: Ste Eulalie-de-Cernon – Le Rouquet (4 km).

Gauge: Standard.

Contact details: Vélorail de Larzac, SARL Rando-Rail, La Gare, 12230 Ste Eulalie-de-Cernon. Telephone: 05 65 58 72 10

Website: www.domaine-barraque.com/VeloRail.htm

Operating dates: Contact the tourist office to make a reservation.

Comments: When visiting this vélorail do not miss the opportunity to see the recently constructed magnificent viaduct on the A75 autoroute at Millau designed by Norman Foster, it is truly a work of art. It is best viewed from below on the southern outskirts of Millau to appreciate the technical merit of this wonderful feat of engineering.

Local Tourist Office: 12230 Ste Eulalie-de-Cernon. Telephone: 05 65 62 77 33 Fax: 05 65 62 77 44. E-mail: infos@domaine-barraque.com website: www.domaine-barraque.com/index.htm

A 1909-built motrice, No. 420, formerly ELRT.   *Amitram*

Nord – Pas-de-Calais

Nord-Pas-de-Calais is in the north of France bordering Belgium with just one regional neighbour, Picardie in the south. It comprises just two departments, Nord (59) and Pas-de-Calais (62). The regional capital is Lille and there are major centres at Dunkirk and Calais. This region has three heritage/tourist railways, one discontinued railway, one location where there is preserved traction and two museums.

Railways

Tramway Touristique de la Vallée de la Deûle also known as AMITRAM

Member: FACS-UNECTO
Location: Marquette-lez-Lille, 77 km south-east of Dunkirk.
Department: Nord (59).
Getting there: By train (TGV) to Lille then local bus No. 9. By road from Lille's ring road A25/A22 exit at 10 for Marquette-lez-Lille.
Route: Marquette - Wambrechies (3 km).
Journey time: 40 minutes.
Gauge and type of traction: Metre; motrices (variously built between 1897 and 1949), autobuses, a trolley bus and a diesel locotracteur.
Rolling stock: For a long and comprehensive list of stock visit the official website.
Contact details: AMITRAM Secrétariat, BP45, 59520 Marquette-lez-Lille. Telephone: 03 28 38 84 21 Fax: 03 28 38 84 22. E-mail: amitram@amitram.assoc.fr and also tourisme59118@wambrechies.fr
Website: www.amitram.asso.fr
Operating dates: From the beginning of April to end of September on Sunday afternoons between 1430 and 1900 hours and running every 20 minutes. Public holiday afternoons operating between the same times but only every 40 minutes. Group reservations are possible.
Tariff: An adult ticket is 4€, senior citizens, the handicapped, etc. 2€, groups of 10 persons+ 3€ each and children younger than 15 years go free (2006).
History: AMITRAM was formed in 1968. In 1984 the depot was built and in 1995 a line was established between the Town Hall (Hôtel de Ville) in Marquette-lez-Lille and the bridge at Wambrechies.
Comments: The Lavoisier depot is an active workshop for the tramway but unfortunately it is not open to visitors. However, it is possible by making special arrangements beforehand to visit on the last Saturday of each month between 1400 to 1600 hours from the end of March to the end of October. The collection of trams can also be viewed without prior arrangement on the last Saturday afternoon of each month from April to September.
Local Tourist Office: 23, rue des Martyrs, 59520 Marquette-lez-Lille. Telephone: 03 20 06 42 84 Fax: 03 20 51 20 08.

Chemin de Fer Touristique de la Vallée de l'Aa (CFTVA)

Picasso autorails Nos. X 3853 and X 3817 at Blendecques station.   *François Coin*

Member: FACS-UNECTO
Location: Arques, 53 km south-east of Calais.
Department: Pas-de-Calais (62).
Getting there: By SNCF to St Omer. By road take the autoroute A26 and exit at 3 (St Omer) and then follow the RN42.
Route: Arques to Lumbres (17 km).
Journey time: 49 minutes.
Gauge and type of traction: Standard; steam, autorail.
Rolling stock: Autorail Picassos Nos. X 3853, X 3817 and autorail carriages (remorques) Nos. XR 7888, XR 8161 and XR 8270 (to be restored), a steam locomotive 150 type 52 Kriegslok No. 6690, a 1925 Moyse locotracteur (to be restored) and several carriages and wagons.
Contact details: Chemin de Fer Touristique de la Vallée de l'Aa, 3 rue des Cuvelots, 62380 Bayenghem-les-Senighem. Telephone-Fax: 03 21 12 19 19 or 03 21 93 45 46. E-mail: cftva@free.fr
Website: http://cftva.free.fr This site is well worth visiting.
Operating dates: On Saturdays, Sundays and public holidays from 1st May to the last weekend in September with departures from Arques at 1400 and 1600 hours and from Lumbres at 1500 and 1700 hours. In July and August departures from Arques are at 1015, 1430 and 1630 hours and from Lumbres at 1115, 1530 and 1730 hours.
Tariff: An adult return ticket is 6€ and for a child (4-14 years) 4€ (2005).

Comments: A comprehensive programme of operations throughout the year including special events at Halloween and Christmas.
Local Tourist Office: Office de Tourisme de St Omer, place Roger Salengro, 62510 Arques. Telephone: 03 21 88 59 00 Fax: 03 21 88 59 00.
E-mail: arques.tourisme@wanadoo.fr website: www.ville-arques.fr

Chemin de Fer Touristique de la Vallée de la Scarpe also known as Amicale Amandinoise de Modelisme Ferroviaire et de Chemin de Fer Secondaire (AAMCS)

Member: FACS-UNECTO
Location: St Amand-les-Eaux, 43 km south-east of Lille.
Department: Nord (59).
Getting there: By SNCF train to St Amand-les-Eaux. By road take the autoroute A25 (Lille – Valenciennes) and exit at 4 to St Amand-les-Eaux.
Route: St Amand-les-Eaux (2 km).
Journey time: 45 minutes.
Gauge and type of traction: 600 mm; steam, diesel.
Rolling stock: DFB 1535 steam locomotive, several locotracteurs comprising a 1917 Deutz MLH 332 mono-cylinder, a Deutz OMZ 122 No. 3, Decauville TMB45 No. 4, a 1941 Jung ZL 114, a Ruston DL20, a Plymouth and a Whitcombe. There is also an assortment of open carriages.
Contact details: Chemin de Fer Touristique de la Vallée de la Scarpe, Maison du Tourisme et du Thermalisme, 89 Grand Place, 59230 St Amand-les-Eaux. Telephone: 03 27 48 39 65 or 03 27 48 14 55 (after 1800 hrs CET). E-mail: aamcs@saint-amand-les-eaux.com
Website: http://ffmf.nord.free.fr/pagesclubs/aamcs/aamcs.htm
Operating dates: From May to September on most Sundays (but not all so check beforehand) with departures every hour from 1430 hours.
Tariff: Steam-hauled trips for an adult return ticket is 3€ and for a child (5-12 years) 1.5€. Diesel-hauled trips for an adult return ticket is 2€ and for a child 1€ (2005).
History: The Association, Amicale Amandinoise de Modelisme Ferroviaire et de Chemin de Fer Secondaire, was formed in 1985 for scale modellers of standard and 600 mm gauge locomotives and other rolling stock. However, the 'real railway' followed later in 1988 with the development of the line and the acquisition of a 1917 German-built Henschel and a number of locotracteurs and carriages.
Local Tourist Office: 89 Grand Place, BP 191, 59734 St Amand-les-Eaux. Telephone: 03 27 48 39 65 Fax: 03 27 45 20 91. E-mail: gvalembois@agglo-porteduhainaut.fr website: www.tourisme-porteduhainaut.fr

Discontinued Railway

Train de Pays des Morins (TPV)

Location: Boulogne-sur-Mer.
Department: Pas-de-Calais (62).
Comments: This railway operated autorail No. X 2431 on a route between Boulogne-sur-Mer and Desvres, a distance of 18 km, between 1990 and 1993. It is said that France's Prime Minister of the time was the *Président d'Honneur!* Sadly the autorail was scrapped at Boulogne-Outreau in 1998. (Source: FACS-UNECTO.)

Preserved Locomotives and Other Traction

AAATV-Lille

Location: Lille-Acsq Depot, on the outskirts of Lille and 78 km south-east of Dunkirk.
Department: Nord (59).
Getting there: Lille can be reached by the autoroutes A1, A23, A25 and A27.
Exhibits: 141 TC 51 and BB 12144.
Contact details: AAATV-Lille, Dépôt d'Acsq, 59002 Lille.
Comments: Both locomotives are preserved as static exhibits and not registered for use on RFF (SNCF) tracks.
Local Tourist Office: Palais Rihour, place Rihour, BP 205, 59002 Lille.
Telephone: 08 91 56 20 04 Fax: 03 59 57 94 14. E-mail: info@lilletourism.com website: www.lilletourism.com

Museums

Musée de la Mine also known as Centre Historique Denis Papin (CMCF)

Location: Oignies, 26 km south of Lille.
Department: Pas-de-Calais (62).
Getting there: By road take the autoroute A1 and exit at 18 and then follow the RN17 to Oignies.
Gauge and type of traction: Standard and 600 mm; steam, electric.
Rolling stock: A 1931 Pacific 231 C 78, a diesel locomotive No. 62094, electric locomotives BB 12068 and BB 12125 and CC 40101 and a variety of fast coaches.
Contact details: Centre Historique Denis Papin, rue Emile Zola, 62590 Oignies. Telephone: 03 21 69 60 46.
Website: http://perso.wanadoo.fr/nord-est/musee.html
Operating dates: The museum is open from April to October on the second and fourth Sundays of each month from 1400 to 1900 hours.
Tariff: Not advised.

Local Tourist Office: 89 Grand'Place, BP 191, 59734 St Amand-les-Eaux. Telephone: 03 27 48 39 65 Fax: 03 27 45 20 91. E-mail: gvalembois@agglo-porteduhainaut.fr website: www.tourisme-porteduhainaut.fr

Cercle d'Etudes Ferroviaires Nord (CefNord)

Location: Denain, 51 km south-east of Lille.
Department: Nord (59)
Getting there: By road take the autoroute A2 and exit at 18 on to D40 to Denain. *Exhibits*: A varied collection of steam locomotives including a 1923 020 T Cockerill, an 1886 020 T *L'Union* constructed at the workshops of the Mine Company of Anzin, a 1913 020 T Cail classed as *Monument Historique*, a 1910-built 020 T Cockerill and a 030 T Fives-Lille. Diesel locomotives include a BDR, a Gaston Moyse 20 TDE No. 100, a Gaston Moyse 20 TDE No. 181, a 1955 Gaston Moyse 20 TE No. 69 and an ex-USINOR locotracteur No. 282 in the course of restoration. The association's depot is large containing a considerable collection of carriages, wagons, cranes etc. in all sorts of condition.
Contact details: CefNord, rue de Turenne, 59220 Denain. E-mail: cefnord@free.fr
Website: http://cefnord.free.fr/actus/index.htm This website is kept up to date and is most comprehensive. It now includes a forum for discussions on railway matters in French!
Operating dates: Guided tours are only by prior arrangement with the President of the Association who can be contacted by e-mail.
Tariff: An entry ticket is 2.30€ per person (2005).
Comments: The Association was formed with the following objectives: to create a museum of railways with services that operated in the Nord - Pas-de-Calais region; to safeguard rolling stock which either circulated in the area or was built there; to restore some items back to operating order; to safeguard documents in relation to the railway; to organize as well as participate in exhibitions; and, to organize visits including photographic ventures to railways elsewhere. There is also a desire to resurrect Train Touristique du Hainaut which ran between the depot in rue de Turenne in Denain and the site of a former mine 7 km away at Wallers-Aremberg. It last ran in January 1990 when a Picasso autorail No. 4046, owned by CefNord, carried 12 passengers.
Local Tourist Office: 1 rue Askièvre, 59300 Valenciennes. Telephone: 03 27 46 22 99 Fax: 03 27 30 38 35. E-mail: valenciennes.tourisme@wanadoo.fr or tourismevalenciennes@wanadoo.fr

Pays de la Loire

Pays de la Loire is in the north-west of France and has regional borders with Bretagne to the north-west, Basse-Normandie to the north, Centre to the east and Poitou-Charentes to the south. It comprises the departments of Loire-Atlantique (44), Maine-et-Loire (49), Mayenne (53), Sarthe (72) and Vendée (85). Its regional capital is Poitiers and other cities include Angoulême, La Rochelle and Niort. This region has four heritage/tourist railways, one location where preserved traction is stored, one museum and two vélorail services.

Railways

Chemin de Fer de la Vendée (CFV)

Member: FACS-UNECTO
Location: Mortagne-sur-Sèvre, 66 km south-east of Nantes.
Department: Vendée (85).
Getting there: By road take autoroutes A10, A11 and A87 (Paris – Angers) and exit at 27 then follow the RN160 to Mortagne-sur-Sèvre.
Route: Mortagne-sur-Sèvre to Les Herbiers (22 km).
Journey time: One hour.
Gauge and type of traction: Standard; steam, autorail and diesel.
Rolling stock: Two steam locomotives comprising a Fives-Lille 030T No. 6 and a 1945-built 030 T *Hannibal* which is in the course of restoration. There is also a Picasso autorail No. X 3823 and an XR carriage, a diesel locomotive No. 61042 ex-SNCF, a locotracteur Baudet-Donon-Roussel No. 560 and a 1934 Moyse locotracteur 20tDE. A number of carriages, and in particular the ex-CIWLT No. 2750 restaurant car formerly operating on the Orient-Express, complete the collection.
Contact details: Chemin de Fer de la Vendée, BP 10, La Gare, 85290 Mortagne-sur-Sèvre. Telephone: 02 51 63 02 01 Fax: 02 51 63 08 39.
E-mail: chemindefer.Vendée@wanadoo.fr
Website: www.trains-fr.org/unecto/cfvendee/cfv.htm
Operating dates: The services operate on every Sunday in June, in July and August on Wednesdays, Fridays and Sundays and in September on the first two Sundays. Departures from Mortagne-sur-Sèvre are at 1530 hours and departures from Les Herbiers at 1700 hours.
Tariff: An adult return ticket is 12€ and for a child (5-13 years) 8€. An adult single ticket is 9€ and for a child 6€. A family return ticket is 45€ and a family single ticket is 35€ (2006).
History: The St Christophe-du-Bois–Chantonnay line was initially brought into service in 1914 carrying goods and passengers. The passenger services were terminated in 1939 but the carriage of goods continued until 1992 and it was also in that year that the tourist railway services were begun.
Comments: From 1st April to 31st October lunch and/or dinner is possible by reservation on the 'Orient-Express' restaurant carriage hauled by a diesel from Mortagne-sur-Sèvre. Menus range between 31€ and 48.50€. The 22 km line

crosses three magnificent viaducts as well as the restored station at Les Herbiers where a Bistro is located allowing travellers to enjoy the pleasures of a meal if not taken on the train.
Local Tourist Office: 2 Grande Rue St Blaise, 85500 Les Herbiers. Telephone: 02 51 92 92 92 Fax: 02 51 92 93 70. E-mail: contact@ot-lesherbiers.fr website: www.ot-lesherbiers.fr

Chemin de Fer de la Sarthe (TRANSVAP)

Member: FACS-UNECTO
Location: Connerré-Beillé, 25 km east of Le Mans.
Department: Sarthe (72).
Getting there: By SNCF train to Connerré-Beillé on the Paris to Le Mans line. By road take autoroutes A10 and A11 and exit at 5 and then the D261 and the RN23 to Connerré-Beillé.
Route: Connerré-Beillé to Bonnétable (17 km).
Gauge and type of traction: Standard; steam, autorail and diesel.
Rolling stock: There are two steam locomotives comprising a 1917 British-built 020 T saddle tank and a 1924 Corpet-Louvet (ex Houillères des Cévennes). There are also two Billard autorails Nos. 901 and 903, a Picasso autorail No. X 3953, three locotracteurs and two 1869-built cranes.
Contact details: Chemin de Fer de la Sarthe (TRANSVAP) La Gare, 72160 Beillé. Telephone: 02 43 89 00 37 Fax: 02 43 89 00 37.
Website: http://membres.lycos.fr/transvap/ and
http://mail.trains-fr.org/unecto/transvap/index.html
Operating dates: Every Sunday and public holiday in July and August departing Connerré-Beillé at 1045, 1145 and 1500 hours and departing Bonnetable at 1150 and 1330 hours.
Tariff: An adult return ticket is 9€ and for a child (4-12 years) 6€ (2006).
History: Since 1979 the association TRANSVAP has been operating the 17 km of departmental line which was finally closed to traffic by SNCF two years earlier.
Local Tourist Office: Hôtel des Ursulines, rue de l'Etoile, 72000 Le Mans. Telephone : 02 43 28 17 22 Fax: 02 43 28 12 14. E-mail: OfficeDuTourisme@ville-lemans.fr

Chemin de Fer de Semur-en-Vallon (CCFSV)

Location: Semur-en-Vallon, 41 km east of Le Mans.
Department: Sarthe (72).
Getting there: By road take the autoroute A11 and exit at La Ferte Bernard and travel to Vibraye and there follow the direction signs 'Museotrain et Train Touristique'.
Route: Semur-en-Vallon (3 km).
Journey time: Allow 40 minutes for the trip and visit to the museum.
Gauge and type of traction: 600 mm; diesel.

Decauville steam locomotive awaiting departure at Semur-en-Vallon station.

Sebastien/Collection CCFSV

Rolling stock: Two Decauville steam locomotives together with Decauville, Yung, Slanzy and Paltry diesel locotracteurs, plus a wide selection of wagons and carriages including one offering 12 seats and originally constructed in 1850. There is a host of other items stored or in the course of restoration including 10 other locotracteurs.

Contact details: Chemin de Fer de Semur-en-Vallon, c/o Christian Pottier, 72390 Semur-en-Vallon. Telephone: 02 43 60 76 89 or 02 43 93 67 86 Fax: 02 43 63 14 16. E-mail: c.d.tx@wanadoo.fr

Website: http://ccfsv.free.fr/historique.html

Operating dates: From the first Sunday in June to mid-September on Sundays and public holidays with departures every half hour between 1430 and 1830 hours. Group bookings are taken for May to September.

Decauville TPC 15 No. 0351 locotracteur.   *Sébastien, Collection CCFSV*

Tariff: An adult ticket is 3€ and for a child (4-12 years) 2€. There are reductions for groups (2005).
Comments: Founded in 1966 by Robert Pottier it is also has a small agricultural museum.
Local Tourist Office: Centre Culturel et Touristique de la Gare, avenue Michel Verdier, 72320 Vibraye. Telephone: 02 43 60 76 89.
E-mail: otvaldebraye@wanadoo.fr

Train d'Union (AAFVDL)

Location: Château-du-Loir, 52 km north-west of Tours.
Department: Sarthe (72).
Getting there: By road take autoroutes A10, A11 and A28 then the RN138 to Château-du-Loir.
Route: Château-du-Loir to Besse-sur-Bray (35 km).
Gauge and type of traction: Standard; autorail.
Rolling stock: Autorail No. X 3953 on loan from TRANSVAP.
Contact details: Train d'Union, c/o Monsieur Claude Saurel, 1 impasse du Ruisseau, 72390 Dissay-s/s-Courcillon. Telephone: 02 43 79 43 14.
Website: No official website has been identified but a picture of the autorail No. X 3953 can be seen at: http://jpmk.chez.tiscali.fr/Sarthe1.htm
Local Tourist Office: parc Henri Goude. 2, avenue Jean Jaurès, BP 51, 72500 Château-du-Loir. Telephone: 02 43 44 56 68 Fax: 02 43 44 56 95. E-mail: ot.loir.berce@wanadoo.fr
website: http://www.tourisme.fr/office-de-tourisme/chateau-du-loir.htm

Preserved Locomotives and Other Traction

Loco Vapeur 141 R 1199

Member: FACS-UNECTO
Location: Basse-Goulaine depot, on the eastern side of Nantes.
Department: Loire Atlantique (44)
Getting there: By SNCF train to Nantes. By road take the autoroute A11 to Nantes.
Rolling stock: Mikado No. 141 R 1199.
History: This Mikado, No. 141 R 1199, is one of the 12 in France that has been preserved for posterity. Towards the end of World War II, the railways of France and their rolling stock were in a very poor state. After D-Day in 1944, an order was placed with United States industry to supply 1,340 Mikado steam locomotives. 141 R 1199 was built by the Baldwin Locomotive works in Philadelphia in February 1947 and in July of that year was delivered to France where it began work at Le Mans depot; indeed the locomotive spent all of its career at that depot being one of only 21 machines to hold that distinction in France. During its career, 141 R 1199 completed 1,628,351 km. It was renovated

Mikado 141 R 1199 stands at Rochefort station in Poitou-Charentes. *Marine Chereau*

in 1992 at the Nantes-Blottereau depot and came to its present location in 1995. It weighs 192 tonnes and running on heavy fuel oil (rather than coal) she delivers 2,900 hp and has a maximum speed of 100 km per hour.

Contact details: Reservations and enquiries can be made by writing to the Association Loco Vapeur R 1199, Secrétariat, 9 rue de Kerlédé, 44100 Nantes (the Secretary is Monsieur Philippe Guéry). The association's principal address is 9, rue de la Jarnigarnière, 44115 Basse-Goulaine Telephone: 08 71 72 33 17. E-mail: info@r2nantes.org

Website: http://www.r2nantes.org

Comments: A well-preserved Mikado approved for use on RFF (SNCF) tracks. In 2005, it undertook four excursions. Places are limited on the train so advance bookings are essential.

Local Tourist Office: 7 rue de Valmy, BP 64106, 44041 Nantes. Telephone: 02 40 20 60 00 Fax: 02 40 89 11 99. E-mail: office@nantes-tourisme.com

Museum

Association des Amis du Petit Anjou (AAPA)

Location: St Jean-de-Linières, 10 km west of Angers and 96 km south-west of Le Mans.

Department: Maine-et-Loire (49).

Getting there: By SNCF train to Angers. By road take the autoroute A11 to Angers.

Exhibits: The association has safeguarded a significant amount of material from the former Chemin de Fer de l'Anjou including a number of ANF Blanc-Misseron carriages and wagons constructed in the last decade of the 19th century. There is also a considerable collection of locomotive power including locotracteurs, both electric and diesel, draisines, cranes and an 1899-built Pinguely 030 T steam locomotive believed to be from the former Chemin de Fer du Beaujolais (CFB) and used there until 1934. Material from the former Electric Tramways of Angers is also preserved.

Contact details: Association des Amis du Petit Anjou (AAPA), 86 rue de la Madeleine, 49000 Angers. Telephone: 02 41 88 80 88. E-mail: info@petit-anjou.org The workshops are at St Jean-de-Linières.

Website: www.petit-anjou.org

Comments: The objective of the association, with the support of its 30 active members, eventually is to create a 'living museum of the Petit Anjou'. In the meantime, the association is very active preserving and restoring material, producing newsletters, giving exhibitions and encouraging visitors by prior arrangement. Exhibitions and open days occur from time to time so it is well worth contacting them beforehand to see what can be seen, where and when. Generally speaking, though, the workshops are usually active every Saturday and groups of interested railway enthusiasts, no more than 30 in number, are particularly welcome to visit by making a pre-booking. Monsieur Olivier Simonin of AAPA is most helpful. The website is also well worth visiting.

Local Tourist Office: Angers Tourisme, 7, place Kennedy, BP 15157, 49051 Angers. Telephone: 02 41 23 50 00 Fax for information: 02 41 23 50 09. E-mail: accueil@angers-tourisme.fr

LKM V10C locotracteur No. 10 with second class coach No. B111 built in 1892 by ANF stands at AAPA's workshop. *Patrick Voisine*

Vélorails

Le Relais Fleuri

Member: FACS-UNECTO
Location: St Loup-de-Gast, 57 km west of Alençon.
Department: Mayenne (53).
Getting there: By road take the autoroute A81 on to the RN162 to St Loup-de-Gast.
Route: St Loup-de-Gast to Ambrières-les-Vallées (3 km).
Gauge: Standard.
Contact details: Le Relais Fleuri, rue de Gare, 53300 St Loup-de-Gast.
Telephone: 02 43 08 88 67. E-mail: marie-de-st-loup-du-gast@wanadoo.fr
Operating dates and tariff: Contact the Mairie at St Loup-de-Gast.
Local Tourist Office: Base de Vaux, 53300 Ambrières-les-Vallées. Telephone: 02
43 04 90 25 Fax: 02 43 08 93 28. E-mail: otsiambrieres@wanadoo.fr

Les Draisines de Commequiers

Location: Commequiers, 65 km south-west of Nantes.
Department: Vendée (85).
Getting there: By road take autoroutes A10, A11 and A83 and exit at 5 and
follow the RN160, D948 and D94 to Commequiers.
Route: Commequiers to Coex (9 km).
Journey times: Choice of 2, 3, or 4 hours.
Gauge: Standard.
Contact details: Les Draisines de Commequiers, Gare de Vélorail 85220
Commequiers. Telephone: 02 51 54 79 99.
Operating dates: From the third week in March to the third week in September. In
the months of March, April, May and September operating on Wednesdays and at
weekends, in June, July and August on every day except Mondays. There may be
some variations to this programme so check first. Operating hours are always in the
afternoons from 1400 to 1900 hours and to 2100 hours at the height of the summer
season. In 2005, for school mid-term holidays, an extra week was inserted in the
programme at the end of October, again operating every day except Mondays but
given the shorter daylight hours, operated only from 1200 to 1600 hours.
Tariff: Vélorail hire for 2 hours is 16€ (22€ in July and August) for 3 hours 24€
(33€ in July and August) for 4 hours 32€ (44€ in July and August). There are
reductions for groups. There are also reductions for schoolchildren but not in
July and August (2005).
Local Tourist Office: Communauté de Communes Atlancia, 85220 Commequiers.
Telephone 02 51 55 55 55.

Picardie (Picardy)

Is located in the north of France and is close to the frontier with Belgium and has regional borders with Nord - Pas-de-Calais to the north, Haute-Normandie to the west, Île-de-France to the south and Champagne-Ardenne to the east. It comprises just three departments, Aisne (02), Oise (60) and Somme (80). Its regional capital is Amiens with other cities at Beauvais and Laon. This region has four tourist railways, one TER-SNCF tourist service, one discontinued railway and one museum.

Railways

Chemin de Fer du Vermandois (CFTV)

No. 140 C 314 built by North British of Glasgow in 1917 coupled to 1913-built tender No. 18 C 428 by Marine-Homécourt. *CFTV*

Member: FACS-UNECTO
Location: St Quentin, 178 km east of Calais.
Department: Aisne (02).
Getting there: By SNCF to St Quentin. By road take the autoroute A26 (Calais-Reims Autoroute des Anglais) and exit at 10 on to the RN44 or take the autoroute A29 (Amiens-St Quentin) and exit at 11 then local roads to the SNCF station at St Quentin.
Route: St Quentin to Origny-Ste-Benoîte via Ribemont and Mézières-sur-Oise (22 km).
Journey time: An hour each way but longer on 'restaurant' trains.
Gauge and type of traction: Standard; steam, diesel and autorail.

Rolling stock: Steam locomotives comprise a 140 C 314 (1917), an 18 C 428 (1913) and a 030 T Fives-Lille (1933). There are also a diesel locomotive No. CC 61041 (1952), an ABJ 4 autorail No. X 3623 and a Picasso No. X 3866. There are four locotracteurs comprising a Moyse (1950), a BDR (1954), a Y 2400 (1968 ex-SNCF) and Y 2498 *Olivier* (1968). The railway also holds a large collection of passenger carriages most dating from around 1928.

Contact details: Chemin de Fer du Vermandois, BP 152, 02140 St Quentin. Telephone: 03 23 64 88 38 Fax: 03 23 64 88 38. E-mail: cftv.actu@tiscali.fr

Website: www.trains-fr.org/cftv/

Operating dates: Every Sunday in July and August departing at 1030 and 1435 and returning at 1230 and 1715 hours. From April to December there are 'specials' on many weekends including lunches in the Orient-Express restaurant car. There are other excursions and theme events including Christmas specials.

Tariff: An adult third class return ticket is 13€ and for a child (4-12 years) 8€. A family ticket is 33€. First class restaurant car travel costs 18€ for adults and 12€ for children without meals. The return train journey and a four-course lunch (including wine and coffee) on 'special weekends' will cost an adult 40€ and a child 27€. Reservations are essential (2005).

History: Tourist services began in August 1979 initially with Régie Departementale de Transport de l'Aisne until October 1981 and then in collaboration with SNCF and the local communes. It has now become the premier tourist railway in France operating on RFF (SNCF) track. Since 1995 an authentic restaurant car and bar has been added to the Vermandois Express.

Comments: Steam locomotive driving courses are available (telephone or see internet site for detailed booking arrangements). From time to time special excursions are arranged on RFF (SNCF) tracks using trains which have been approved for such use. This is likely to include a trip to the Steam Festival on the Bay of Somme railway in 2006. The CFTV is twinned with the South Devon Railway Trust in England who can be reached on their website at www.southdevonrailway.org Events are run throughout the year for special occasions such as Halloween and Christmas. This is a 'must-do' railway visit.

Local Tourist Office: espace Victor Basch, BP 80, 02102 St Quentin. Telephone: 03 23 67 05 00 Fax: 03 23 67 78 71. E-mail: accueil@tourisme-saintquentinois.fr website: www.tourisme-saintquentinois.fr

Chemin de fer de la Baie de Somme (CFBS)

Member: FACS-UNECTO

Location: St Valéry-sur-Somme, 109 km south of Calais.

Department: Somme (80).

Getting there: By SNCF train to Noyelles-sur-Mer where the tourist train makes a stop. By road take autoroutes A16 or A28 to Abbeville and then follow the D940 to Le Crotoy or St Valéry-sur-Somme.

Route: St Valéry-sur-Somme to Le Crotoy via Noyelles-sur-Mer and St Valéry-sur-Somme – to Cayeux-les-Bains Brighton-Plage (27 km).

Robatel-Buffaud 031 T No. 3714 *Beton* leaves Noyelles-sur-Mer for Le Crotoy.   *Author*

Journey time: St Valéry-sur-Somme to Le Crotoy - one hour; St Valéry-sur-Somme to Cayeux - 45 minutes.

Gauge and type of traction: Metre gauge; mixed gauge St Valéry-sur-Somme to Noyelles-sur-Mer, and has been known to have taken standard gauge traffic for special events including a visit from a Southern Railway (UK) locomotive. Traction is both steam and diesel.

Rolling stock: Eight steam locomotives including four in operation, an 020 T, a 130 T Corpet-Louvet, a 130 T Haine St-Pierre and an 031 T Robatel-Buffaud. There are five diesel locotracteurs of which three are in service, five autorails awaiting restoration, 19 passenger carriages and 42 wagons of various descriptions.

Contact details: Chemin de fer de la Baie de Somme, BP 80031, 80230 St Valery-sur-Somme. Telephone: 03 22 26 96 96 Fax: 03 22 26 95 66.

E-mail: cfbs@neuronnexion.fr

Website: www.chemin-fer-baie-somme.asso.fr

Operating dates: From Easter to 1st November on most days from April to September except Mondays. Mainly a Sunday service in October. Departure times from St Valéry-sur-Somme vary according to type of traction used and direction of travel but popular services leave St Valéry-sur-Somme at 1045, 1530 and 1730 hours and return from Le Crotoy at 1200, 1530 and 1730 hours. The St Valéry-sur-Somme to Cayeux-les-Bains only operates in July and August. Special group excursions can be booked. It is also possible to enjoy evening meals on board the trains on certain days in the season. Before making a visit check the times (*horaires*) of train operations as well as details of special events and evening meal services.

Tariff: An adult return ticket is from 7.50€ to 13.50€ according to journey taken and a child (4-18 years) from 5.70€ to 10.30€ (2006).

History: During the summer of 1887 the Société Générale des Chemin de Fer Économiques opened this metric gauge railway for two prime purposes, the carriage of tourists to the beaches of the Bay of the Somme and the movement of local products such as beet, *galets* and cockles. However, it was in the 1960s that the use of the railway declined in favour of road transport. It was then, in 1970, like the story of many railways throughout France, and for that matter, throughout the world, that a group of volunteer railway enthusiasts came together to form the l'Association du Chemin de Fer de la Baie de Somme and once again opened up the line, this time to tourism. Since the re-opening of the service there has been a rapid expansion in the number of visitors; the railway with its interesting and varied collection of locomotives and carriages now welcomes more than 80,000 visitors every year.

Comments: The railway is twinned with the Kent & East Sussex Railway in the UK. More information about the history of this railway can be found in *Railways of the Baie de Somme* by Philip Pacey with Roland Arzul and Guy Lenne (Oakwood Press - *see Bibliography*). A visit to this railway is a 'must-do'.

Local Tourist Office: 2, place Guillaume le Conquérant, 80230 St Valéry-sur-Somme. Telephone: 03 22 60 93 50 Fax: 03 22 60 80 34. E-mail: officetourismestvalery.80@wanadoo.fr website: www.saint-valery-sur-somme.fr

Tourisme Ferroviaire de la Brie Champenoise à l'Omois (TFBCO)

Location: Condé en Brie, 36 km west of Épernay.
Department: Aisne (02).
Getting there: By road take the autoroute A4 and exit at 18 and then follow the RN3, D407 and D933 to Montmirail in the department of Marne (51).
Route: Mézy to Montmirail (24 km).
Journey time: 1 hour 10 minutes each way.
Gauge and type of traction: Standard; autorail.
Rolling stock: A 1955-built autorail Picasso No. X 3926, one of 251 constructed and which has recently undergone some restoration work. This autorail was formerly used on the Chemin de Fer Touristique de la Seudre also known as Le Train des Mouettes (*see entry under the Poitou-Charentes region*).
Contact details: c/o Mairie de Condé en Brie, 02330 Condé en Brie. Telephone: 03 23 71 46 05. E-mail: david.maine@wanadoo.fr
Website: http://tfbco.free.fr/
Operating dates and tariff: Services will recommence in 2006.
Comments: This railway is very much in its infancy having only begun operations with the Picasso at the end of June 2005.
Local Tourist Office: rue Gare, 02330 Condé en Brie. Telephone: 03 23 82 05 38 Fax: 03 23 82 05 38 or 03 23 82 90 91. E-mail: sicondeenbrie@wanadoo.fr

Diesel locotracteur No. T24 hauls tourist train alongside the Somme Canal.   *Author*

Le Petit Train de la Haute Somme also known as Association Picardie pour la Préservation et l'Entretien des Véhicules Anciens (APPEVA)

Location: Froissy, 44 km south of Amiens.
Department: Somme (80).
Getting there: By TGV to Amiens then local transport. By road take the autoroute A1 and exit at Péronne or take the A29 and exit at 'Gare TGV', then the RN29 and D329 to Froissy.
Route: Froissy – Cappy – Dompierre (7 km).
Journey time: 45 minutes.
Gauge and type of traction: 600 mm; steam, diesel.
Rolling stock: Steam locomotives include a 1922-built 020 T Neumeyer, a 1937 Henschel 020 T, a 1928 Decauville 030 T type Progrès, a 1918 Krauss 040 T type DFB, a 1918 Borsig 040+T, a 1925 Vulcan-Werke 040+T, a 1917 Alco-Cooke 131 T, a 1945 Franco-Belge 040+T type KDL11, a 1915 Orenstein and Koppel 030 T and a 1917 Orenstein and Koppel 050 T. Diesel locotracteurs include a 1937 Billard type T75D, a 1960 Orenstein and Koppel, a 1946 Plymouth (USA), two 1941 three-axle Coferna, a 1935 Arn-Jung, two 1917 twin-axle Baldwins (USA), another 1939 Plymouth, a 1968 Socofer, two 1958 Billards, a 1917 Simplex (GB), two 1916-18 Simplex, a 1917 Fairbanks-Morse 'Speeder' draisine, etc.
Contact details: Association Picardie pour la Préservation et l'Entretien des Véhicules Anciens (APPEVA), BP 106, 80001 Amiens (NB: the museum and railway are located at Froissy). Telephone: 03 22 83 11 89 Fax: 03 22 83 11 89. E-mail: appeva@club-internet.fr
Website: www.appeva.org
Operating dates: From May to September with services in May, June, early July and September on Sundays and public holidays with departures from 1415, 1515, 1615 and 1715 hours. The museum is open from 1345 to 1900 hours. From mid-July to the end of August it also operates every weekday except Mondays with departures at 1430 and 1600 hours. The museum is open on these weekdays from 1345 to 1730 hours.
Tariff: An adult return ticket is 8.50€ and for a child (5-12 years) 5.50€. There is a reduced tariff every day except on Sundays in July and August (2006).

Orenstein & Koppel prototype 050 T of 1917, No. 8285, one of a class of 35 most powerful steam locomotives ordered by the German Army in World War I. *Author*

History: It was in 1969-1970 that a group of enthusiastic volunteers discovered that much of the old line left over from World War I and the following decades was still in existence albeit in a poor state of repair. After many months of negotiations followed by much hard work the first tourist passenger trains operated in 1971 on the line as it was then named Chemin de Fer Froissy-Cappy-Dompierre (CFCD). The railway's 600 mm gauge had its origins in 1870 when an industrialist, Paul Decauville, teamed up with a French Army artillery officer, Colonel Péchot, and an engineer, Monsieur Bourdon, to create a track way with a new narrow gauge. About the same time the Germans were developing their 600 mm tracks which they called *Deutsch Feld Bahn* (lit. German countryside railway). Then came World War I and it was locomotives running on this track in the Somme that played a vital part in supplying the trenches with artillery and other supplies. For example, in the preparation for the Battle of the Somme in 1916, 1,500 tonnes of ammunition were conveyed every day on the railway! After the war the whole area from Amiens to the Ardennes was desolated and reconstruction work had to begin. The narrow gauge trains on this network from Péronne played an important part in the recovery of the area. The development and use of the narrow gauge railway continued between the wars with many local enterprises taking advantage of the railway transport. Sugar beet (*betteraves*) are an example and from 1927 onwards this locally grown crop was carried to a local sugar refinery. However, the line Dompierre–Cappy was eventually closed to general traffic in 1954 but the carriage of sugar products continued on the railway until 1972 when their transport was finally transferred to the roads.

Comments: APPEVA is twinned with the UK's Leighton Buzzard Railway. The journey is particularly attractive starting its journey at Froissy and running alongside the Somme canal for almost half of its route. The museum (entrance free) is fascinating – *see entry page 148.*

Local Tourist Office: 1, rue Louis XI, BP 146, 80200 Péronne. Telephone: 03 22 84 42 38 Fax: 03 22 84 51 25. E-mail: accueil@ot-peronne.fr website: www.ot-peronne.fr

TER-SNCF - Les Trains à la Mer

Location: Mers-les-Bains and Le Tréport, 37 km west of Abbeville.
Department: Seine-Maritime (76).
Getting there: These seaside special TER-SNCF trains travel to Le Tréport and St Valéry-sur-Somme railway stations from the main cities of Laon, Amiens and Paris.
Route and journey time: To Le Tréport from Laon is 1 hour 50 minutes, from Amiens 1 hour 5 minutes and from Paris 2 hours 34 minutes.
Gauge and type of traction: Standard; modern autorail.
Contact details: Information can be obtained from the railway stations of departure, local tourist offices or by the website.
Website: www.trainstouristiques-ter.com/trains_mer.htm
Operating dates: These trains operate every Sunday and on public holidays from the beginning of July to the beginning of September departing about 0800 hours from the three locations (Laon, Amiens and Paris Nord) for Le Tréport and leaving there for Laon at 1736 hours, Amiens at 1905 hours and for Paris Nord at 2028 hours. On the same operating days a separate special service travels from Paris to St Valéry-sur-Somme at 0804 or 1007 hours and returns from St Valéry-sur-Somme at 1723 or 1923 hours - this journey takes 1 hour 57 minutes.
Tariff: Up to 50% reductions on the normal SNCF fares (2005).
Comments: These specials are 'day-out' events to the seaside for inhabitants of nearby cities.
Local Tourist Offices: esplanade de la Plage, Quai Sadi Carnot, 76470 Le Tréport. Telephone: 02 35 86 05 69 Fax: 02 35 86 73 96. website: www.ville-le-treport.fr or 2, place Guillaume Le Conquérant, 80230 St Valéry-sur-Somme. Telephone: 03 22 60 93 50. website: www.saint-valery-sur-somme.fr

Discontinued Railway

Chemin de Fer du Val de Bray (CFVB)

Location: Goincourt.
Department: Oise (60).
Contact details: were Chemin de Fer du Val de Bray (CFVB) 60390 Auneuil or 9 rue Marie Curie, 60000 Goincourt (if still applicable).
Comments: The Project was begun in 1996 with one of the objectives being to develop a tourist line between Beauvais and Auneuil, a distance of 12 km. In spite of 160,000 francs being voted by the Regional Council of Picardie for a feasibility study, the project was unfortunately abandoned in 2004. One day, perhaps, the phoenix will rise…! (Source: FACS-UNECTO.)

Part of the railway museum at Froissy.   *Author*

Museum

Musée d'Association Picardie pour la Préservation et l'Entretien des Véhicules Anciens (APPEVA)

Operating dates: In May, June, early July and September the museum is open on Sundays and public holidays from 1345 to 1900 hours. From mid-July to the end of August, it is open every weekday (except Mondays) from 1345 to 1730 hours (2005).

Tariff: Free.

History: Between 1970 and 1971, the founders of the Association Picardie pour la Préservation et l'Entretien des Véhicules Anciens (APPEVA) cleared the line from Froissy to Dompierre and at the same time searched for locomotives, carriages and wagons which were lying derelict or about to be scrapped. It is to their credit that over the following 25 years they have been able to assemble an important collection of over 30 locomotives, including 10 steam-driven, and more than a hundred carriages and wagons. A number of these have been restored to full working order, others are stored in purpose built railway sheds or are on display in the museum. Opened in 1996 the museum adjoins the departure platform at Froissy. Many of these items have been classified as of being of historical interest; indeed, it is thought that this collection of 600 mm material is probably the most important in Europe.

Comments: This is a most interesting museum which has free admission but donations are appreciated. Trains operate on the local line from a platform alongside the museum.

Local Tourist Office: 1, rue Louis XI, BP 146, 80200 Péronne. Telephone: 03 22 84 42 38 Fax: 03 22 84 51 25. E-mail: accueil@ot-peronne.fr website: www.ot-peronne.fr

Poitou-Charentes

Poitou-Charentes is located on the western side of France and borders the regions of Pays-de-la-Loire to the north, Centre to the north east, Limousin to the east and Aquitaine to the south. It comprises the departments of Charente (16), Charente-Maritime (17), Deux-Sèvres (79) and Vienne (86). Its regional capital is Poitiers and other cities include Angoulême, La Rochelle and Niort. This region has two heritage/tourist railways and one vélorail service.

Railways

Le Train des Mouettes formerly run as the Chemin de Fer de la Seudre

030 T No. 3 le Progrès.   *Didier Lebrun and Xavier Léoty*

Member: FACS-UNECTO
Location: La Tremblade, 92 km south-west of Niort and close to another tourist railway service at St Trojan-les-Bains.
Department: Charente-Maritime (17).
Getting there: By road take the autoroute A10 and exit at 22 on to the RN150 and then follow the D14 to La Tremblade.

Route: La Tremblade to Saujon (21 km).
Journey time: The round trip is 2 hours 30 minutes.
Gauge and type of traction: Standard; steam
Rolling stock: A 030 T No. 3 *le Progrès* (built in 1891) and various carriages.
Contact details: Le Train des Mouettes, Gare du Train Touristique, rue de la Resinerie, 17390 La Tremblade. Telephone: 05 46 75 11 10 or 08 92 39 14 28 Fax: 05 46 75 41 36. E-mail: contact@traindesmouettes.com
Website: www.traindesmouettes.com
Operating dates: From the middle of April to early October operating mainly from Thursdays to Sundays inclusive with extra services from mid-July to the end of August on most days. Departures are both in the mornings and afternoons. Consult the railway or tourist office to obtain exact operating days and hours.
Tariff: An adult return ticket is 13€ and for a child (4-11 years) 6€. An adult single ticket is 10€ and for a child 6.50€. Dogs and cycles go free (2006).
History: A study was undertaken in 1865 to build a line between Saujon and La Tremblade but it was not until 1875 that the building of the line was completed and operations began. The prime purpose was originally to provide passenger services but later the carriage of goods was embraced notably resin, vinegar and oysters from the Seudre estuary, the latter especially being popular in France from the end of the Franco-Prussian War in 1871 to the beginning of World War I in 1914. Initially the railway was in private hands but by 1878 financial difficulties were encountered leading to the state purchasing the line as part of the Chemin de fer d'Orléans network. Closures of parts of the line to passengers began in 1932 and again in 1939 after SNCF had been formed. The year 1965 saw the end of most of the goods traffic with the exception of oysters but that eventually ended in 1980. Two years later a volunteer association - Chemin de Fer de la Seudre - was formed to run tourist trains, some steam-driven but later diesel. In 2003 the association ended its days after 19 years and their services stopped. CFTA (Connex-Tradition) has now taken over operations.
Comments: This railway is one of the Connex-Tradition services.
Local Tourist Office: 1, boulevard Pasteur, BP 141, 17390 La Tremblade. Telephone: 05 46 36 37 71 Fax: 05 46 36 37 30. E-mail: ot@la-tremblade.com website: www.la-tremblade.com

Le P'tit Train de St Trojan also known as Société du Tramway Touristique de St Trojan (STTST)

Location: St Trojan-les-Bains, 99 km south-west of Niort.
Department: Charente-Maritime (17).
Getting there: By road take the autoroute A10 and exit at 33 then follow the RN248, RN11, D911 and D123 to Île d'Oléron.
Route: St Trojan-les-Bains to Maumusson (6 km).
Journey time: 1 hour 30 minutes round trip.
Gauge and type of traction: 600 mm; steam, autorail and diesel.

Rolling stock: A 1916-built Deutsch Feldbahn (DFB) 040 T steam locomotive, a 1926 Crochat-Decauville petro-electric X AT3 autorail and its trailer carriage No. XR AT3, a 1937 Billard type 75P and three 1932-built Deutz OMZ 117 locotracteurs, two of which are operational. There is also a variety of carriages and goods wagons.

Contact details: Société du Tramway Touristique de St Trojan, avenue du Débarquement, 17370 St Trojan-les-Bains. Telephone: 05 46 76 01 26 Fax: 05 46 76 07 13. E-mail is via the website.

Website: www.le-ptit-train.com

Operating dates: From mid-April to mid-September with departures at 1100, 1430, 1515, 1600, 1645 and 1730 hours except in July and August when there are departures every 45 minutes from 1000 to 1815 hours.

Tariff: An adult ticket is 10€ and for a child 7€. There are special rates for groups and families (2005).

History: The idea of developing this railway was that of a military medic, Doctor Pol Gala in 1959. Construction began in 1962 and the railway was opened to the public in June 1963. The line was extended between 1963 and 1965. Over the years there have been problems with erosion leading to some difficulties. For example, this railway has the unenviable distinction of having the only railway station in France, Maumusson, which has had to have been rebuilt 18 times in 41 years!

Comments: This line is the only tourist line on the Île d'Oléron. It travels through the woods and the sand dunes along the Bay of Gasteau. On Monday evenings in July and August there are the 'Sunset Trains', two-hour-long journeys at dusk. This trip is a 'must-do'.

Local Tourist Office: Bureau Municipal de Tourisme, Carrefour du Port, 17370 St Trojan-les-Bains. Telephone: 05 46.76 00 86 Fax: 05 46 76 17 64. E-mail: ot-st-trojan-les-bains@wanadoo.fr website: www.st-trojan-les-bains.fr

Vélorail

Chemin de Fer de Charente Limousine also known as Vélorail de Charente (CFCL)

Member: FACS-UNECTO

Location: Manot-Roumazières, 46 km north-west of Angoulême.

Department: Charente (16).

Getting there: The nearest SNCF station is at Confolens. By road take the autoroute A28 and exit at 28 on to the RN141 to Roumazières.

Route: Roumazières to Confolens (17 km).

Gauge: Standard.

Contact details: Vélorail de Charente, CFCL, PN5, 16500 Manot. Telephone-Fax: 05 45 71 16 64. E-mail: velorail16@wanadoo.fr

Website: www.velorail16.com

Operating dates: It operates at weekends in June and September and every day in July and August. The hours of the services do vary, so check first. From October to the end of May, this service is available on request.

Tariff: Vélorail hire for 3 hours is 25€ with special prices for groups, one member of whom must be an adult (2005).
Comments: A full three hours is needed to enjoy the journey.
Local Tourist Office: place des Marronniers, 16500 Confolens. Telephone: 05 45 84 22 22 Fax: 05 45 85 98 09. E-mail: otconfolentais@wanadoo.fr website: www.tourisme-confolens.com

A vélorail.   *Vélorail de Charente*

Provence-Alpes-Côte d'Azur

Provence-Alpes-Côte d'Azur is in the south-east of France and has a frontier with Italy and regional borders with Rhône-Alpes to the north and Languedoc-Roussillon to the west. It comprises the departments of Alpes-de-Haute-Provence (04), Hautes-Alpes (05), Alpes-Maritimes (06), Bouches-du-Rhône (13), Var (83) and Vaucluse (84). Its regional capital is Marseille and other important cities are Nice, Gap, Digne, Avignon and Toulon. This region along with the Rhône-Alpes region is the most active for railway enthusiasts. It has three heritage/tourist railways, four TER-SNCF tourist services, one discontinued railway, three locations where traction is preserved, three museums and one vélorail service.

Railways

Régie Départementale des Transports des Bouches-du-Rhône (RDT13) operating Le Petit Train des Alpilles and Train à Vapeur du Val de Provence

An RDT13 diesel locotracteur and carriages heading for Arles. *Author*

Member: FACS-UNECTO
Location: Arles, 36 km south of Avignon and 66 km south of Orange.
Department: Bouches-du-Rhône (13).
Getting there: By SNCF train to Arles. By road from Orange take the autoroutes A9 and A54 to Arles.
Routes: RDT13, as part of its tourist services, delivers a diesel-hauled service between Arles and Fontvielle (10.5 km). It also operates the Train a Vapeur du Val de Provence which is a steam service between Châteaurenard, near Avignon and Barbentane (10 km). RDT13 also operates several freight lines near Arles, Tarascon and more recently Montpellier as well as local bus services.
Journey time: Both journeys take about 40 minutes each way.

Gauge and type of traction: Standard; steam, autorails and diesel.
Rolling stock: Autorails No. X 584 (ex-Hyères-Salin) and No. X 3824 (ex-Comité Cannes-Grasse), an 030 T steam locomotive No. 8157 (returned to service in September 2002) and several diesel locotracteurs.
Contact details: Régie Départementale des Transports des Bouches-du-Rhône (RDT 13), 17 bis, avenue de Hongrie, 13200 Arles. Telephone: for RDT 13 diesel services call 04 90 18 81 31 and for RDT 13 steam services call 06 98 16 55 33 (mobile) Fax: 04 90 18 18 41. E-mail: letraindesalpilles@rdft13.fr
Website: www.rdt13.fr
Operating dates: From mid-June to mid-September diesel-hauled services run on Wednesdays and Thursdays departing Arles at 1000, 1330 and 1510 hours and Fontvielle at 1050, 1420 and 1600 hours. Steam services when running leave Chateaurenard on Sundays at 1500 hours but it is very important to check first and confirm it is operating.
Tariff: An adult ticket is 8€ and for a child 5€ (2005).
History: The railway line in its founding days was originally operated by the former Compagnie des Chemin de Fer des Bouches du Rhône (BDR). Between 1978 and 1981 the line between Arles and Fontvielle was run by l'AJECTA-Provence. In 2000, RDT13 took over the tourist services on the line with the co-operation of APPAF (*see separate entry on page 162*). APPAF owns a variety of locomotives based at their SNCF depot at Miramas, notably two autorails which operate on this line in the high season.
Comments: It is possible to charter the steam service for any time in the year.
Local Tourist Office: boulevard des Lices, 13200 Arles. Telephone: 04 90 18 41 20 Fax: 04 90 18 41 29. E-mail: ot-arles@visitprovence.com

Association du Chemin de Fer Touristique du Centre Var (ATTCV)

Member: FACS-UNECTO
Location: Carnoules, 38 km north-east of Toulon.
Department: Var (83).
Getting there: By road takes the autoroutes A6, A7 & A8 and exit at 13 on to RN97 to Carnoules.
Route: Carnoules – Brignoles (24 km).
Journey time: Not yet advised.
Gauge and type of traction: Standard: autorail.
Rolling stock: Picasso autorail No. X 3800 and a second Picasso autorail No. X 3976.
Contact details: Association du Chemin de Fer Touristique du Centre Var, Le Bastidon, route de Nice, 83390 Cuers. Telephone : 04 94 48 62 40.
Website: http://attcv.ifrance.com/
Operating dates: Autorail services resumed in August 2005 and are set to continue in 2006 on Sundays and some Wednesdays.
Tariff: An adult ticket is 8.50€ and for a child (4-10 years) 5€ (2006).
History: Founded in 1994 L'Association du Chemin du Train Touristique du Centre Var worked hard for seven years to seek approval to operate its Picasso

Picasso autorail No. X 3976 of ATTCV. *Phillipe Granata*

autorail between Carnoules and Brignoles. So it was, in August 2001, that a service again operated after a break of more than 60 years! However, there was and still is much to be done and the 50 or so volunteers need more help, physical and financial, to realise their objectives. The early 2005 season did not see services operating due to continuing administrative problems in seeking approvals with the Réseau Ferré de France (RFF) on track issues. Fortunately, after many months of discussions, these were overcome in the August 2005 thus allowing services to resume.

Comments: In addition to the restored tourist services on Sundays and some Wednesdays, every Saturday morning ATTCV members meet either at the railway shed near to the SNCF station at Carnoules or at their development site at Besse-sur-Issole. They very much appreciate interest and support that visitors give to their railway. It is good news that a tourist service is now able to operate regularly on this route in what is a most attractive area of Provence.

Local Tourist Office: Hôtel de Ville, place Gabriel Péri, 83660 Carnoules. Telephone: 04 94 28 32 96. E-mail: contact@carnoules.org website: www.carnoules.org

Le Train de Pignes also known as the Groupement d'Etudes des Chemin de Fer de Provence (GECP)

The 1909 Fives-Lille 230 T No. E-327 undergoing pre-season maintenance at Puget-Theniers. *Author*

Member: FACS-UNECTO
Location: Puget-Théniers, 87 km west of Digne and 66 km north-west of Nice.
Department: Alpes-Maritimes (06).
Getting there: Take the RN202 from Nice or Digne to Puget-Théniers.
Route: Puget-Théniers to Annot (20 km) and in high season continuing to Le Fugeret (a further 5.6 km).

Journey times: Puget-Théniers to Annot takes 1 hour 40 minutes including a 35 minute stop at Entrevaux. The journey from Annot to Le Fugeret takes 15 minutes. Return journeys back from Le Fugeret and Annot are slightly quicker.
Gauge and type of traction: Metre; steam, diesel.
Rolling stock: There are two steam locomotives comprising a 1909 230 T Fives-Lille No. E-327 formerly of the Brittany rail network (owned by FACS and on loan to GECP) and a 1923 120+030 T Mallet No. E-211 formerly of the Portuguese Railways. There is also a CFD diesel locotracteur bought from the Chemin de Fer Touristique du Bas-Berry (*see entry under Centre region*), seven passenger carriages and 12 wagons (fourgons) variously constructed between 1888 and 1912.
Contact details: Le Train de Pignes, Dépôt des Locomotives, 06230 Puget-Théniers. Telephone: Puget-Théniers – 04 93 05 04 82 and Nice - 04 97 03 80 80 Fax: Nice - 04 97 03 80 81. E-mail: gecp@libertysurf.fr
Website: www.gecp.asso.fr
Operating dates: On Sundays from early June to late October leaving Puget-Théniers at 1000 and returning from Annot at 1600 hours. In July and August, extra steam trains run from Annot at 1400 to Le Fugeret and returning from there at 1450 hours.
Tariff: An adult return ticket from Puget-Théniers to Annot is 17.50€ and for a child 14.50€, and from Annot to Le Fugeret for an adult is 5.70€ and for a child 4.20€ (2005).
History: A group of volunteers formed the Groupement d'Etudes des Chemin de Fer de Provence in 1980 and by linking with the Connex-Tradition Nice – Digne service have successfully operated this steam-driven section ever since.
Comments: This part of the route links with Chemin de Fer de la Provence (Nice to Digne route) at Puget-Théniers, Annot and sometimes Le Fugeret (*see next entry*). The steam service was variable in 2005 owing to steam locomotive maintenance difficulties. This is a 'must-do'.
Local Tourist Office: boulevard St Pierre, BP 54, 04240 Annot. Telephone: 04 92 83 23 03 Fax: 04 92 83 30 63 or 04 92 83 32 82.
E-mail: otsi.annot@wanadoo.fr or annot.mairie@wanadoo.fr

TER-SNCF - Chemin de Fer de la Provence (CP) operated by Connex-Tradition

Member: FACS-UNECTO
Location: Nice is on the Côte d'Azur in the south-east of France on the Mediterranean coast.
Department: Hautes-Alpes (05) and Alpes-Maritimes (06).
Getting there: By SNCF rail services to Nice. By road, take the autoroute A8 and exit at 50 for Nice. To Digne via Grenoble take the autoroute A51 and exit on to RN75 and then follow RN85 (route Napoléon) to Digne.
Route: Nice to Digne (151 km).
Journey time: Usually about 3 hours 12 minutes.
Gauge and type of traction: Metre; diesel.
Contact details: Chemin de Fer de la Provence, 4 bis, rue Alfred Binet, 06000 Nice. Telephone: Nice station on 04 97 03 80 80, Digne on 04 92 31 01 58 Fax: Nice station on 04 97 03 80 81, Digne on 04 92 32 08 56. E-mail: train.pigne@connex.net

Diesel-powered car standing at Digne station. *Author*

Website: www.trainprovence.com
Operating dates: All year with four return journeys per day from Nice to Digne. Departures from Nice at 0642, 0900, 1243 and 1700 hours and from Digne at 0700, 1033, 1358 and 1725 hours.
Tariff: The cost of tickets vary but in 2005 a single journey from Nice to Digne (or the other way) was 17.65€ with 50% reduction for children (4-12 years) and 25% for those aged 55+ but check current fare at a station or on the internet (2006).
History: This railway route, famous the world over, had its origins in 1891 during the steam era. It is a magnificent example of engineering given the nature of the terrain and the heights (more than 1,000 m) to be crossed. In all, 50 tunnels, bridges and viaducts had to be built.
Comments: It is without doubt one of the longest and most beautiful railway routes in France and is enhanced on Sundays from mid-June to mid-September with Le Train de Pignes (steam-driven) operating on part of the route between Puget-Théniers and Annot and return (*see previous entry*). This railway is one of the Connex-Tradition services and is definitely a 'must-do'.
Local Tourist Office: place du Tampinet, BP 201, 04000 Digne-les-Bains. Telephone: 04 92 36 62 62 Fax: 04 92 32 27 24. E-mail: info-digne.les.bains@wanadoo.fr website: www.ot-dignelesbains.fr and 5 promenade des Anglais, BP 4079, 06302 Nice. Telephone: 08 92 70 74 07. E-mail: info@nicetourisme.com website: www.nicetourisme.com

TER-SNCF – Train des Merveilles

Location: Nice on the Côte d'Azur in the south-east of France on the Mediterranean coast.
Department: Alpes-Maritimes (06).
Getting there: By SNCF to Nice. By road, take the autoroute A8 and at exit 50 for Nice.
Route: Nice-St Roche to Tende-Val-des-Merveilles (73 km).
Journey time: 1 hour 50 minutes each way.
Gauge and type of traction: Standard; autorail.
Rolling stock: Autorails type X 2200 with XR 6000 remorques (unpowered carriages) specially renovated for this service. The autorails and carriages are colourfully painted in the livery of Haut Pays Niçois.
Contact details: via the tourist office in Nice.
Website: www.trainstouristiques-ter.com/provence.htm
Operating dates: Departs from Nice at 0900 hours on Saturdays, Sundays and public holidays from the beginning of April to the beginning of July then every day until September.
Tariff: An example of a fare for an adult return ticket is 21.20€ or with a *Carte Isabelle* it is reduced to 11€ (2006).
History: The desire by the French authorities in Nice to have this railway line built goes back to mid-19th century. However, it was the Italians who first began the work in 1879 but there were many delays as the military authorities on both sides of the frontier were unhappy with the project from a national security point of view. In 1895, the French Government gave their approval for the work to re-commence leading to the first train arriving at Tende-Val-des-Merveilles in 1913, albeit an Italian one! The onset of World War I led to the work being halted and it was not re-started until 1920. In 1928 the line eventually was formally opened, 72 years after the idea had first been mooted! It was electrified in part in 1935. Unfortunately, three-quarters of the line was destroyed between 1940 and 1945 in World War II, ironically perhaps the military authorities eventually had their way! After the end of hostilities the French side of the line was re-built and re-opened in 1947 but it was not until 1979, 51 years after the original opening, that the Italian section was re-established.
Comments: A guide gives a commentary on the train in French! The line travels the border between France and Italy. The mountainous scenery is outstanding especially when viewed from the train, which, in three separate *boucles* (loops), spirals its way up the mountains. With a length of 5,938 metres the line has the longest railway tunnel in France under the Col de Braus. This is a 'must-do' journey.
Local Tourist Office: 5 promenade des Anglais, BP 4079, 06302 Nice. Telephone: 08 92 70 74.TER- E-mail: info@nicetourisme.com or avenue du 16 septembre 1947, 06430 Tende-Val-des-Merveilles. Telephone: 04 93 04 73 71 Fax: 04 93 04 35 09. E-mail: info@tendemerveilles.com

TER-SNCF – La TER de la Côte Bleue

Location: Marseille
Department: Bouches-du-Rhône (13).
Getting there: By TGV services direct to Marseille. The autoroutes A7, A50 and A55 all terminate in Marseille.
Route: Marseille Saint-Charles to Miramas (60 km).
Journey time: 1 hour 10 minutes.
Gauge and type of traction: Standard; modern autorail.
Contact details: via the tourist office in Marseille.
Website: www.trainstouristiques-ter.com/Côte_bleue.htm
Operating dates: On Sundays in July, August and September, eight services operate each way each day with the first departure from Marseille at 0618 and the last from Miramas at 1935 hours. Reservations are essential in the high season.
Tariff: The *Carte Bermuda* includes the train journey and a mini cruise and for adults is 15€ and for a child (4-12 years) 10€ (2006).
Comments: It is possible to view the *calanques* (rocky coastline and bays) from a small cruise boat, *l'Albatros*, which is included in the trip's itinerary.
Local Tourist Offices: 4, la Canebière, 13000 Marseille. Telephone: 04 91 13 89 00 Fax: 04 91 13 89 20. E-mail: info@marseille-tourisme.com or 24, place Jean Jaurès, 13140 Miramas. Telephone: 04 90 58 08 24 Fax: 04 90 50 11 05. E-mail: ot.miramas@free.fr

TER-SNCF – Le Train des Alpages

Location: Marseille.
Department: Bouches-du-Rhône (13).
Getting there: TGV services direct to Marseille. The autoroutes A7, A50 and A55 all terminate in Marseille.
Route: Marseille Saint Charles to Briançon (260 km).
Journey time: 4 hours 10 minutes.
Gauge and type of traction: modern autorail.
Contact details: Telephone 04 42 37 14 08, or visit one of the railway stations at Marseille Saint-Charles, Marseille Blancard, Aubagne, Aix-en-Provence or Manosque.
Website: www.trainstouristiques-ter.com/train_alpage.htm
Operating dates: On Saturdays in July and August the train departs from Marseille at 0600, Aix-en-Provence at 0629 and Manosque at 0713 arriving at Briançon at 1010 hours. It returns from Briançon at 1724 and arrives at Manosque at 2016, Aix-en-Provence at 2100 and Marseille at 2133 hours.
Tariff: An adult return is 20€ and for a child (4-12 years) 10€ (2006).
Comments: On many of the Saturdays in July and August special excursions are arranged in conjunction with the running of this train.
Local Tourist Offices: 4, la Canebière, 13000 Marseille. Telephone: 04 91 13 89 00 Fax: 04 91 13 89 20. E-mail: info@marseille-tourisme.com or
1, place du Temple, 05100 Briançon. Telephone: 04 92 21 08 50 Fax: 04 92 20 56 45. E-mail: OFFICE-TOURISME-BRIANCON@wanadoo.fr

Discontinued Railway

Chemin de Fer Hyères-les-Palmiers

Location: Hyères.

Department: Var (83).

Comments: This railway, related to the former and now defunct Chemin de Fer des Alpilles, ran a service between Hyères and Les Salins-d'Hyères in the summer of 1982 using autorail No. X 5845. Unfortunately the service did not make it into a second season. (Source: FACS-UNECTO.)

Preserved Locomotives and Other Traction

Société Ferroviarie du Grand Delta (SFGD)

Autorail No. X 2403 owned by M. J-M Henry.   *Author*

Location: Avignon, 97 km north of Marseille.

Department: Vaucluse (84).

Getting there: By rail on the TGV to Avignon. By road take the autoroute A7 and exit at 23 then the RN7 to Avignon.

Gauge and type of traction: Standard; autorail.

Rolling stock: Autorails Nos. X 2403 and X 3824 from Comité Cannes-Grasse (CCG - *see page 162*).

Contact details: Société Ferroviarie du Grand Delta, c/o Monsieur J-M Henry, 16 rue des Muriers, 84000, Avignon. Telephone: 04 90 85 25 98.

Comments: These autorails are preserved and approved for use on RFF (SNCF) tracks.
Local Tourist Office: 41 cours Jean Jaurès, BP 8, 84000 Avignon. Telephone: 04 32 74 32 74 Fax: 04 90 82 95 03. E-mail: information@ot-avignon.fr website: www.ot-avignon.fr

APPAF

Location: Miramas, 57 km north-west of Marseille.
Department: Bouches-du-Rhône (13).
Getting there: By SNCF train to Miramas. By road take the autoroute A54 and exit at Salon-en-Provence and then follow the RN569 to Miramas.
Gauge and type of traction: Standard; steam and electric.
Exhibits: Electric locomotive BB 4177 and a Mikado steam locomotive 141 R 1298.
Contact details: APPAF, Dépôt de Miramas, 7 ave du Mai-Juin, 13140 Miramas.
Website: http://appaf.free.fr/ is in the course of design.
Comments: No. 141 R 1298, built by Montreal, began its career at the Sotteville depot near Rouen and concluded its duties at Narbonne in November 1973. During its career it completed 1,546,715 kilometres fuelled by heavy oil. Still in the ownership of SNCF, it is now preserved as a static exhibit and not approved at present for use on RFF (SNCF) tracks. No. BB 4177 is also a static exhibit at the Miramas depot.
Local Tourist Office: 24, place Jean Jaurès, 13140 Miramas. Telephone: 04 90 58 08 24 Fax: 04 90 58 08 24. E-mail: ot.miramas@free.fr
website: www.miramas.org/tourisme

Comité Cannes-Grasse (CCG)

Location: Le Cannet
Department: Alpes-Maritimes (06).
Getting there: By road take the autoroute A8 and exit at 42 on to RN285 to Le Cannet.
Gauge and type of traction: Standard; autorail.
Rolling stock: A Unifié 300 hp Picasso autorail No. X 3824. The Committee also has a Corpet-Louvet 030 No. 8 steam locomotive, listed as a *Monument Historique*, and which is currently on loan to AGRIVAP in Ambert in the Auvergne (*see page 33*).
Contact details: Comité Cannes-Grasse (CCG), 1 rue Casimir Reynard, 06110 Le Cannet. E-mail: lescatj-p@azur.fr
Website: www.trains-fr.org/ccg/
History: The Committee was formed in June 1973 to pressure for the re-establishment of a passenger railway service between Cannes and Grasse, a line which had originally opened by the PLM in 1871. Passenger services were stopped on this line in 1938 and freight was halted in 1991. The first success of the pressure group was achieved in 1978 when the line from Cannes to Ranguin

Corpet-Louvet 030 No. 8 *Ilena* currently on loan to AGRIVAP at Ambert in the Auvergne.
Author

was opened and a railcar, No. X 94630, was allocated to the duty. Unfortunately, a further extension of the line was not achieved. Sadly, this service operated for the last time on the eve of what turned out to be a long-running SNCF strike in November 1995; the service was not re-instated after the strike ended. Notwithstanding this setback, the four main objectives continued to be promoting the re-opening of the Cannes-Grasse railway line, representing the interests of the local public on transport issues, to save historical rolling stock and to organize excursions mainly on Sundays to tourist locations. Matters started to look up when the Region published in its 2000-2006 Development Plan its desire to re-open the line to relieve the road congestion in the area. Work began in 2002 and was concluded with the official opening of the line on 26th March, 2005 when regular passenger services first returned to the Cannes-Grasse line after an absence of 67 years. The success has been not only to restore the local line but also to integrate it into the TER network; for example, of the services running each day from Grasse, four terminate at Cannes, three continue on to Nice, two reach Menton and 10 end their journey at Ventimiglia just over the border in northern Italy.

Comments: An enthusiastic group in spite of the setbacks but one which has now triumphed. A journey on the 15 km line (between 35 and 45 minutes) is well worth taking not only for the superb scenery but to lend continuing support to a hard fought and won project.

Local Tourist Office: avenue du Campon, 06110 Le Cannet. Telephone: 04 93 45 34 27 Fax: 04 93 45 28 06. E-mail: tourisme@lecannet.com or tourisme@mairie-le-cannet.fr website: www.mairie-le-cannet.fr

Museums

Ecomusée des Transport et des Techniques

Location: Breil-sur-Roya, 50 km north of Monaco.
Department: Alpes-Maritimes (06).
Getting there: By TGV to Nice. By road, take autoroutes A8 and A10 into Italy then the SS20 north back into France where the road number changes to RN204 for Breil-sur-Roya. The exhibition is on display at the station in Breil-sur-Roya.
Gauge and type of traction: Standard; steam, electric.
Exhibits: A selection of steam and electric locomotives, locotracteurs, trams and trolleybuses; electric locomotive CC 7140 is exhibited there as is a BB 8100 and other interesting material but check first that none has been re-located! Also said by FACS-UNECTO to be there at one time, as a static exhibit, was Mikado 141 R 1108 which was built by LIMA and introduced into service at Nevers in May 1947 and retired at Vierzon in December 1975 having completed 1,653,150 kilometres. It was fired by heavy oil.
Contact details: Ecomusée du Haut-Pays Nicois, c/o Office de Tourisme, 06540 Breil-sur-Roya.
Local Tourist Office: 17 place Bianchéri, 06540 Breil-sur-Roya. Telephone: 04 93 04 99 76 Fax: 04 93 04 99 76. E-mail: tourismebreilsurroya@wanadoo.fr website: http://www.breil-sur-roya.fr

Musée Provençal des Transports de la Barque (MPTUR)

Location: Fuveau, 33 km north-east of Marseille.
Department: Bouches-de-Rhône (13).
Getting there: By TGV to Marseille. By road take autoroute A8 from Aix-en-Provence and exit on to the RN96 then follow the D6 and D46 to Fuveau.
Gauge and type of traction: Standard and 600 mm; steam, trams.
Contact details: Musée Provençal des Transports de la Barque, Gare SNCF de La Barque, 13710 Fuveau, and communications c/o Monsieur Noël Mailliary, Lou Souleou C1, boulevard Bazile Barrelier, 13014 Marseille. Telephone: 04 91 98 15 91. E-mail: cppva@referentiel.com
Website: www.fuveau.fr/loisir/tourisme/musees.asp?page=2c3a
Operating dates: The museum opened its doors for the first time at the beginning of June 2005. It now encourages visits by individuals on Sundays between 1400 and 1800 hours. However, the months of opening have not been publicised but are likely to be from June to September. Groups can visit at any time by prior appointment (2006).
Tariff: Not announced for 2006.
Comments: The museum traces the local history of transport through its interesting collection of locomotives, trolley buses, trams and wagons.
Local Tourist Office: 2, place du Général de Gaulle, BP 160, 13100 Aix-en-Provence. Telephone: 04 42 16 11 61 Fax: 04 42 16 11 62. E-mail: infos@aixenprovencetourism.com

L'Ecomusée du Veynois

Location: Veynes, 27 km west of Gap.
Department: Hautes-Alpes (05).
Getting there: By SNCF to Veynes. From Gap take the D994 to Veynes.
Exhibition: This *ecomusée* celebrates the history and traditions of Veynes and its surrounding area. Veynes has a strong link with the development of the railways not least of all it being the birthplace of the 19th century engineer Adrien Ruelle. Monsieur Ruelle (1815-1887) known locally as *l'Étoile de Veynes* (star of Veynes) became a director of the PLM company and was instrumental in the design and construction of the railway lines in the Alps. In addition, he built homes on housing estates for railway workers and a depot for the locomotives including a *rotonde* (roundhouse). He was also a regional councillor when the first train entered Veynes in 1875. His life and works, and that of a developing railway town in the late 19th century, are the focus of this most interesting museum.
Contact details: Ecomusée du Veynois, 3 rue du Jeu de Paume, 05400 Veynes. Telephone: 04 92 58 00 49 Fax: 04 92 58 19 17. E-mail: henri.favier@wanadoo.fr
Website: http://perso.wanadoo.fr/henri.favier/fichiers/musee.html
Operating dates: From June to the end of September operating on Wednesdays and Saturdays from 1500 to 1900 hours with guided tours at 1600 hours.
Tariff: An adult is charged 3.50€ and a child (4-10 years) 1.50€ (2006).
Comments: The website for the L'Ecomusée du Veynois was written by Monsieur Henri Favier, a local newspaperman and a mine of information. A visit to this *ecomusée* could be usefully combined with a trip on the TER-SNCF service Le Train des Alpes which travels to Veynes from Grenoble (*see page 178*).
Local Tourist Office: avenue Commandant Dumont, 05400 Veynes. Telephone: 0 4 92 57 27 43 Fax: 04 92 58 16 18. E-mail: Tourisme.Veynois@wanadoo.fr website www.tourisme.fr/office-de-tourisme/veynes.htm

Vélorail

Ventoux Rail Nostalgie

Location: Aubignan, 33 km north-east of Avignon.
Department: Vaucluse (84).
Getting there: By SNCF train to Carpentras. By road take the autoroute A7 and exit at 9 and follow the D950 to Aubignan.
Route: Aubignan to Carpentras (7 km).
Gauge: Standard.
Contact details: Ventoux Rail Nostalgie, 84810 Aubignan. Telephone: 08 71 13 60 07 Fax: 04 90 40 22 60. E-mail: contact@ventoux-rail-nostalgie.com
Website: www.ventoux-rail-nostalgie.com/fr.htm
Operating dates: Selected Sundays in the summer but check with the operator first as it is necessary beforehand to make a reservation.
Local Tourist Office: boulevard Louis Guichard, route de Caromb, 84810 Aubignan. Telephone: 04 90 62 65 36 Fax: 04 90 62 65 36.
E-mail: ot.aubignan@wanadoo.fr website: www.tourisme.fr

Rhône-Alpes

Rhône-Alpes is located in the south-east of France with frontiers with Switzerland and Italy and regional borders with Franche-Comté to the north, Auvergne to the west, Languedoc-Rousssillon to the south-west and Provence-Alpes-Côte-d'Azur to the south. It comprises the departments of Ain (01), Ardèche (07), Drome (26), Isère (38), Loire (42), Rhône (69), Savoie (73) and Haute-Savoie (74). Its regional capital is Lyon and other important centres are Bourg-en-Bresse, Privas, Valence, Grenoble, Saint Etienne, Chambèry and Annecy. This region with Provence-Alpes-Côte d'Azur is the most active for railway enthusiasts. It has seven heritage / tourist railways, two TER-SNCF tourist services, one tourist railway where operations have been temporarily suspended, one projected railway, two discontinued railways, two locations where preserved traction is stored and two museums.

Railways

Chemin de Fer d'Anse also known as Association de la Voie 38cm (AV38)

Miniature autorails at Anse.   *Chemin de Fer d'Anse*

Member: FACS-UNECTO
Location: Anse, 26 km north of Lyon.
Department: Rhône (69).
Getting there: By road take the autoroute A6 and exit at 32 on to the RN6 to Anse. Follow the signs for Camping – Les Portes du Beaujolais.
Route: Anse to Pont St Bernard (2.5 km).

Gauge and type of traction: 380 mm; autorail, steam and locotracteur all miniature in size.

Rolling stock: Three reproduction (open-topped) autorails powered by 425 cc Citroën two-cylinder engines. One reproduction locotracteur and a number of carriages and wagons. A reproduction type 131 steam locomotive on a design of Jean Villette is in the course of construction, is almost completed and likely to be ready for service for the 2006 season.

Contact details: Association de la Voie 38cm, 8 avenue de la Libération, 69480 Anse. Telephone: 04 74 60 26 01. E-mail: cft.anse@wanadoo.fr

Website: www.trains-fr.org/anse/

Operating dates: From April to October on Sundays and public holidays from 1430 to 1830 hours and from mid-June to late August also on Saturday afternoons from 1430 to 1830 hours.

Tariff: An adult return ticket is 4€ and for a child (2-12 years) 2€ (2005).

Comments: A miniature railway perhaps only of novelty interest to true railway enthusiasts but certainly an interesting and popular family attraction. The railway is twinned with the Romney, Hythe & Dymchurch Railway in England.

Local Tourist Office: place du 8 Mai 1945, 69480 Anse. Telephone: 04 74 60 26 16 Fax: 04 74 67 29 74. E-mail: contact@tourismepierresdorees.com website: www.tourismepierresdorees.com

Chemin de Fer du Vivarais (CFV) also known as Chemin de Fer Touristique - Le Mastrou (CFTM)

Member: FACS-UNECTO

Location: Tournon-sur-Rhône, 95 km south of Lyon.

Department: Ardèche (07).

Getting there: By SNCF train to Tournon-sur-Rhône (TGV and TER). By road take the autoroute A7 to Tain l'Hermitage then the RN86 and D216 over the River Rhône to Tournon-sur-Rhône. When crossing over the Rhône note the first suspension bridge ever to be built on a design of Marc Seguin's, the French inventor who also designed the tubular boiler (*see page 96*).

Route: Tournon-sur-Rhône to Lamastre (33 km).

Journey time: Two hours each way.

Gauge and type of traction: Metre gauge running off standard gauge at the SNCF main line at Tournon-sur-Rhône; steam, diesel and autorail.

Rolling stock: The CFV with over 141 items listed in stock holds one of the most interesting and varied collection of narrow gauge material in the country. The inventory includes five 48-tonne Mallet 030 steam locomotives variously built between 1904 and 1932, a 1903 Pinguely 030 two-cab steam locomotive originally used on the tramways of Lyon's streets, another single-headed 030 Pinguely originally from Morbihan, two 1924 Corpet-Louvet 040 steam locomotives, and a 1906 Mallet 020 + 020 steam locomotive from the Corrèze region. Two 1948 diesel units, 'X' and 'Y', would not be of particular interest other than for the fact that they are constructed on former chassis belonging to

Mallett 020-020 No. 104 of 1906 (*foreground*) and a 1903-built Mallet 030-030 No. 403 take water.   *Author*

St Leonard steam locomotives originally constructed in 1887. Autorails are also well represented with a 1935 De Dion-Bouton type ND, two Billard type A-150Ds (built 1937 and 1940), two Billard type A-80Ds (1937 and 1939) and a 1938 Brissonneau et Lotz articulated railcar. There a number of unpowered railcars (remorques). A number of passenger carriages have been preserved from the original railway including three referred to as *cages à poules* (hen-houses!). Also preserved is a beautiful Voiture de Salon built by De Dietrich in 1902 which is available to be used on the line for special charters.

Contact details: Chemin de Fer du Vivarais, avenue de la Gare, 07300 Tournon-sur-Rhône. Telephone: 04 75 08 20 30 Fax: 04 75 07 01 77. E-mail: contact@ardeche-train.com

Website: www.ardeche-train.com

Operating dates: Services, both steam-hauled and autorails, operate from April to October. In April and October, on Saturdays and Sundays, there are three services each way per day. In May, June and September, it operates on every day except Monday and Wednesday with three services each way on most days, but check beforehand. In July and August, services operate every day with departures from Tournon-sur-Rhône at 0905 (Tuesdays only), 1000, 1400 and 1815 hours and from Lamastre at 0800, 1230, 1430 and 1630 hours (2006).

Tariff: An adult return ticket is 20€ and for a child (4-15 years) 10€. An adult single is 17€ and for a child 10€. A family ticket, single or return (2 adults and 2 children) is 50€. NB: credit and debit cards are accepted (2006).

History: Construction of the 33 km of line between Tournon-sur-Rhône and Lamastre began in 1886 and was completed five years later. Construction was particularly arduous with much of the excavation having to be done by hand. Gunpowder was also used extensively to blast a way through the rock. By 1903, the entire line of 202 km creating a link between the Rhône and the Loire rivers via the Boutière Mountains was completed. The line, locally named in the Franco-Provençal patois as Le Mastrou, brought a new prosperity to an area which hitherto had been hard to access there being only a few difficult and dangerous roads. The transport of felled wood was the prime product but livestock, agricultural provisions and people were also carried. Autorails, which were much faster and cheaper to run than steam locomotives, were introduced to the line in 1935. After World War II had ended railway operations continued successfully including the carriage of tourists to the area. However, it was the original choice of the narrow metre gauge which eventually led to the demise of the commercial operations on the railway. The demand for wood increased after the war throughout France but this meant that loads had to be transferred from narrow gauge to standard gauge wagons in order to move swiftly over long distances to other parts of France. Double loading, unloading and re-loading was both costly and time-consuming and so towards the end of the 1950s there came a serious decline in rail traffic. This decline came as a direct result of the greater use of heavy lorries especially as by that time the roads had been significantly improved. Eventually and inevitably, the decision was taken to close the line at the end of 1968. Much to the surprise of the locals, a group of railway enthusiasts formed an association - Sauvegarde et Gestion des Véhicules Anciens (SVGA) - with the aim of saving the line and its rolling stock. This they did the following year and in the June the line re-opened and the first tourists were carried. Since then, the railway has gone from strength to strength and it is now probably one of the best heritage railways in all of France.

Comments: This is one of the prime 'must-do' heritage railways in France. Of course, it will be of special interest to rail enthusiasts but the line itself, tracing its path along the beautiful Doux Valley, makes for a most enjoyable day out for all the family. Tournon-sur-Rhône and Lamastre are well worth visiting as are many of the pretty villages on the way. The association SVGA also guarantees the operation of the Chemin de Fer du Haut-Rhône (CFHR) railway in the department of Isère (*see the next entry*).

Local Tourist Office: Hôtel de la Tourette, BP 47, 07301 Tournon-sur-Rhône. Telephone: 04 75 08 10 23 Fax: 04 75 08 41 28. E-mail: tournon-sur-rhone@fnotsi.net ot.tournon@wanadoo.fr website: www.ville-tournon.com and www.valleedudoux.com

Chemin de Fer du Haut-Rhône (CFHR)

Member: FACS-UNECTO
Location: Montalieu-Vallée Bleue, 61 km east of Lyon.
Department: Isère (38).
Getting there: The nearest SNCF station is at Ambérieu-en-Bugey. By road take the autoroute A42 and exit at junction 7 and follow the D124, later the D62 and finally the RN7 south to Montalieu-Vallée Bleue.
Route: Montalieu-Vallée Bleue to le Pont de Sault-Brenaz (5 km).
Journey time: 50 minutes round trip.

A 1922 Decauville 030 T preparing to leave on its afternoon excursion. *Author*

Gauge and type of traction: 600 mm; steam.
Rolling stock: A Decauville 030T built in 1922 and a Krauss 040 DFB built in 1914. An interesting range of colourful carriages including Nos. 103 and 104 (ex-Tramways of Neufchatel built in 1892), Nos. 142 and 160 (ex-Tramways of Valenciennes built in 1911) and No. 51 (built in 1917 and used by the German Army).
Contact details: Chemin de Fer du Haut-Rhône, c/o Office de Tourisme, 69440 Montalieu. The President is Monsieur J. Hoos. Telephone: 04 78 81 84 30 Fax: 04 78 81 67 45. E-mail: jcthoos@aol.com
Website: www.trains-fr.org/unecto/cfhr/
Operating dates: In May, June, September and October operates on Sundays at 1530 hours and in July and August on Saturdays at 1530 hours and on Sundays at 1530 and 1630 hours.
Tariff: An adult return ticket is 6.50€ and for a child (4-12 years) 5€ (2005).
Comments: A short but nevertheless enjoyable journey through the Bois de Corniolay along the banks of the River Rhône to the station alongside the hydro-electric scheme at Sault-Brenaz. The Musée du Cheminot is not far away at Ambérieu-en-Bugey (*see page 183*).
Local Tourist Office: 1 rue du Rhône, 38390 Montalieu-Vercieu. Telephone: 04 74 88 48 56 Fax: 04 74 88 67 96. E-mail: ot.montalieu@wanadoo.fr website: www.paysdelapierre.org

Chemin de Fer de la Brévenne (CFTB) also known as
  Train Touristique des Monts du Lyonnais

Member: FACS-UNECTO
Location: L'Arbresle, 27 km north-east of Lyon.
Department: Rhône (69).
Getting there: By SNCF train from Lyon Part-Dieu to L'Arbresle. By road from Lyon north on the autoroute A6 to junction 33 (Porte de Lyon) and then on the RN6 and D160 to L'Arbresle.
Route: L'Arbresle to La Giraudière to Ste Foy l'Argentière (19 km).

No. 130 T 157 of 1914 (awaiting restoration) with 1954-built 030 DH4 diesel at Ste Foy
l'Argentière station.   *Author*

Journey time: 1 hour 10 minutes.
Gauge and type of traction: Standard; steam (awaiting attention), diesel.
Rolling stock: A 1914-built steam locomotive 130 T 157 (ex-FS series 880) in
need of restoration, a 1954-built 030 DH4 diesel locomotive (ex-Est de Lyon),
five locotracteurs, five passengers carriages and a variety of wagons.
Contact details: Chemin de Fer de la Brévenne, 5 place de la Gare, 69610 Ste Foy
l'Argentière. Telephone: 04 74 70 90 64. E-mail: cftb@club-internet.fr
Website: http://cftb.free.fr
Operating dates: Operates on Sundays only from mid-June to mid-September
departing from L'Arbresle (SNCF station) at 1015 and 1515 hours and returning
from Ste Foy l'Argentière at 1320 and 1735 hours. An extra service operates on
Saturday afternoons from 15th-31st August.
Tariff: An adult return ticket is 10€ and for a child 5€ (2005).
History: In 1869 the company of Dombes du Sud-Est (DSE) was given approval
to construct a railway line of 80 km between Lyon (gare St Paul) and
Montbrison as part of a link to Bordeaux via Clermont-Ferrand. In 1876, the
section to Montbrison was opened to traffic. In 1882, DSE was taken over by the
company Paris-Lyon-Méditerranée (PLM). There was much local interest at the
time in visiting the area, indeed so much, that a metre gauge line was begun for
a route between Ste Foy l'Argentière and Feurs via St Laurent de Chamousset.
Its construction was well advanced by 1914 with many of the required bridges
and platforms completed. However, with the onset of World War I the project
was abandoned and never re-started. By 1923 the l'Arbresle – Ste Foy
l'Argentière line was very active for its time with four return journeys per day
between Lyon and l'Arbresle and three between Lyon and Montbrison. The

decline began in 1938 when SNCF was formed and, like many other lines throughout France, the new company set about closures or reduced services. Initially, passenger services were stopped but World War II brought their return in 1940 between l'Arbresle and St Foy l'Argentière and they continued until 1955 with goods traffic remaining until 1990. Today, passenger services continue between Lyon and Sain–Bel just 3.5 km beyond l'Arbresle. Goods traffic (*granulats*) is also carried from local quarries to l'Arbresle. The Lyon to Roanne line is still very active with SNCF services branching off at l'Arbresle. In 1993, steam trains returned to the line and the tourist line was begun. Unfortunately, the steam locomotive 130 T 157 is out of service and awaits funds for its restoration but the former Est de Lyon diesel delivers a reliable service.

Comments: The route of line today follows the beautiful la Brévenne, a river much appreciated by local anglers. The railway architecture is also of interest. Local places to visit of transport interest are a Mine Museum at St Pierre-la-Palud and wildlife at the Parc de Courzieu near to la Giraudière. There is a minature railway at Ste Foy l'Argentière station.

Local Tourist Office: 18 place Sapéon, 69210 l'Arbresle. Telephone: 04 74 01 48 87 Fax: 04 74 01 48 87. E-mail: ot.paysdelarbresle@wanadoo.fr

Chemin de Fer de la Mure (Connex-Tradition)

Member: FACS-UNECTO
Location: St Georges-de-Commiers, 23 km south of Grenoble.
Department: Isère (38).
Getting there: By SNCF train to St Georges-de-Commiers. By road take the autoroute A480 from Grenoble and exit at 12 to Vif and then on to the SNCF station at St Georges-de-Commiers.
Route: St Georges-de-Commiers (alt. 316 m) to La Mure (alt. 882 m) (30 km).
Journey time: 1 hour 50 minutes each way.
Gauge and type of traction: Metre; motrices electrified 2400V dc.
Rolling stock: Five Thury electric (368 kw) locomotives original to this railway, four automotrices (rail-cars) built 1916-18 and from the Franco-Swiss line Nyon-St Cergue, two automotrices originally from the Chemin de Fer Rhétiques network, 15 passenger carriages and a great number of goods wagons.
Contact details: Chemin de Fer de la Mure (Connex-Tradition) La Gare, 38450 St Georges-de-Commiers. Telephone: 04 76 73 57 35 or 08 92 39 14 26 Fax: 04 76 73 57 36. E-mail: trainmure@aol.com
Website: www.trainlamure.com
Operating dates: In April and October operates on Wednesdays, Saturdays and Sundays departing from St Georges-de-Commiers at 1430 hours and returning from La Mure at 1700 hours. In May, June and September it operates daily with departures from St Georges-de-Commiers at 0945 and 1430 hours and returning from La Mure at 1430 and 1700 hours. In July and August services are daily departing from St Georges-de-Commiers at 0945, 1200, 1430 and 1730 hours and returning from La Mure at 0945, 1200, 1430 and 1700 hours.

An afternoon train crossing the viaduct near to the village of Le Villaret.   *Author*

Tariff: An adult return ticket is 18€ and for a child (4-16 years) 12€. An adult single ticket is 15€ and for a child 10€. A family ticket (5 persons) is 50€. A combined ticket for a train return journey and a mine visit is 20.60€ for an adult and 12.80€ for a child (2005).

History: The line from St Georges-de-Commiers to La Mure was originally part of a 114 km line towards Gap. Construction began in 1882 and the La Mure section was opened to traffic in 1888 having cost 12 million (ancient) francs. Its prime purpose was to transport coal (anthracite) from the pits at and near La Mure down to St Georges-de-Commiers just south of the city of Grenoble. One of 12 Five-Lille steam locomotives was used to haul up to 10 fully-loaded wagons on each journey. There was a large complement of rolling stock including 24 carriages and closed wagons (fourgons), 260 coal wagons and a mobile crane; sadly, none of this has survived. Between 1903 and 1911 the railway set about a programme of electrification replacing the steam engines with five Swiss-Franco-built electric locomotives capable of hauling up to 20 fully-loaded wagons. The railway worked well for many years; for example, in 1955 620,917 tonnes of anthracite were transported, in 1945 51,015 tonnes of other products were carried including 14,543 tonnes of cement and, in 1943, 458,127 passengers were conveyed. However, as was the experience throughout much of Europe, after World War II the growth of road transport on better roads saw the beginning of the decline of the railway. In 1950 all passenger traffic ceased, by 1952 goods traffic was practically finished and October 1988 saw the end of the rail transport of anthracite. The local mines were finally closed in March 1997. Happily for the line, tourism has brought a new life to the

railway and to the area. Passenger traffic began again in 1968 and today, operated by Connex-Tradition, thousands of tourists enjoy the natural beauty of the area and marvel at the achievements of this 120-year-old railway.
Comments: Said to be the most beautiful railway line in the Alps it was the first electrified railway in the world that is still operating today, albeit with a different form of 'cargo'. The route of the line is an outstanding feat of engineering with 142 *ouvrages d'art* (construction works of art) including 18 tunnels and 12 bridges and viaducts. The most outstanding structure is the viaduct suspended 150 metres above the gorge at the Monteynard Barrage, a dam which flooded the River Drac valley. Also worth seeing from the road rather than the train are Les Viaducs de Loulla, two viaducts one above the other in the same cutting. It is possible, in July and August, to combine the train journey with a cruise on the lake by leaving St Georges-de-Commiers at 0945, taking a special bus from La Mure at 1200 hours and embarking on *La Mira* at 1230 and after the cruise returning to La Mure by 1645 in time for the 1700 hours train back to St Georges-de-Commiers. All in all it is a super day out. The railway, during its operating year, organizes a number of days with special themes; for example, an armed gang attack on the train, a 'crime on the Mure Express', a musical festival and a special event at Halloween. Other local attractions include La Mine Image at La Motte d'Aveillans which traces the history of mining in the area and L'Écomusée de l'Abeille (bee museum) at the railway station in La Motte d'Aveillans. This railway is definitely a 'must-do'.
Local Tourist Office: 43, rue de Breuil, 38350 La Mure. Telephone: 04 76 81 05 71 Fax: 04 76 81 65 87. E-mail: tourisme.lamure@wanadoo.fr website: www.ville-lamure.com

Chemin de Fer de Chamonix au Montenvers (CM)

Location: Chamonix, 90 km south-east of Geneva.
Department: Haute-Savoie (74).
Getting there: By SNCF train to St Gervais-les-Bains then the Mont Blanc Express (*see entry below*) to Chamonix. By road take the autoroutes A6 and A40 then the RN205 and RN506 to Chamonix. Be aware of winter weather conditions as wheel chains will more than likely be required.
Route: Chamonix to Montenvers and Montenvers to Mer-de-Glace (5.14 km).
Journey time: 20 minutes.
Gauge and type of traction: Metre; trams electrified 11kV 50Hz and diesel.
Rolling stock: Six electrically-driven rack and pinion (*crémaillère*) autocars and three diesel locomotives. There is a retired 1923-built Winterthur steam locomotive on static display on the platform at Chamonix station.
Contact details: Chemin de Fer de Chamonix au Montenvers, 74401 Chamonix. Telephone: 04 50 53 12 54 or 04 50 53 22 75 Fax: 04 50 53 83 93. E-mail: sales@compagniedumontblanc.fr
Website: http://www.compagniedumontblanc.fr/en/index.html
Operating dates: Services operate throughout the year except between 3rd and 16th October. In winter, departures are every day from 0900 with last journey

A tram about to leave Chamonix station. *Author*

down at 1630 hours. In summer, departures are from 0830 with the last return at 1730 hours. These times are extended from 0800 to 1830 hours in July and August.

Tariff: An adult return ticket from Chamonix to Montenvers is 14.50€, for a junior 12.30€ and for a child 10.20€. An adult single ticket from Chamonix to Montenvers is 11€, for a junior (12-15 years) 9.40€ and for a child (4-11 years) 7.70€. An adult and junior return from Montenvers to Mer-de-Glace is 3.50€ and for a child 3€. An adult, junior and child single ticket from Montenvers to Mer de Glace is 2.50€ (2005).

History: The line took its first passengers in the summer of 1909 and at that time the carriages were hauled by steam locomotives with the journey taking about 55 minutes. Just after the end of World War II, a *grotte* (cave) was cut into the famous Mer-de-Glace (at seven kilometres long France's largest glacier) so that visitors could safely see inside. In 1953, the line became the first electrified rack and pinion train in the world. However, it was not until 1993 that the railway was first opened for winter services.

Comments: This venue is immensely popular throughout the year, as much in summer for the walking as it is for sports in the winter. Indeed the road to Chamonix, the town and its car parks are always congested so the best advice is to take the Le Mont Blanc Express train from St Gervais-les-Bains (Le Fayet) to Chamonix. The Chamonix-Montenvers tram, hauled by electric self-propelling railcars or diesel locomotives, travels at a speed of 14-20 km/h and rises from an altitude of 1,042 metres to 1,913 metres. Each train carries between 160 and 200 passengers up gradients which vary between 11% and 22%. The journey includes a passage over a viaduct 152 metres in length. This journey is a 'must-do'.

Local Tourist Office: 85 place du Triangle de l'Amitié, BP 25, 74401 Chamonix-Mont-Blanc. Telephone: 04 50 53 00 24 Fax: 04 50 53 58 90.
E-mail: info@chamonix.com website: www.chamonix.com

Tramway du Mont Blanc (TMB)

Anne leaving Le Fayet (St Gervais-les-Bains station).   *Author*

Location: Le Fayet at St Gervais-les-Bains, 79 km east of Annecy.
Getting there: By SNCF rail to St Gervais-les-Bains (Le Fayet). By road take the autoroute A40 then the RN205 to St Gervais-les-Bains (Le Fayet) but be aware of winter weather conditions, wheel chains may be required.
Route: Le Fayet to the Nid d'Aigle at the foot of Le Glacier de Bionnassay (12 km).
Journey time: Approximately 1 hour 10 minutes each way.
Gauge and type of traction: Metre; rack and pinion trams (motrices) electrified 11kV 50Hz.
Rolling stock: Three electric rack and pinion trams, named *Anne, Marie* and *Jeanne* after the then owner's three daughters, were supplied in 1956 replacing the previous steam-driven motor carriages.
Contact details: Tramway du Mont Blanc, rue de la Gare, 74190 Le Fayet, St Gervais-les-Bains. Telephone : 04 50 47 51 83. E-mail: sales@compagniedumontblanc.fr
Website: www.compagniedumontblanc.com
Operating dates: Every day throughout the year with regular services running every 90 minutes.
Tariff: An adult return ticket is 23€, for a junior (12-15 years) 19.60€ and for a child (4-11 years) 16.10€. An adult single ticket is 16€, for a junior 13.60€ and for a child 11.20€. A family return ticket is 69€ (2005).
History: Between 1885 and 1904 many ideas came and went for the building of some kind of mechanised route up Mont Blanc, le Toit d'Europe (Roof of Europe) as it is known to the French. The original idea of a railway up Mont Blanc was that of the engineer Issartier who wanted to take his route right to the

summit where he intended to build a terminus! However, it was Henri Duportal, an engineer who had been responsible for the PLM line from Cluses to Le Fayet, who wished to build a tramway from Le Fayet to l'Aigulle du Goûter, 1,000 m short of the summit. His idea was accepted as the cost of his proposal was considerably less than that of his competitors. Work began on building the railway in 1904 with Col de Voza (1,653 metres) being reached in 1907, Bellevue (1,800 metres) in 1911, Nid d'Aigle (2,372 metres) in 1912 and finally to the foot of the Glacier de Bionnassay in 1914 where it was then decided to terminate the tramway. In 1923, the line was opened for the first time in winter to the Bellevue station. The traction was originally steam-driven trams but these were replaced in 1956 with electrically-driven vehicles which still continue to run today.

Comments: This tramway is the highest altitude rack and pinion train in France. It rises a total of 1,788 metres from Le Fayet to Nid d'Aigle. If it is intended to use the tramway to access the high altitude footpaths always check the weather beforehand (winter and summer) on 08 92 68 02 74. The mountain rescue services can be contacted on 04 50 53 16 89. This journey is a 'must-do'.

Local Tourist Office: 115, avenue du Mont Paccard, 74170 St Gervais-les-Bains Mont Blanc. Telephone: 04 50 47 76 08 Fax: 04 50 47 75 69. E-mail: welcome@st-gervais.net website: www.st-gervais.net

TER-SNCF - Le Mont Blanc Express

Location: St Gervais-les-Bains, 77 km south-east of Geneva in Switzerland.
Department: Haute-Savoie (74).
Getting there: By SNCF rail to St Gervais-les-Bains (Le Fayet). By road take the autoroutes A6 and A40 from Paris then the RN205 to Le Fayet (NB: be aware of winter weather conditions, as wheel chains may be required).
Route: St Gervais-les-Bains to Chamonix to Vallorcine (all in France) and then to Martigny in Switzerland. It is 38 km from St Gervais-les-Bains to Vallorcine, the last main station in France, and a further 31 km to Martigny.
Journey time: Le Fayet to Vallorcine – 1 hour 20 minutes; Le Fayet to Martigny – 2 hours 18 minutes.
Gauge and type of traction: Metre; electrified.
Contact details: TER-SNCF, Gare de St Gervais-les-Bains, 74170. Telephone: 04 50 53 12 98 or 08 91 67 68 00.
Website: www.trainstouristiques-ter.com/mont_blanc.htm
Operating dates: All year
Tariff: There are three types: *Le Tarif Mont Blanc* - if tickets are bought at one of the stations on the route there is a 50% reduction; *Le Passeport pour les Cimes* gives the traveller for 20€ a seven day pass for as many second class trips as required on all TER trains and buses on this route on the French side, i.e. terminating at the Franco-Swiss frontier at Le Châtelard; and finally, *Les cartes locales* which allows passengers to travel free of charge with either a Guest Pass, a Holiday Home Pass or a Seasonal Worker pass all available from one of the municipal authorities at Servoz, les Houches, Chamonix or Vallorcine (2006).

A St Gervais Express standing at Chamonix station.   *Author*

Comments: This is the best way to travel up the valley to Chamonix to visit the town and travel on the Chemin de Fer de Chamonix au Montenvers to see the world famous Mer-de-Glace glacier, France's biggest glacier at seven kilometres long.
Local Tourist Office: 115 avenue du Mont Paccard, 74170 St Gervais-les-Bains Mont Blanc. Telephone: 04 50 47 76 08 Fax: 04 50 47 75 69. E-mail: welcome@st-gervais.net website: www.st-gervais.net

TER-SNCF – Le Train des Alpes

Location: Grenoble, 106 km south-east of Lyon.
Department: Isère (38).
Getting there: SNCF services run to Grenoble. By road take the autoroutes A43 and A48 from Lyon to Grenoble.
Route: Grenoble to Veynes (110 km) and Grenoble to Gap (137 km).
Journey time: Grenoble to Veynes takes 2 hour 30 minutes.
Gauge and type of traction: Standard; modern diesel-powered autorail.
Rolling stock: Autorail type X 73500, 700 hp capable of 140 km per hour, seating 79 persons, heated, air conditioned and with panoramic windows.
Contact details: Telephone: 08 92 35 35 35 or visit one of the railway stations, consult www.ter-sncf.com/rhone_alpes/default.htm or visit a local tourist office.
Website: www.trainstouristiques-ter.com/train_alpes.htm
Operating dates: Throughout the year with six journeys each way between Grenoble and Gap on weekdays (including Saturdays) and five on Sundays (2005).

Tariff: An adult second class single ticket for Grenoble to Veynes is 15.20€ and an adult second class single for Grenoble to Gap is 18.20€ (2005).

History: The line was planned as early as 1856 and built between 1870 and 1880. The geographical and geological characteristics of the area presented many problems requiring the construction of 27 tunnels varying in length between 50 metres and 1,175 metres, 15 viaducts from 48 to 285 metres high and five bridges between 30 and 60 metres in height. During its time it has seen most forms of traction – steam (030s, series 4000, 242 TD, 140 A, B, J, etc.) diesel (AIA 68000, BB 67000, 67300, 67400, CC 72000 etc.) and autorails (Micheline in the 1930s, Decauville, X 2400, V 2800, X 4200 Panoramiques, RGP etc.).

Comments: This train travels through the beautiful natural parks of the Vercors and des Ecrins with as many as seven mountains either side rising over 2,000 metres and passing through many attractive villages on the way. The train itself starts its journey at an altitude of 210 m rising 1,167 m with some of the inclines on the route being as much as 2.5 per cent. Some trains continue beyond Gap to Briançon, another beautiful route.

Local Tourist Offices: 14, rue de la République, BP 227, 38019 Grenoble. Telephone: 04 76 42 41 41 Fax: 04 76 00 18 98. E-mail: welcome@grenoble-isere.info or 2a, cours Frédéric Mistral 05002 Gap. Telephone: 04 92 52 56 56 Fax: 04 92 52 56 57. E-mail: office.TourismeGap@wanadoo.fr, or avenue Commandant Dumont, 05400 Veynes. Telephone: 04 92 57 27 43 Fax: 04 92 58 16 18. E-mail: Tourisme.Veynois@wanadoo.fr

Railway Operations Temporarily Suspended

Train touristique de l'Ardèche Méridionale also known as Association Viaduc 7

Member: FACS-UNECTO
Location: Vogüé, 10 km south of Aubenas.
Department: Ardèche (07).
Getting there: By road take the autoroute A7 to Montelimar then follow the RN102 and D979 to Vogüé.
Route: Vogüé to St Jean-le-Centenier (17 km).
Journey time: 30 minutes each way.
Gauge and type of traction: Standard; autorail, diesel.
Rolling stock: Two Picasso autorails (used extensively on French railways between 1950 and 1988) No. X 3865 (ex-Bordeaux) and No. X 3989 (ex-Mohon), two autorail carriages (ex-Bordeaux) and one diesel Decauville locotracteur No. Y 6482 (ex-SNCF).
Contact details: Association Viaduc 7, BP 23, 07203 Aubenas. Telephone: Gare de Vogüé on 04 75 37 03 52 and at St Jean-le-Centenier on 04 75 36 70 32.
Website: www.viaduc07.com
Operating dates: May to September (excluding July and August) on Wednesday afternoons departing at 1445 hours, and on Sundays and public holidays with departures from Vogüé at 1030, 1445 and 1700 hours and from St Jean-le-Centenier at 1135, 1550 and 1800 hours. In July and August trains operate every day with the same scheduled departure times as listed above.

Picasso autorail No. X 3989 with diesel Decauville locotracteur No. Y 6482 standing near to Vogüé station. *Author*

Tariff: An adult return tickets is 6.5€ and for a child (4-12 years) 4€; an adult single ticket is 4.5€ and for a child 3€ (2005).

History: The line was originally built for the transport of basalt from local quarries, a service which has since been revived with the re-establishment of this line by Viaduc 07. Viaduc 07 was created in 1987 on the closure of the old line known as *l'Etoile de Vogüé* (Star of Vogüé). Originally the association organized model railway exhibitions but eventually, with the help of 4,500 contributors, 700,000FF (106,870€) was raised which with a further 210,000FF (32,610€) from the local council allowed the line to re-open for tourism in 1996.

Comments: The line has interesting railway architecture set in beautiful unspoilt countryside. There is a model railway exhibition at the station at St Jean-le-Centenier. Owing to technical problems towards the end of the 2005 season the service was not operating until advice had been sought on the condition of the rolling stock. It is believed that the service is likely to resume in due course. Check first before travelling any great distance to make a visit.

Local Tourist Office: quartier de la Gare, 07200 Vogüé. Telephone: 04 75 37 01 17 Fax: 04 75 37 01 17. E-mail: vogue@fnotsi.net

Railway Project

Les Amis du Chemin de Fer Teillois (ACFT)

Location: Le Teil, 6.6 km west of Montélimar.
Department: Ardèche (07).
Getting there: By road, take the autoroute A7 and exit at 17 if coming from the north and exit 18 from the south and take the RN 7 and the RN 102 to Le Teil.
Proposed Route: Le Teil, close to the River Rhône, to St Jean-le-Centenier (15.6 km).
Gauge and type of traction: Standard.

Rolling stock: None as yet.
Contact details: Association des Chemins de Fer Teillois, Gare du Teil, 07400 Le Teil. (The President is Albert Gobbato, Le Rac, 26780 Malataverne. The Treasurer is Michel Gerlat, Rue Pablo Picasso, 26200 Montélimar. Telephone: 04 75 51 21 04). E-mail of the webmaster is bacterius@aol.com
Operating dates: To be announced.
Comments: This project to recover the disused railway line would extend the Viaduc 7 line which runs from Vogüé to St Jean-le-Centenier, already a distance of 17 km, by a further 15.6 km. The area above the River Ardèche is a popular holiday destination. The countryside is outstandingly beautiful and there is little doubt this extended railway would further enhance its attractiveness to tourists, not least of all, with the improved accessibility to the area. The line originally travelled from Le Teil to Alès in Gard. The section from Vogüé to Alès is in a poor state and there are no plans to recover it for a tourist railway. Much of it can still be walked, however, and there is a considerable amount of interesting PLM built architecture to observe.
Local Tourist Office: Allées Provençales, 26200 Montélimar. Telephone: 04 75 01 00 20 Fax: 04 75 52 33 69. E-mail: info@montelimar-tourisme.com

Discontinued Railways

Chemin de Fer Touristique de Meyzieu

Location: Meyzieu.
Department: Rhône (69).
Comments: The route of 1.4 km on 600 mm gauge track was originally constructed in 1961 in the commune of Meyzieu by the future founders of the Vivarais Railway (CFV-CFTM – *see earlier entry*). The project closed after 10 years when the opportunity arose to develop what is now the Vivarais Railway about the same time as the local commune wished to build a leisure park on the existing Meyzieu site. Given the success of the Vivarais Railway over the past 30 years, this tourist railway is unlikely to be reintroduced. (Source: FACS-UNECTO.)

Chemin de Fer Touristique du Breda

Location: La Rochette.
Department: Isère (38) and Savoie (73).
Comments: This railway was inaugurated in 1979 by a group of railway modellers who wanted to and did develop an authentic railway using standard gauge material. It ran for 10 years but the line was eventually de-classified and closed in 1989. Some of the members later founded the Chemin de Fer de la Brévenne (CFTB) also known as Train Touristique des Monts du Lyonnais (*see earlier entry*). (Source: FACS-UNECTO.)

Preserved Locomotives and Other Traction

APMFS de Chambéry

2CC2-3402 at Chambéry depot in June 2005.   *Alain and Thomas Gallé*

Location: La Motte Servolux, Chambéry, 54 km north of Grenoble.
Department: Savoie (73).
Getting there: By road take the autoroutes A6 and A46 and then on to RN346 followed by autoroute A43 and exit at 14 to La Motte Servolux, Chambéry.
Rolling stock: Electrically-driven locomotives, 2CC2 3402, CC20001 and others.
Contact details: Dépôt de SNCF, 136 rue Auguste Renoir, 73290 La Motte Servolux, Chambéry. Telephone: 04 79 61 87 32 Fax: 04 79 61 87 33. E-mail: info@apmfs.org

Website: www.apmfs.org
Comments: An excellent website to learn more about the technical detail of these interesting preserved locomotives.
Local Tourist Office: 24, boulevard de la Colonne, 73000 Chambéry. Telephone: 04 79 33 42 47 Fax: 04 79 85 71 39. E-mail: info@Chambéry-tourisme.com website: www.Chambéry-tourisme.com

L'Association des Amis du Rail au Forez (ARF)

Location: St Etienne.
Department: Loire (42).
Getting there: By SNCF to St Etienne. By road take the autoroute A47 from Lyon or the A72 from Clermont Ferrand to St Etienne.
Contact details: ARF, c/o Gare SNCF de Bellevue, 42100 St Etienne. Telephone: 04 77 80 40 60. E-mail arforez@cegetel.fr
Website: http://arforez.free.fr
Operating dates: Annual excursions.
History: The association was formed in 1973 to pursue interests in railways, both full size and in model form. Conservation is also a priority and acting as a pressure group, they have had a number of notable successes. Most recently, after a year's struggle, they have had a major role in securing an agreement from the St Etienne Municipal Council to preserve the Pacific 231 K 82. The association has about 60 active members.
Comments: ARF qualifies for an entry because it regularly organizes trips on RFF (SNCF) tracks with preserved locomotion including steam and electricity-powered as well diesel driven autorails. This programme began in 1975 and there have since been 42 excursions. In 2005, for example, the electric locomotive CC 7102, sister to the electric locomotive CC 7107 (the 1955 world speed record holder pictured overleaf) took an excursion from Dijon to St Etienne. Such outings are open to non-members on prior application.
Local Tourist Office: 16, avenue de la Libération, 42000 St Etienne. Telephone: 04 77 49 39 00 Fax: 04 77 49 39 03. E-mail: information@tourisme-st-etienne.com

Museums

Musée du Cheminot d'Ambérieu

Member: FACS-UNECTO
Location: Ambérieu-en-Bugey, 57 km north-east of Lyon.
Department: Ain (01).
Getting there: By road take the autoroutes A6, A40 and A42 and then the D77 to Ambérieu-en-Bugey.
Exhibits: Electric locomotives CC 7002, CC 7102 and CC 7106.
Contact details: Musée du Cheminot d'Ambérieu, 01500 Ambérieu-en-Bugey,

No. CC 7107, which achieved the Blue Riband world record on 28th March, 1955 at a speed of 331 km/h, is pictured here at the Cité du Train, Mulhouse. *Author*

46, rue Aristide Briand, 01500 Ambérieu-en-Bugey. Telephone: 04 74 46 84 67 (answerphone) or 04 74 38 23 24 or 04 74 38 43 65. E-mail: musee.cheminot@free.fr
Website: http://musee.cheminot.free.fr/
Operating dates: The museum is open all the year round on Saturdays from 0900 to 1200 and 1400 to 1800 hours and on Sundays from 1400 to 1800 hours. Between 15th June and 15th September it is also open from Tuesdays to Fridays between 1400 and 1800 hours.
History: The museum, Musée du Cheminot, is a member of the association 'Patrimoine des Pays de l'Ain' and was founded in 1987 to preserve the history of the local railway network. It rapidly built an important collection which is now preserved and displayed in the museum close to the centre of Ambérieu-en-Bugey.
Comments: The museum is well worth a visit and can be combined with an enjoyable ride on the nearby Chemin de Fer du Haut-Rhône at Montalieu-Vallée Bleue, 23 km to the south (*see earlier entry*).
Local Tourist Office: Pavillon du Tourisme, Hôtel de Ville, place Robert Marcelpoil, 01500 Ambérieu-en-Bugey. Telephone: 04 74 38 18 17 Fax: 04 74 34 01 90. E-mail: tourisme@ville-amberieuenbugey.fr   website: www.ville-amberieuenbugey.fr

Musée de l'Automobile de Rochetaillée-sur-Saône
also known as Musée Henri Malartre

Location: Rochetaillée-sur-Saône, 11 km north of Lyon.
Department: Rhône (69).
Getting there: By road take the autoroute A46 and exit on to D433 to Rochetaillée-sur-Saône. The museum is situated 11 km north of Lyon on the banks of the River Saône, which is about 20 minutes drive from the centre of Lyon. Bus services operate from the centre of Lyon – Nos. 40 and 70 – stop at Rochetaillée (Intermarché).
Contact details: Musée Henri Malartre, 645, rue du Musée, 69270 Rochetaillée-Sur-Saône. Telephone: 06 78 78 29 83 or 04 78 68 10 30. E-mail: musee-malartre@mairie-lyon.fr
Website: www.musee-malartre.com/malartre/sections/fr
Operating dates: Every day except Mondays (unless a public holiday) from 0900 to 1800 hours and staying open an hour longer in July and August. Last admissions are an hour before closing. The museum is closed on 1st January, the last week of January and 25th December each year.
Tariff: An adult ticket is 5.30€, and for a student, a disabled person, a family member and a group member 2.30€ per person. Younger than 18s enjoy free admission.
Comments: Principally this is a museum of automobiles, motor-cycles and cycles. There are a few items of railway interest but nonetheless the museum is well worth a visit in its own right.
Local Tourist Office: Pavillon du Tourisme, place Bellecour, BP 2254, 69214 Lyon. Telephone: 04 72 77 69 69 Fax: 04 78 42 04 32. E-mail: info@lyon-france.com

Glossary of French Railway Terms

abonnement	season ticket
aiguillage	point
aller-retour	return ticket
aller-simple	single ticket
arrêt	stop
autorail	railcar
bénévolé	volunteer
billet	ticket
billet de quai	platform ticket
chauffeur	fireman
chef de gare	station master
chef de train	guard
cheminot	railwayman
crémaillère	rack and pinion
composteur	machine for validating a ticket
cyclo-draisine	rail cycle
draisine	rail vehicle for inspecting track
écartement	gauge
employé(e) de wagons-lit	train attendant
essieu(x)	axle(s)
ferroviaire	railway (noun) rail (adj.)
fourgons	wagons (goods)
gare	station
grue	crane
guichet	ticket office
horaires	(train) times
ligne	line
locomotive à vapeur	steam locomotive
matériel roulant	rolling stock
mécanicien	driver (Mechanic)
minieresbunn (German)	mining train
musée	museum
motrice	tram
obliteration	term used for validating a ticket
ouvrages d'art	works of art often used to describe outstanding railway constructions
parcours	route
passage à niveau	level crossing
passionnée	enthusiast
patrimoine	heritage
poste d'aiguillage	signal box
quai	platform
rail conducteur de contact	live rail
rame	string (of carriages)
RATP	Régie Autonome de Transports Parisien (Umbrella organization in the Île de France looking after local train, tram, metro and bus services)
remorque	trailer; unpowered carriage
réseau	network
RER	Reseau Express Régional
RFF	Réseau Ferré de France
SNCF	Société Nationale des Chemins de Fer Français
strapontin	fold-down seat
TER	Transports Express Régional
tête de ligne	railhead
TGV	*train grande vitesse*
thermique	thermal; heated
trajet	journey
tronçon	section
voyages	journeys or voyages
vélo	cycle
vélorail	rail cycle
voie	track, line or way (often used at stations to indicate platform of departure or arrival)
voiture	carriage or coach

Bibliography

All references are to books, journals, brochures and other documentation published in the French language unless otherwise stated.

Encyclopédie du matériel moteur SNCF – Tome 1: Les locomotives à courant continu 1500V by Olivier Constant. Editions Publitrain eurl, 2004 F-Betschdorf. (ISSN 1267 – 5008)

Encyclopédie du matériel moteur SNCF – Tome 2: Les locomotives à vapeur depuis 1938 by Olivier Constant. Editions Publitrain eurl, 2005 F-Betschdorf. (ISSN 1267 – 5008)

Les Archives de l'Ouest-Etat – Tome 1: L'histoire de la compagnie de l'Ouest by Pierre Laederich and Bruno Moret. Editions Publitrain eurl, F-Betschdorf. (ISSN 1267 – 5008)

Les Archives de l'Ouest-Etat – Tome 2: L'histoire de la Reseau de l'Eta (1878-1909) by Bruno Moret. Editions Publitrain eurl, F-Betschdorf. (ISSN 1267 – 5008)

Les Archives de la DEV – Tome 1: voitures DEV acier ordinaire et inox, rames Michelin by Jean-Marc Dupuy. Editions Publitrain eurl, F-Betschdorf. (ISSN 1267 – 5008)

Les Archives de la OCEM: voitures, wagons, fourgons, automotrices, locomotives à vapeur by Jean-Marc Dupuy. Editions Publitrain eurl, F-Betschdorf. (ISSN 1267 – 5008)

Les Panoramiques et autres autorails touristiques by Olivier Constant. Editions Publitrain eurl, 2004 F-Betschdorf. (ISSN 1267 – 5008)

Les ABJ – Les ABJ 1,2,3, 4 – Les ABJ à l'export – Les ABJ préservés et des CFSNE … by Olivier Constant. Editions Publitrain eurl, 2003 F-Betschdorf. (ISSN 1267 – 5008)

Les automotrices Z2 by Olivier Constant. Editions Publitrain eurl, 2002 F-Betschdorf. (ISSN 1267 – 5008)

Les autorails unifiés- Tome 6: Les X 2100/X 2200, XR 6100/XR 6200 by Olivier Constant. Editions Publitrain eurl, 2001 F-Betschdorf. (ISSN 1267 – 5008)

Les autorails unifiés - Tome 4: Les X 4300, X 4500, X4630, X 4750, X 4790, X 94630 by Olivier Constant. Editions Publitrain eurl, 1999 F-Betschdorf. (ISSN 1267 – 5008)

Les autorails unifiés - Tome 3: Les X 2700, RGP 2, RGP 1 TEE, RGP modernisées by Olivier Constant. Editions Publitrain eurl, 1996 F-Betschdorf. (ISSN 1267 – 5008)

Les autorails unifiés - Tome 2: Les X 2051 Budd,, X 2800, by Olivier Constant et autres. Editions Publitrain eurl, 1995 F-Betschdorf. (ISSN 0986 – 6663)

Paris et l'Ile-de-France - Tome 1: Les reseaux Esr, Nord et Saint-Lazare by Jean Tricoire and Jean-Paul Geal. Editions Publitrain eurl, 2002 F-Betschdorf. (ISSN 1267 – 5008)

Les « Mountain » de l'Est – Les 241.101, 242 A 1, 241 A SNCF ex-241-000 de l'Etat et de l'Est by Olivier Constant. Editions Publitrain eurl, 1997/8 F-Betschdorf. (ISSN 1267 – 5008)

Les BB 15000 by Jean-Marc Dupuy. Editions Publitrain eurl, 2005 F-Betschdorf. (ISSN 1267 – 5008)

Le Train, No. 195. Editions Publitrain eurl, July 2004 Betschdorf. (ISSN 0986 – 6663)

Le Train, No. 207. Editions Publitrain eurl, July 2005 F-Betschdorf. (ISSN 0986 – 6663)

Musée français du Chemin de Fer Mulhouse. Editions La Nuée Bleue / DNA, Strasbourg 1991. (ISBN 2-7165-0173-4)

Musée français du Chemin de Fer Mulhouse – Histoire, Projets, Collection – Numéro spécial 24 ans du Musée No 438-96/3. Editions AFAC, 1996 Paris. (ISSN 1252 – 9907)

Musée français du Chemin de Fer Mulhouse by M. Jean Renaud et autres. Mulhouse Musée, 1989. (ISBN 2-9501041-0-X)

Connaissance des Arts – Cité du Train edited by Guy Boyer. SPFA, 2005 Paris. (ISSN 1242 – 9198)

Cité du Train – Le Catalogue edited by Philippe Mirville. Editions La Vie du Rail, 2005. (ISBN 2-915 034-34-6)

The Story of the Train, Board and Trustees of the Science Museum (National Rail Museum), GB-London 1999. (ISBN 1 872826) (**English language**).

Railways of the Baie de Somme – A Landscape with Trains by Philip Pacey with Roland Arzul and Guy Lenne. The Oakwood Press, 2000 Usk, UK. (ISBN 0-85361-554-3) (**English** and French languages).

Tramways à Vapeur du Tarn, by Sarah Wright. The Oakwood Press, 2001 Usk, UK. (ISBN 0 85361 570) (**English** language).

La France Vue du Rail – Cartes des Chemins de Fer Touristiques. UNECTO, 2005.

The Yellow Cerdagne Train. Editions Mimosa for SNCF Montpellier.

La Lettre du Projet de Parc naturel régional des Pyrénées Catalanes – No. 4 Spécial Train Jaune. Agence Méditerranéenne de l'Environnement, July 2001 Montpellier.

Sauvegarder Le Patrimoine. Edition APPEVA, 2001 Amiens.

Le p'tit train de la haute Somme et son Musée des C.F. Militaires & Industriels. Edition APPEVA, 1996 Amiens.

Le Chemin de Fer de la Mure. SOFITEC, undated Paris.

The Vivarais Railway by Jean Arrivetz. Edition SAEP, 1993 Ingersheim. (**English** language).

Chemin de Fer du Vivarais. Société Chemins de Fer Touristiques et de Montagne, undated Lyon.

Once upon a time… le petit train d'artouste by Sophie Ponsol. Bihet ; 2000 Pau-Bizanos. (ISBN 2-9514106-2X) (**English** language).

AGRIVAP – Historique et Descriptif de la Ligne – Bon Voyage à bord des Autorail de la Découverte. AGRIVAP 2002, unpublished commentary.

Commentaires du Train Touristique Gentiane Express - de la Dordogne au Puy Mary. CFHA undated. (**English** language).

Du Rhône à La Loire – L'Aventure des CFD. Association Patrimoine du Plateau Vivarais-Lignon, undated F-Le Chambon sur Lignon.

The History of Trains by Colin Garratt. Chancellor Press, 1998 London. (ISBN 0 7537 0630 X) (**English** language).

The Encyclopaedia of Trains and Locomotives edited by David Ross. Amber Books, 2003 Leicester. (ISBN 1-85605-792-5) (**English** language).

Named Trains of France by Derek Wilde. The SNCF Society, 2004 (**English** language).

Journal of The SNCF Society, editions 92, 113, 114, 115, 116, 117, 118, 119 and 120 (ISSN 1358 – 6238) (**English** language).

Relevant Websites

www.trains-fr.org FACS-UNECTO

www.trains-fr.org/ahicf/ Association pour l'histoire des chemins de fer en France (French railway history).

http://users.skynet.be/sky34004/repfer.html Répertoire des sites ferroviaires is a most comprehensive list of website references for Railways in France, Belgium and elsewhere in the world prepared by Michel Marin.

www.railfrance.org Most comprehensive site on French Railways.

http://voiemetrique.org Narrow gauge railways.

www.railpassion.org An enthusiast site.

www.ratp.fr Paris rail transport.

http://www.transilien.com SNCF-Transilien for transport in Paris area.

http://fret.sncf.com/fr SNCF's freight business.

www.connex.net Connex rail company.

http://lwdr.free.fr The French Railway's website.

www.webvdr.com *La Vie du Rail* weekly magazine's website.

www.sncf.com The official SNCF website.

www.voyages-sncf.com The SNCF site to book journeys by rail in France. If the criteria selected are flexible some excellent deals are to be had. The site can be accessed in English, French, Spanish, Dutch, German and Italian languages.

www.ter-sncf.com Rail travel within the regions of France.

www.adminet.com/comp/sncf.html Unofficial site on matters SNCF.

www.railfaneurope.net Excellent site for pictures, stock lists and liveries on French and other railways.

http://www.tgv.com/EN/index.htm Official SNCF booking site for TGV services.

www.raileurope.co.uk UK site for booking rail journeys in Europe

www.espacetrain.com A comprehensive site run by Frenchman Frédéric Parrot in French but always a good starting point.

www.raileurope.com Rail Europe Group is a US-based company of which SNCF and SBB (Swiss Federal Railroads) are the majority shareholders.

www.greatrail.com Great Rail Journeys is a York (UK) based company offering rail tours in France and elsewhere.

www.railtravelcenter.com/index.htm Rail Travel Centre is a USA company running tours in Europe.

www.sncfsociety.org UK-based organization

Useful Addresses

FACS-UNECTO, Gare de l'Est, 75475 Paris. Telephone and Fax +33 (0)1 40 38 39 07. Website: www.trains-fr.org   This is the key organization in France representing the interests of Heritage and Tourist Railways – it is a mine of useful information.

The SNCF Society, c/o J. Rowcroft, 5 Middle Furlong, Seaford, Sussex BN25 1SR, England. Website: www.sncfsociety.org

Rail Europe is located at the French Travel Centre, 178 Piccadilly, London W1. Telephone: 08708 371 371.
Website: www.raileurope.co.uk E-mail: reservations@raileurope.co.uk

The Railway Touring Company, 4A Tuesday Market Place, King's Lynn PE30 1JN Tel: 01553 661500 Fax: 01553 661800. Website: www.railwaytouring.co.uk e-mail: n.dobbing@btconnect.com British company which frequently runs excursions in France (and elsewhere) using heritage locomotives on SNCF lines.

Railtrail Tours Ltd, 43 St Edward Street, Leek, ST13 5DN.
Tel: 01538 38 23 23 Fax: 01538 38 25 25. Website: www.railtrail.co.uk E-mail: enquiry@railtrail.co.uk Another British company which runs excursions to France and elsewhere.

Travelsphere Ltd, Compass House, Rockingham Road, Market Harborough, Leicestershire LE16 7QD Telephone: 0870 240 2426.
Website: www.travelsphere.co.uk/website/intros/rail-intro.aspx

Venice-Simplon Express Ltd, Sea Containers House, 20 Upper Ground, London SE1 9PF. Telephone 020 7805 5060 www.orient-express.com

French Railway Magazines (*Revues*)

Le Train, Editions Publitrain eurl, BP 10, F-67660 Betschdorf. ISSN 0986-6663 (monthly).

Connaissance du Rail, Editions de l'Ormet, BP 12, F-03330 Valignat. ISSN 0222-4844 (monthly).

La Vie du Rail et des Transports, 11, rue de Milan F-75440 Paris. Published weekly in four regional editions - ISSN 0042-5478 (édition générale) 0042-5478, Atlantique - 1145-4466, Nord-Est - 1145-4474, Sud-Est - 0243-6752.

Voie étroite, Edited by l'APPEVA, BP 106, F-8001 Amiens (bi-monthly).

Voies Ferrées, Published by Presses et Editions Ferroviaires, 4, avenue Albert premier de Belgique F-38000 Grenoble. ISSN 0249-4917 (bi-monthly).

Voie Libre, Editions Loco-Revue, 12, rue du Sablen, BP 104, F-56401 Auray. ISSN 1277-3646 (monthly).

Rive Droite, Rive Gauche, Edited by l'association Sauvegarde de la Petite Ceinture, 11, rue Oswaldo-Cruz F-75016 Paris (monthly).

Revue Générale des Chemins de Fer, 19, rue d'Amsterdam F-75008 Paris. ISSN 0035-3183 (monthly).

RATP Savoir Faire, Edited by RATP, LAC A85, 54, quai de la Rapée, 75599 Paris (quarterly).

Rail Passion, Published by La Vie du Rail.com, 11, rue de Milan, 75440 Paris. ISSN 1261-3665 (bi-monthly).

Rail Miniature Flash, Rigel Editions, 82, rue Curial, 75019 Paris ISSN 033-8737 (monthly).

Objectif Rail, Le Villard F-48230 Chanac. ISSN M 07296 RD (bi-monthly).

Le train du Sud, Edited by Groupe d'Etude sur le Chemin de Fer de Provence, Dépôt des Locomotives F-06260 Puget Théniers. ISSN 0152-7940 (quarterly approximately).

Loco-Revue, Editions Loco-Revue, 12, rue du Sablen, BP 104, F-56401 Auray. ISSN 0024-5739 (monthly).

Le Rail, Editions du Groupe Actis, 3, avenue Hoche F-75008 Paris. ISSN 0989-8220 (monthly).

L'Echo du Rail, Edited by Les Editions du Cabri, quartier Giandola, F-06540 Breil sur Roya. ISSN 0764-4566 (monthly).

Chemins de Fer régionaux et urbains, Edited by FACS-UNECTO.

Gare de l'Est Cour souterraine, Place du 11 Novembre 1918, F-75475 Paris. ISSN 1141-7447 (bi-monthly).

Correspondances - Revue d'histoire ferroviaire, Editions Loco-Revue, 12, rue du Sablen, BP 104, F-56401 Auray (bi-monthly).

Entre les lignes, Edited by RATP, LAC A85, 54, quai de la Rapée F-75599 Paris (monthly).

Fret Magazine, Edited by Direction du Fret de la SNCF, 10, place de Budapest F-75436 Paris (monthly).

Key to Map Locations